T0353435

Impact of Digital Transformation on Security Policies and Standards

Sam Goundar
The University of the South Pacific, Fiji

S. Bharath Bhushan
School of SCSE, VIT Bhopal University, India

Vaishali Ravindra Thakare
Atria Institute of Technology, India

A volume in the Advances in
Information Security, Privacy, and
Ethics (AISPE) Book Series

Published in the United States of America by
  IGI Global
  Information Science Reference (an imprint of IGI Global)
  701 E. Chocolate Avenue
  Hershey PA, USA 17033
  Tel: 717-533-8845
  Fax: 717-533-8661
  E-mail: cust@igi-global.com
  Web site: http://www.igi-global.com

Library of Congress Cataloging-in-Publication Data

Names: Goundar, Sam, 1967- editor. | Bhushan, Bharat (Software specialist),
    editor. | Thakare, Vaishali Ravindra, 1991- editor.
Title: Impact of digital transformation on security policies and standards
    / Sam Goundar, Bharath Bhushan and Vaishali Ravindra Thakare, editors.
Description: Hershey, PA : Information Science Reference, an imprint of IGI
    Global, 2020. | Includes bibliographical references and index. |
    Summary: "This book summarizes the policies, standards, and mechanisms
    for security in all sort of digital applications. It also focuses on
    blockchain and its imminent impact on financial services in making a
    smart government along with bitcoin and the future of digital
    payments"-- Provided by publisher.
Identifiers: LCCN 2019039178 (print) | LCCN 2019039179 (ebook) | ISBN
    9781799823674 (hardcover) | ISBN 9781799823681 (paperback) | ISBN
    9781799823698 (ebook)
Subjects: LCSH: Computer networks--Security measures--Standards. | Data
    protection. | Electronic information resources--Access control. |
    Electronic data interchange--Security measures.
Classification: LCC TK5105.59 .I43 2020 (print) | LCC TK5105.59 (ebook) |
    DDC 005.8--dc23
LC record available at https://lccn.loc.gov/2019039178
LC ebook record available at https://lccn.loc.gov/2019039179

This book is published in the IGI Global book series Advances in Information Security, Privacy, and Ethics
(AISPE) (ISSN: 1948-9730; eISSN: 1948-9749)

British Cataloguing in Publication Data
A Cataloguing in Publication record for this book is available from the British Library.

All work contributed to this book is new, previously-unpublished material.
The views expressed in this book are those of the authors, but not necessarily of the publisher.

For electronic access to this publication, please contact: eresources@igi-global.com.

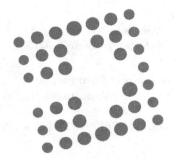

Advances in Information Security, Privacy, and Ethics (AISPE) Book Series

ISSN:1948-9730
EISSN:1948-9749

Editor-in-Chief: Manish Gupta, State University of New York, USA

MISSION

As digital technologies become more pervasive in everyday life and the Internet is utilized in ever increasing ways by both private and public entities, concern over digital threats becomes more prevalent.

The **Advances in Information Security, Privacy, & Ethics (AISPE) Book Series** provides cutting-edge research on the protection and misuse of information and technology across various industries and settings. Comprised of scholarly research on topics such as identity management, cryptography, system security, authentication, and data protection, this book series is ideal for reference by IT professionals, academicians, and upper-level students.

COVERAGE

- Computer ethics
- Security Classifications
- Network Security Services
- Data Storage of Minors
- IT Risk
- Internet Governance
- Security Information Management
- Privacy-Enhancing Technologies
- Tracking Cookies
- Global Privacy Concerns

IGI Global is currently accepting manuscripts for publication within this series. To submit a proposal for a volume in this series, please contact our Acquisition Editors at Acquisitions@igi-global.com or visit: http://www.igi-global.com/publish/.

Titles in this Series

For a list of additional titles in this series, please visit:
http://www.igi-global.com/book-series/advances-information-security-privacy-ethics/37157

Cyber Security of Industrial Control Systems in the Future Internet Environment
Mirjana D. Stojanović (University of Belgrade, Serbia) and Slavica V. Boštjančič Rakas (University of Belgrade, Serbia)
Information Science Reference • © 2020 • 374pp • H/C (ISBN: 9781799829102) • US $195.00

Digital Investigation and Intrusion Detection in Biometrics and Embedded Sensors
Asaad Abdulrahman Nayyef (Sultan Qaboos University, Iraq)
Information Science Reference • © 2020 • 320pp • H/C (ISBN: 9781799819448) • US $235.00

Handbook of Research on Intrusion Detection Systems
Brij B. Gupta (National Institute of Technology, Kurukshetra, India) and Srivathsan Srinivasagopalan (AT&T, USA)
Information Science Reference • © 2020 • 400pp • H/C (ISBN: 9781799822424) • US $265.00

Applied Approach to Privacy and Security for the Internet of Things
Parag Chatterjee (National Technological University, Argentina & University of the Republic, Uruguay) Emmanuel Benoist (Bern University of Applied Sciences, Switzerland) and Asoke Nath (St. Xavier's College, University of Calcutta, India)
Information Science Reference • © 2020 • 315pp • H/C (ISBN: 9781799824442) • US $235.00

Internet Censorship and Regulation Systems in Democracies Emerging Research and Opportunities
Nikolaos Koumartzis (Aristotle University of Thessaloniki, Greece) and Andreas Veglis (Aristotle University of Thessaloniki, Greece)
Information Science Reference • © 2020 • 200pp • H/C (ISBN: 9781522599739) • US $185.00

For an entire list of titles in this series, please visit:
http://www.igi-global.com/book-series/advances-information-security-privacy-ethics/37157

701 East Chocolate Avenue, Hershey, PA 17033, USA
Tel: 717-533-8845 x100 • Fax: 717-533-8661
E-Mail: cust@igi-global.com • www.igi-global.com

Table of Contents

Singh Indraprastha University, India

Detailed Table of Contents

Chapter 1

    Hima Bindu P., Sri Krishnadevaraya University, India
    John Samuel K., Srinivasa Ramanujan Institute of Technology, India
    Bhaskar Reddy T., Sri Krishnadevaraya University, India

It is a known fact that technology drives the nation. Day by day more disruptive technologies emerge that enable a nation to strive for massive growth in its GDP. The digital India is a high priority programme from the Indian government in order to make India a digitally literate nation. This project mainly provides the services offered by the government to common public through electronic means. This is done by enhancing the operational setup of the existing services. The digitalization of many aspects in India make it a better contender to become a global leader by creating digital empowerment in technology with cumulative internet connectivity. The chapter identifies some of the core areas where the concept of digitalization enhances its operational processes. The changes reflected in each individual sector by adopting digital transformation are discussed in detail.

Chapter 2

    Syed Muzamil Basha, Sri Krishna College of Engineering and
        Technology, India
    Ravi Kumar Poluru, Vellore Institute of Technology, India
    J. Janet, Sri Krishna College of Engineering and Technology, India
    S. Balakrishnan, Sri Krishna College of Engineering and Technology,
        India
    D. Dharunya Santhosh, Sri Krishna College of Engineering and
        Technology, India
    A. Kousalya, Sri Krishna College of Engineering and Technology, India

Software security has become a very critical part of our lives. A software developer who has a fundamental understanding of software security can have an advantage in the workplace. In the massive Equifax breach that occurred in 2017 that exposed data of roughly 140 million people, attackers exploited a vulnerability in Apache Struts, CVE-2017-5638, which allows remote attackers to execute arbitrary commands when specially crafting user-controlled data in HTTP headers. Sensitive data exposure issues are essential to know to protect customer data. It is fascinating to understand how attackers can exploit application vulnerabilities to perform malicious activities. The authors also want the reader to be aware of the fact that we should always be thinking about how our applications handle user-controlled data so that we can put guards in place to minimize security issues in the development of new applications.

Sam Goundar, The University of the South Pacific, Fiji
Bettylyn Chandra, The University of the South Pacific, Fiji
Akashdeep Bhardwaj, University of Petroleum and Energy Studies, India
Fatemeh Saber, University of Malaya, Malaysia
Subhash Appana, The University of the South Pacific, Suva, Fiji

This chapter seeks to examine the digital transformation (digitalisation) of diplomacy and how such digital transformations can be used to positively influence and improve a country's foreign services. The chapter further explores how the country's diplomats and their Foreign Service counterparts at Ministry of Foreign Affairs (MFA) can utilize the tools provided by digitalisation to advance the country's interests. Given the critical intelligence data, diplomatic protocols, and confidential information exchanged at the diplomatic level between countries, it is equally important to evaluate and assess the cyber security measures that are being taken to secure the digital network of the diplomatic missions. Scholarly research was initially conducted to position the field of research amongst pertinent literature to ascertain the use of digital tools in diplomacy and present key deliberations that exist.

Dasari Kalyani, VNR Vignana Jyothi Institute of Engineering and
Technology, India

In today's digital e-commerce and m-commerce world, the information itself acts as an asset and exists in the form of hardware, software, procedure, or a person. So the security of these information systems and management is a big challenging issue for small and large-scale agencies. So this chapter discusses the major role and responsibility of the organization's management in identifying the need for information security policy in today's world of changing security principles and controls. It focuses on various policy types suitable for all kinds of security models and procedures with the background details such as security policy making, functionality, and its impact on an agency culture. Information security policies are helpful to identify and assess risk levels with the available set of technological security tools. The chapter describes the management strategies to write a good policy and selection of the right policy public announcement. The agencies must also ensure that the designed policies are properly implemented and ensure compliance through frequent intermediate revisions.

Chapter 5

Pooja Kaplesh, Chandigarh University, India

This chapter gives an overview about the need for computer security and different types of network securities. Different types of attacks like active and passive are discussed that can harm system resources. This chapter also provides the basics of the cryptography system and basic terms used in cryptography. Security services provided by cryptography are also discussed such as data integrity, privacy/confidentiality, user authentication, message authentication, authorization, digital signatures, validation, access control, and non-repudiation along with their mechanisms.

Chapter 6

Sam Goundar, The University of the South Pacific, Fiji
Alvish Pillai, The University of the South Pacific, Fiji
Akashdeep Bhardwaj, University of Petroleum and Energy Studies, India

Healthcare is a vital portion of today's medical environment, and it is necessary for medical providers to do their work in an efficient and effective manner. Everyday, hundreds of thousands of patients visit medical amenities stimulating the administration to run smoothly. Almost all hospitals and the health centers in Fiji are now heavily dependent on a patient information system (PATISplus) that helps the employees to manage all the medical and administrative information. In this chapter, the authors analyse the ethical issues of a patient information systems (PATIS) using the PAPA model. This is in terms of privacy, accessibility, accuracy, and property. This chapter reviews current policies within the Ministry of Health and Medical Services in Fiji and also if there is a need of development of standard operating procedures in view of the PAPA model.

Chapter 7

Lavanya Lingareddy, Sree Vidyanikethan Engineering College, India
Parthiban Krishnamoorthy, Sree Vidyanikethan Engineering College,
India

Like other new generation information technologies such as IoT, big data, AI, and cloud, cryptocurrency and blockchain became buzz words in both industry and academia due to their advantageous features. With the features like decentralization, transparency, immutability, blockchain technology became more famous and is emerging in almost all fields like banking, education, healthcare, government, and real estate. Blockchain technology was introduced in the year 1991. It came into existence after this technology was created for bitcoin, a digital cryptocurrency by Santoshi Nakamoto in the year 2008. Since then, the blockchain is evolving rapidly. Even though blockchain usage is in high demand in all the sectors and it has received attention from many international organizations, most of the people lag in knowledge of blockchain technology and Cryptocurrency and how exactly they work. This chapter explores more in detail what blockchain technology is, how it works, and its applications.

Chapter 8

Shanthi Makka, Birla Institute of Technology, Ranchi, India
Gagandeep Arora, ITS Engineering College, India
B. B. Sagar, Birla Institute of Technology, Mesra, India

Blockchain technology makes use of a centralized, peer-to-peer (P2P) network of databases, also called nodes, to validate and record digital transactions between individual users located anywhere across the globe. These transactions often take place through the exchange of cryptocurrencies such as bitcoins, Ethereum, and Ripple, etc. The security and transparency that is inherently present in digital transactions place blockchain technology in high demand across various industrial applications. Each node updates its database in real-time as and when transactions occur. The transaction gets authorized only when a majority of the nodes in the network validate the transaction. Once the verification is complete, a block, consisting of hash and keys, is generated for each new transaction and is linked to previous transactions in every database. Every node updates its database with the new block. A hacker would have to break down every node in the system to commit fraud. Blockchain could play a major role in maintaining the cyber security of digital transactions in the future.

Chapter 9

Sam Goundar, The University of the South Pacific, Fiji

Abraham Colin Chongkit, The University of the South Pacific, Fiji
Shalvendra Kumar, The University of the South Pacific, Fiji
Akashdeep Bhardwaj, University of Petroleum and Energy Studies, India

Companies have realized the need to have the competitive edge over their rivals. Enterprise systems provide this competitive edge. But with implementing enterprise system software (ESS), companies have to invest in the networking of their various business offices to interconnect to ESS. This chapter investigates the various ways two companies in Fiji do this and the various disadvantages they face from lack of knowledge of ESS to infrastructure limitations and issues faced in a developing country like Fiji. This chapter focuses on the network security issues of enterprise systems deployed in two companies in Fiji. It compares the information gathered to published papers on network infrastructure, network security issues, and threat assessments. It also proposes solutions to mitigate the security issues faced by enterprise systems networks.

Chapter 10

    Manjula Raghav, Indira Gandhi National Open University, India
    Nisha Dhanraj Dewani, Maharaja Agrasen School of Law, Guru Gobind
        Singh Indraprastha University, India

Development and advancement in information technologies have paved the path for many challenges for the intellectual property rights holders. There are several forms of cybercrimes such as pornography, stalking, cyber fraud, cyber terrorism, etc., that are affecting people, hurdling e-commerce, challenging law, and disturbing the channel of information and communication. No doubt that cybercrimes are offences where the computer is the means of the commission of the offence as well as a target of the offence. Apparently, such offences are generated through electronic means where mens rea has no role to play. This unruly horse is creating several problems in the world of intellectual property, which has the capacity to affect global commerce. This chapter will focus on Indian case laws to showcase the interface between IPR and cyberspace. Also the dealing of issues like cybersqatting, cyberbullying, cyber theft will be discussed in order to check the competency of IPR.

Chapter 11

    Anilkumar Chunduru, Rajiv Gandhi University of Knowledge
        Technologies, India

Gowtham Mamidisetti, Presidency University, India

Cloud computing is a highly demanding zone in the present IT enterprise. The key characteristics are adaptability, productivity, pay-per-utilize, and cost viability. Access control and information security are the significant issues in cloud computing. Various access control strategies are present. The major problems of storing data in expandable access control and access rights from users are not used in this scheme. This chapter presents a generic survey on scalable and secure access control systems and schemes in cloud computing with a key focus on cloud security. Research gaps in the existing literature on cloud security are presented.

Preface

INTRODUCTION

We have entered the era of the Fourth Industrial Revolution (4IR). The Fourth Industrial Revolution is building on the Third (the digital revolution). The digital revolution has been occurring since computers came into existence. It is characterized by a fusion of technologies that is blurring the lines between the physical, digital, and biological spheres. The digital revolution is transforming the world as we know it at unprecedented speed. Digital technologies have changed the way businesses operate, how people connect and exchange information, and how they interact with the public and private sectors. Businesses and citizens alike need to be aware of and possess appropriate skills and infrastructures to capture the enormous value created by the digital economy and make a success of digital transformation.

The digital revolution enabling the Fourth Industrial Revolution that the world is witnessing. It will manifest a significant impact on how we live, work and interact with people and machines. Organizations have no other alternatives, but to step into digital world for their survival and to sure sustainable competitive edge. The governments across the world came up with an initiative to amplify the scope of e-Governance by floating so many digital programmes and undergoing digital transformations. The objective of digital transformation is to provide the necessary infrastructure as a basic utility for every citizen of their country to provide on demand services with superior governance and empowering their citizens digitally.

Security and privacy are the major barriers in adopting the digital mechanisms. Organizations and individuals are concerned about their private and financial data. The security mechanisms that safeguards and monitors the sensitive information should be standardized and the security policies should be assessed on a regular basis. Nowadays more and more innovative applications are using standardized cryptographic mechanisms to explore many new innovative digital financial applications and various decentralized applications that eliminate the need for third party intermediaries, such as identity management, credit management, distrusted ledger, crowd-funding, P2P insurance, smart contracts, supply chain management, online voting, medical records, to name a few.

Digital transformation marks a radical rethinking of how an organization uses technology, people and processes to fundamentally change business performance. Digital transformation is a foundational change in how an organization delivers value to its customers. According to (Negreiro & Madiega, 2019), Internet and digital technologies are transforming our world. For decades, societies and economies have been experiencing a radical digital transformation, fostered by 'digitalisation' and the speeding up of many kinds of interaction through the increasing number of connected devices and data flows.

Digital transformation covers both the integration of digital technologies by enterprises and the impact on society of new technologies, such as the Internet of Things (IoT), cloud computing, innovative digital platforms and blockchain technologies, writes Negreiro & Madiega, 2019 in their European Union Brief on Digital Transformations. It is becoming an increasingly important condition for modern economies to thrive and has the potential to affect many sectors of the economy (including transport, energy, agri-food, telecommunications, financial services, factory production and health care) and to transform people's lives. According to the OECD, the greater computing power of consumer devices, which are available at ever more affordable prices, is accelerating this transformation. Furthermore, artificial intelligence (AI) and advanced robotics are viewed as an important manifestation of the digital transformation.

THE IMPACT OF DIGITAL TRANSFORMATIONS

As an example, the European Union plays an active role in shaping the digital economy, with cross-policy initiatives that range from boosting investment to reforming EU laws, to non-legislative actions to improve Member States' coordination and exchange of best practices. The 2014-2019 parliamentary term has seen a number of initiatives in the areas of digitalisation of industry and public services, investment in digital infrastructure and services, research programmes, cybersecurity, e-commerce, copyright and data protection legislation. There is a growing awareness among EU citizens that digital technologies play an important role in their everyday lives (Negreiro & Madiega, 2019).

In a 2017 survey, two-thirds of Europeans said that these technologies have a positive impact on society, the economy and their own lives. However, they also bring new challenges. A majority of respondents felt that the EU, Member States' authorities and companies need to take action to address the impacts of these technologies. The European Union will increase its support for digital transformation in the coming years, as illustrated by the recent proposal for the Digital Europe programme (for 2021-2027) – which would be the first ever funding programme dedicated solely to supporting digital transformation in the EU.

Negreiro & Madiega, 2019, states that further EU action will doubtless be needed, notably to increase infrastructure investment, boost innovation, foster digital champions and businesses digitalisation, reduce existing digital divides, remove remaining barriers in the digital single market and ensure an adequate legal and regulatory framework in the areas of advanced computing and data, artificial intelligence, and cybersecurity. The European Parliament, as co-legislator, is closely involved in shaping the policy framework that will help citizens and businesses fully exploit the potential of digital technologies.

Digital transformation is a revolutionary technology that will play a vital role in most of the major industries. Apart from governance, it can be used for a wide variety of applications such as tracking, ownership, physical assets, voting rights, security and encryption of various digital resources and access of online, distributed platforms. Digital transformation encompasses some of the following indexing keywords: Applied Cryptography, Blockchain Technologies, Data Security and Protection, Digital Financial Applications, e-Services, Legal, Regulatory, and Compliance Issues, Cyber-Physical Systems, Security Vulnerabilities, Security and Privacy Applications, and Trust Models. However, this is not an exhaustive list of indexing keywords.

DIGITAL TRANSFORMATION: MYTH VS. REALITY

For many, digital transformations are a hyped word. The word digital transformations are used by everyone without taking into consideration, the context in which it should be used. Everyone is throwing the word around to make themselves and their organisations to appear to be on the cutting edge of the digital technology. It has become keyword for some, while a myth for others. It has been hyped so much that one cannot isolate the reality from the myth. In the article "Five Myths About Digital Transformations", MIT Sloan Management Review Spring 2017 Issue, Andriole (2017) dispels the myth as follows: "If you want to lead your organization's technology transition, the first step is grasping the realities of digital transformations - rather than getting seduced by the hype.

The five myths by Andriole (2017) are below:

Myth #1: Every company should digitally transform. **Reality:** Not every company, process, or business model requires digital transformation.

Myth #2: Digital transformation leverages emerging or disruptive technologies. **Reality:** Most short-term transformational impact comes from "conventional" operational and strategic technology - not from emerging or so-called "disruptive" technology.

Myth #3: Profitable companies are the most likely to launch successful digital transformation projects. **Reality:** If things are going well - defined crassly as employee and shareholder wealth creation - then the chances of transforming anything meaningful are quite low.

Myth #4: We need to disrupt our industry before someone else does. **Reality:** Disruptive transformation seldom begins with market leaders whose business models have defined their industry categories for years.

Myth #5: Executives are hungry for digital transformation. **Reality:** The number of executives who really want to transform their companies is relatively small, especially in public companies.

Successful digital transformation requires an organisation to have an embedded digital culture. As organisations advance from pilot digital transformation programs to wide scale adoption, they often run into unexpected obstacle: culture clash, laments Hemerling et al. (2018). According to the authors of the article "Its Not a Digital Transformation without Digital Culture", being a digital organisation means not only having digital products, services, and customer interactions but also powering core operations with technology. Becoming one, therefore, requires a tectonic change in the activities employees perform as well as in their individual behaviours and the ways they interact with others inside and outside the organisation. Leaders need to acknowledge digital transformation as the fundamental, strategic paradigm shift that it is. Like any major transformation, a digital transformation requires instilling a culture that supports the change while enabling the organisations overarching strategies.

According to Rončević, Golub, and Pluščec (2019), digital transformation involves changing and transforming the business model and adapting the company to market changes using different digital technologies. For companies to survive in the market and become competitive, it is necessary to adapt to the process of digital transformation that can be viewed as a change in all aspects of human life caused by digital technology. Nowadays, in the context of digital transformation, we can talk about the application of robots, artificial intelligence, 3D printing, drones, or so-called "industry 4.0". The concept of Industry 4.0 requires digital transformation and networking of all functions inside and outside of the factory, where robots are used instead of workers in production lines. The development of robotization comes in all spheres of human life and is increasingly paying attention to their development, research and appliance. Robotization has an increasing impact on employment, so accordingly there is a need for new jobs, while today's professions go to oblivion. Robots use sensory and control systems and artificial intelligence that leads them to independence in decision-making and work.

THE IMPACT OF DIGITAL TRANSFORMATIONS ON SECURITY POLICIES

The best practices of security policies and standards are prescribed in Chapter 3: Policies, Standards, Guidelines, and Procedures of the CISSP Security Management and Practices Training Guide. According to the Training Guide, part of information security management is determining how security will be maintained in the organization. Management defines information security policies to describe how the organization wants to protect its information assets. After policies are outlined, standards are defined to set the mandatory rules that will be used to implement the policies. Some policies can have multiple guidelines, which are recommendations as to how the policies can be implemented. Finally, information security management, administrators, and engineers create procedures from the standards and guidelines that follow the policies.

Information security policies are high-level plans that describe the goals of the procedures. Policies are not guidelines or standards, nor are they procedures or controls. Policies describe security in general terms, not specifics. They provide the blueprints for an overall security program. When creating policies for an established organization, there is an existing process for maintaining the security of the assets. These policies are used as drivers for the policies. For other policies in which there are no technology drivers, standards can be used to establish the analysts' mandatory mechanisms for implementing the policy (Bragg, 2002). Regardless of how the standards are established, by setting standards, policies that are difficult to implement or that affect the entire organization are guaranteed to work in your environment. Even for small organizations, if the access policies require one-time-use passwords, the standard for using a particular token device can make interoperability a relative certainty.

It is not surprising that leading cyber security analysts and digital transformations executives think that digital transformation and cybersecurity are inextricably intertwined. As Forrester Research (2018) writes, "As businesses become more digitized and interconnected, the impact cyberattacks have on brand value, customer trust, and physical safety increases." The cyber security analyst views were validated by a 2018 survey of 300 security leaders commissioned by networking vendor Fortinet. Their survey found 92% of Chief Information Security Officers said Digital

Transformation has a large impact on business and 85% said that security is the biggest challenge to Digital Transformation efforts.

An article written online by the Finjan Team (2019), states the following: "with the growth of applications, big data, artificial intelligence, multi-cloud, etc., so too have the opportunities for hackers, attackers and other bad actors to do bad things. The breadth of attacks vectors – the attack surface as it is called – has increased substantially with the growth of digital transformation making it more difficult to provide countermeasures. The increased attack surface means that hackers can infiltrate an organization's environment, move horizontally or laterally through it, or linger for months watching and waiting until the optimum time to strike. The latter example, known as an Advanced Persistent Threat (APT), is particularly difficult to detect and mitigate".

ABOUT THIS BOOK

This edited book addresses the required policies, standards and mechanisms for security in transforming the world towards being a digitally secured one. The aim is to utilize the information from this book, educate the society for improving their quality of life for all its citizens, disseminating knowledge, strengthening social cohesion, generating earnings and finally ensuring that organizations and public bodies remain competitive in the global electronic marketplace. Un-fortunately, such a rapid technological evolution cannot be problem-free.

Concerns are raised regarding the lack of trust in electronic procedures and the extent to which information security and user privacy can be ensured. This book is going to deal with security policies, standards and mechanisms in shaping the digital world. The intention is that the knowledge gained from this book will result in new business applications such as smart contracts, sharing economy, crowd funding, governance, supply chain auditing, file storage, e-hospitals, smart cities, protection of intellectual properties, identity management, anti-money laundering, data management, land title registrations and stock trading.

At the moment, there are very few books which have specifically focused on the required policies, standards and mechanisms for security in transforming the world towards digitally secure. This book will summarize the policies, standards and mechanisms for security in all sort of digital applications. Besides, this book will also focus on the blockchain and its imminent impact on financial services in enabling smart governments along with bitcoin and the future of digital payments. This will help practitioners to manage their works in smart way. In addition, the book will also summarize the recent research developments in the area of blockchain applications and other technologies which are helpful in shaping a digital world.

The primary objective of this book is to enable researchers and practitioner to understand the current research topics, challenges and future directions regarding digital technology and security mechanisms from the technical, management and organisational perspective.

Graduate students, academics, researchers and practitioners in the industry will also find this book quite useful. The other objective of this book is to be a primary source for students, academics, researchers and practitioners to reference the evolving theory and practice related to digital transformation and security policies and standards. It aims to provide a comprehensive coverage and understanding in the management, organisation, technological, and business use. The book intends to provide opportunities for investigation, discussion, dissemination and exchange of ideas in relation to digital transformation and security policies and standards internationally across the widest spectrum of scholarly and practitioner opinions to promote theoretical, empirical and comparative research on problems confronting all the stakeholders.

Organization of the Book

The book is organized into 11 chapters. A brief description of each of the chapters follows:

Chapter 1: Digital Transformation and Its Effects on Various Sectors – Indian Perspective

This chapter focusses on digital transformation in India. It is a known fact that the technology drives the nation. Day by day more and more disruptive technologies emerge which enable a nation to strive for massive growth in its GDP. The digital India is a high priority programme from the Indian government in order to make India a digitally literate nation. This project mainly provides the services offered by the government to common public through electronic means. This is done by enhancing the operational setup of the existing services. The digitalization of many aspects in India make it a better contender to become a global leader by creating digital empowerment in technology with cumulative internet connectivity. The present paper identifies some of the core areas where the concept of digitalization enhances its operational processes. The changes reflected in each individual sector by adopting digital transformation is discussed in detail.

Chapter 2: A Case Study on Data Vulnerabilities in Software Development Lifecycle Model

This chapter looks at data vulnerabilities in the software development life cycle. Moreover, software security has become a very critical part of our lives. A software developer who has a fundamental understanding of software security can have an advantage in the workplace. To address the common data vulnerabilities in web application development. The massive Equifax breach that occurred in 2017 that exposed data of roughly 140 million people. Attackers exploited a vulnerability in Apache Struts which is CVE-2017-5638, which allows remote attackers to execute arbitrary commands when specially crafting user-controlled data in HTTP headers. Sensitive data exposure issues are essential to know so that you can help protect your customer's data. It is fascinating to understand how attackers can exploit application vulnerabilities to perform malicious activities. We also want the reader to know that we should always be thinking about how our applications handle user-controlled data. So that we can put guards in place to minimize security issues in the development of new applications.

Chapter 3: Digital Transformation of Diplomacy – The Way Forward for Small Island States

This chapter seeks to examine the digital transformation (digitalisation) of diplomacy and how such digital transformations can be used, to positively influence and improve a country's foreign services. The chapter further explores how the country's diplomats and their Foreign Service counterparts at Ministry of Foreign Affairs (MFA) can utilize the tools provided by digitalisation to advance the country's interests. Given the critical intelligence data, diplomatic protocols, and confidential information exchanged at the diplomatic level between countries, it is equally important to evaluate and assess the cyber security measures that are being taken to secure the digital network of the diplomatic missions. Scholarly research was initially conducted to position the field of research amongst pertinent literature to ascertain the use of digital tools in diplomacy and present key deliberations that exist.

Chapter 4: Information Security Policies and Procedures Guidance for Agencies

This chapter examines information security policies and procedures for agencies. In today's digital e-commerce and m-commerce world, the information itself acts as an asset exists in the form of hardware, software, procedure or a person. So the security of these information systems and management is a big challenging issue from small to large scale agencies. So, this chapter discusses the major role and responsibility of the organization's management in identifying the need for information security policy in today's world of changing security principles and controls. It focuses on various policy types suitable for all kinds of security models and procedures also with the background details such as security policy making, functionality and its impact on an agency culture. Information security policies are helpful to identify and assess risk levels with the available set of technological security tools also describe the management strategies to write a good policy and selection of the right policy public announcement. The agencies must also ensure that the designed policies are properly implemented and ensure compliance by owing to frequent intermediate revisions.

Chapter 5: Cryptography Security Services – Network Security, Attacks, and Mechanisms

This chapter gives an overview about need of computer security and different types of network securities. Different types of attacks like active and passive are discussed that can harm your system resources. This chapter also provides basics of cryptography system and basic terms used in cryptography. Security services provided by cryptography are also discussed such as data integrity, privacy/confidentiality, user authentication, message authentication, authorization, digital signatures, validation, access control, and non-repudiation along with their mechanisms.

Chapter 6: Analysing Ethical Issues of a Patient Information Systems Using the PAPA Model

This chapter observes at the digital transformations in healthcare. Healthcare is a vital portion of today's medical environment and it is commanding for medical providers to do their work in an efficient and effective manner. Everyday hundreds of thousands of patients visit medical amenities stimulating the administration to run smoothly. Almost all hospitals and the health centres in Fiji are now heavily dependent on Patient Information System (PATISPlus) which help the employees to manage all the medical and administrative information. (HIS: 2013). In this chapter, the authors analyse the ethical issues of a Patient Information Systems (PATIS) using the PAPA model, this is in terms of privacy, accessibility, accuracy and property. This is to find out and review of current policies within the Ministry of Health and Medical Services in Fiji and also if a need of development of standard operating procedures in view of the PAPA model.

Chapter 7: Blockchain Technology and Its Applications

This chapter is about the blockchain technology and its applications. Like other new generation information technologies such as IOT, Big Data, AI and Cloud etc., Cryptocurrency and Blockchain became the buzz words in both industry and academia due to their advantageous features. With the features like decentralization, transparency, immutability etc., the blockchain technology became more famous and is emerging into almost all the fields like Banking, Education, Healthcare, Government, Real estate etc. Blockchain technology was introduced in the year 1991, though it was introduced long back it came into existence after this technology was created for bitcoin, a digital cryptocurrency by Santoshi Nakamoto in the year 2008. Since then the block chain is evolving rapidly. Though the blockchain usage is in high demand in all the sectors and it has received attention from many international organizations, most of the people are in lagging to know about these buzz words (Blockchain technology, Cryptocurrency) and how exactly they work. This chapter explores more in detail about, "what is Blockchain technology?", "How it works?", and its applications.

Chapter 8: Consequent Formation in Security With Blockchain in Digital Transformation

Consequent Formation in Security with Blockchain in Digital Transformation is the focus of this chapter. Blockchain technology makes use of a centralized, peer-to-peer (P2P) network of databases, also called nodes, to validate and record digital transactions between individual users located anywhere across the globe. These transactions often take place through the exchange of cryptocurrencies such as bitcoins, Ethereum, and ripple, etc. The security and transparency that is in inherently present in digital transactions place blockchain technology in high demand across various industrial applications. Each node updates its database in real-time as and when transactions occur. The transaction gets authorized only when most of the nodes in the network validate the transaction. Once the verification is complete, a block, consisting of hash and keys, is generated for each new transaction and is linked to previous transactions in every database. Every node updates its database with the new block. A hacker would have to break down every node in the system to commit fraud. Blockchain could play a major role in maintaining the cyber security of digital transactions in the future.

Chapter 9: Network Security Evaluation and Threat Assessments in Enterprise Systems

This chapter examines the threats posed by digital transformation of enterprise systems. Companies have realized the need to have the competitive edge over their rivals. Enterprise systems provide this competitive edge. But with implementing Enterprise System Software (ESS), companies have to invest in the networking of their various business offices to interconnect to ESS. This paper investigates the various ways two companies in Fiji does this and the various disadvantages they face from lack of knowledge of ESS to infrastructure limitations and issues faced in a developing country like Fiji. This paper focuses on the network security issues of Enterprise systems deployed in two companies in Fiji. It compares the information gathered to published papers namely on network infrastructure, network security issues and threat assessments. It also proposes solutions to mitigate the security issues faced by Enterprise Systems networks.

Chapter 10: Intellectual Property Rights Protection in Cyberspace – An Indian Perspective

This chapter deals with issues faced with digital transformations in regard to intellectual property rights. Development and advancement in information technologies have paved path for many challenges for the intellectual property rights holders. There are several forms of cybercrimes as pornography, stalking, cyber fraud, cyber terrorism etc. which are affecting people, hurdling e- commerce, challenging law and disturbing the channel of information and communication. No doubt that cybercrimes are offences where computer is the means of the commission of the offence as well as target of the offence. Apparently, such offences are generated through electronic means where mens rea has no role to play with. This unruly horse is creating several problems in the world of Intellectual Property which has capacity to affect global commerce. This chapter will focus on Indian case laws to showcase the interface between IPR and Cyberspace. Also, the dealing of issues like cyber-squatting, cyberbullying, cyber theft will be discussed in order to check the competency of IPR.

Chapter 11: Efficient and Secure Data Access Control in Cloud Environment

This chapter is about the efficient and secure data access control in the cloud environment. Cloud computing is a highly demanding zone in the present IT enterprise. The key characteristics are adaptability, productivity, pay-per-utilize and cost viability. Access control and information security are the significant issues in cloud computing. Various access control strategies are present. The major problem of storing data in expandable access control and access rights from users are not used in this scheme. This paper presents a generic survey on scalable and secure access control systems and schemes in cloud computing with a key focus on cloud security. Research gaps in the existing literature on cloud security are presented.

ACKNOWLEDGMENT

I would like to especially acknowledge my Fellow Editors (Dr. Bharath Bhushan and Ms. Vaishali Thakare) for all the hard work they did in managing the chapters of the book. Without them, this book would not have gone to publication. We are proud to present the book on the *Impact of Digital Transformations on Security Policies and Standards*. We would like to thank all the reviewers that peer reviewed all the chapters in this book. We also would like to thank the admin and editorial support staff of IGI Global Publishers that have ably supported us in getting this issue to press and publication. And finally, we would like to humbly thank all the authors that submitted their chapters to this book. Without your submission, your tireless efforts and contribution, we would not have this book.

For any new book, it takes a lot of time and effort in getting the Editorial Team together. Everyone on the Editorial Team, including the Editor-in-Chief is a volunteer and holds an honorary position. No one is paid. Getting people with expertise and specialist knowledge to volunteer is difficult, especially when they have their full-time jobs. Next was selecting the right people with appropriate skills and specialist expertise in different areas of digital transformation, security policies and standards to be part of the Review Team.

Every book and publisher has its own chapter acceptance, review and publishing process. IGI Global uses an online editorial system for chapter submissions. Authors are able to submit their chapters directly through the e-Editorial Discovery system. The Editor-in-Chief then does his own review and selects reviewers based on their area of expertise and the research topic of the article. After one round of peer review by more than three reviewers, a number of revisions and reviews, a chapter and subsequently all the chapters are ready to be typeset and published.

I hope everyone will enjoy reading the chapters in this book. I hope it will inspire and encourage readers to start their own research on digital transformations. Once again, I congratulate everyone involved in the writing, review, editorial and publication of this book.

Sam Goundar
The University of the South Pacific, Fiji

REFERENCES

Andriole, S. J. (2017). Five myths about digital transformation. *MIT Sloan Management Review*, 58(3).

Bragg, R. (2002). *Policies, Standards, Guidelines, and Procedures*. CISSP Security Management and Practices Training Guide.

Finjan Team. (2019). What is Digital Transformations Impact on Cyber Security? *Finjan Cybersecurity – Finjan Blog*. https://blog.finjan.com/what-is-digital-transformations-impact-on-cybersecurity/

Hemerling, J., Kilmann, J., Danoesastro, M., Stutts, L., & Ahern, C. (2018). *It's not a digital transformation without a digital culture*. Boston Consulting Group.

Negreiro, M., Madiega, T. (2019). *Digital Transformations. Briefing – EU Policies – Delivering for Citizens*. European Parliament Research Services. Members' Research Service PE 633.171.

Rončević, A., Golub, M., & Pluščec, M. (2019). The Effects of Digital Transformations and the Impact on Employment in Europe and in the Republic of Croatia. *Journal of Economic and Social Development*, 6(2), 41–50.

Chapter 1
Digital Transformation and Its Effects on Various Sectors:
Indian Perspective

Hima Bindu P.
Sri Krishnadevaraya University, India

John Samuel K.
Srinivasa Ramanujan Institute of Technology, India

Bhaskar Reddy T.
Sri Krishnadevaraya University, India

ABSTRACT

It is a known fact that technology drives the nation. Day by day more disruptive technologies emerge that enable a nation to strive for massive growth in its GDP. The digital India is a high priority programme from the Indian government in order to make India a digitally literate nation. This project mainly provides the services offered by the government to common public through electronic means. This is done by enhancing the operational setup of the existing services. The digitalization of many aspects in India make it a better contender to become a global leader by creating digital empowerment in technology with cumulative internet connectivity. The chapter identifies some of the core areas where the concept of digitalization enhances its operational processes. The changes reflected in each individual sector by adopting digital transformation are discussed in detail.

DOI: 10.4018/978-1-7998-2367-4.ch001

INTRODUCTION

Digitization, digitalization and the digital transformation are the buzz words that are trending in the entire world. One has to know the difference between these three words. The term digitization refers to the process of converting an analog value into a digital value. It can also be stated as the use of digital form in filling up the information of an individual for ordering a product, the use of digital surveys, the usage of digital applications for financial declarations. The word digitalization means the usage of digital means for various sources by an individual, industry or an organization. Information technology sector serves as the key for new business possibilities in place of the traditional business methods. The process of digitalization mainly uses the help of digital technologies which increase customer satisfaction, enhance the customer experiences and increases the cost-saving. Now comes the word digital transformation, it means that creating new strategies which adjust itself for changing demands. It mainly makes use of internet for many things such as selling, manufacturing, marketing, designing etc. Digital transformation necessarily need not be assumed as technological advancement. It doesn't mean just reinventing the software and hardware models. In other words the term digital transformation means the reorganization of the technologies, its process and the business models. This enables a new value for the consumers or customers in steadily changing and growing digital economy. The rate of change in the digital transformation depends mainly on customer needs and demands.

Digital transformation helps in manufacturing industry to reduce the time from raw material to the manufacturing the product, shortens the time for a product to enter into the market, reduces the cost of the product, thereby increasing the productivity of the industry. The traditional business models seems to extinguish and they are substituted with the business models which are flexible, which give real-time response to the customers and which can change instantly according to the demand. Now the present business world runs on Industry 4.0. The main criteria the 4.0 has are the optimum usage of the human resources, produce huge profits with less cost of energy and infrastructure etc. one of the best digital transformation examples can be the solar-powered cars. The general concept of solar cells are implemented on the rooftop of the vehicles which harvest energy from sun and charges the batteries which intern drive the motor. This makes the vehicle to move from the position of rest. The present paper discusses more on the effects of digital transformation on various sectors in Indian perspective.

In these modern days, various companies in different sectors have started initiative activities to search advanced digital technologies as well as to utilize the outcomes. Digital transformation strategies are broadly of two types such as operational and functional where products, markets, processes are operational strategies finance, human resources, and information technologies are functional strategies Digital transformation is in demand to stay connected with the present internet age where many services are delivered both in online and offline mode (Matt, et al. 2015). The digitalization of work related to photo and video technology, wearable sensors and eye-tracking are some notable mentions where different organizations collect the data from these to use it in different ways (Brynjolfsson, 2014). Digital technologies have transformed various organizations and these organizations struggle to cope up with these and the rise of new segments, increase in level of customer satisfaction has made it a transient one. Henriette et al. (2015) conducted a systematic literature review to discuss the opportunities and the vulnerabilities the digital transformation creates. It is concluded that many other things are to be considered before employing digital strategies because enforcing it may cause unexpected outcomes on the organization.

NEED FOR DIGITAL TRANSFORMATION

It is evident to all that India is one of the major economies in the world today. When compared with other major economies India is one or two steps backwards in using these digital means of business. Even though it started late at present the increase in adopting digital technologies is increasing at a rapid rate.

Figure 1 shows the digital trend and its impact in India by the year 2021. One can understand from the figure that there will be a substantialconsiderable growth

Figure 1. Hyper digital growth in India (Arora, 2017)

Hyper Digital Growth in India

Digital Trends	Traffic by 2021	Impact
Rapid adoption of mobility	829 million users	Second largest internet
Growth in social media	2 billion connections	Smart Cities
More citizen services	46 GB average household traffic/month	Increasing number of global startups
Younger workforce		20% of transactions online
Growth in entertainment	Broadband speeds: 18.2 mbps	Digital classrooms
Rapid innovation		Remote healthcare
Broadband in every home	83% traffic is for video viewing	

in the digital technologies and the impact it has on our business and social lives will be huge. Since many digital trends are already in action like smartphones, cloud computing, internet of things, crypto-currencies, speech recognition and many others, they are showing tremendous impact on the society as well as on the business. The best example is the rise of e-commerce. Nowadays, the rate of purchase done by the customer through e-commerce is very high. It is estimated that worldwide e-retail sales will go up to $4.88 trillion when compared with the value of $2.3 trillion which was in the year 2017 (Statista, 2019). Figure 2 shows expected India's digital economy growth by the year 2025. Also, the image shows the expected digital economy from each sector in India by the year 2025. So, with this example one can easily understand that India should be digital transformed so that it can be a global leader.

Figure 2. India's digital transformation statistics by the year 2025 (Kaka et al., 2019)

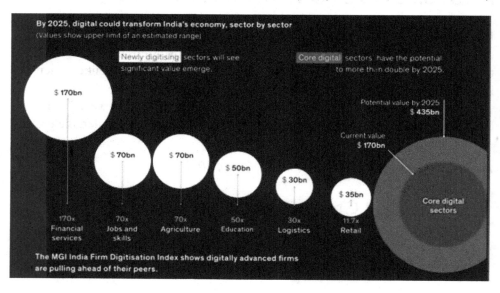

DIGITAL TRANSFORMATION IN DIFFERENT SECTORS

India is one of the developing countries through the destructive step of economic growth towards innovation through crucial sectors, with inspiring government strategies and hostile development in IT.

Agriculture

The complete process from sowing a seed to its yield is ended without the human intervention (by the machine itself) and termed as smart farming. Above 40 per cent of its population in India are workings in agriculture, where it contributes 18 percentage of its countries Gross Domestic Product. Indian agriculturalists (Ulas, 2019) have a scarcity of machines and little information on soil condition, weather conditions, and further variables. From the Government's Online Farmer Advisory Portal, approximately 50 per cent of agriculturalists' enquiries are associated with weather-related information. In 2013, due to poor logistics and warehousing, about $15 billion value of agricultural products are wasted. Nowadays, digital technologies such as Internet, mobile technologies, as well as policies, data analytics, AI, digitally distributed services and apps are altering agriculture. These technologies are transforming India's agriculture environment in numerous ways. With the shortage of written proofs of financial account, every former is often stopped from retrieving banks on the way to assist their fiscal requirements. This problem is cracked by generating certifiable transaction accounts, containing electronic acceptance of unindustrialized supports through digital bank accounts. By these facilities farmer finds financial assistance for buying seeds, manure, as well as insecticides for harvesting or for the upcoming seasons or else formers themselves, participate in digital technologies required for digital agriculture. The essential variables affecting Indian agriculture consist of climate limitations, rainy season, irrigation designs, earth nourishment, administration strategy in national as well as central, product expenses in international as well as Indian and consumption patterns.

Online bank accounts can offer the wages and expenditure documents that farmers must maintain the requirements for economical credit from banks. Crop insurances are available to more number of formers with digital land registry records. Formers can utilize various online markets for transactions on agricultural products and attain further advanced technologies. One of the platform, named government's electronic National Agriculture Market, or eNAM, is accessible in 585 locations. By merging digital technologies, food production improved with progress in population and increments from $50 billion to $65 billion of providence value in 2025. Finally, usage of digital equipment for the agricultural procedure (OECD, 2019), remains comprehensible with the digitalization of agriculture.

Healthcare

In India, particularly in rural areas and poor states healthcare system is exclusive expensive and spends a very low-portion on healthcare sector from its GDP. Globally India stands at 125th rank and has an urban-rural divide. India expends 4.2 percent

Figure 3. Schematic showing the process of digital agriculture (Kaka et al., 2019)

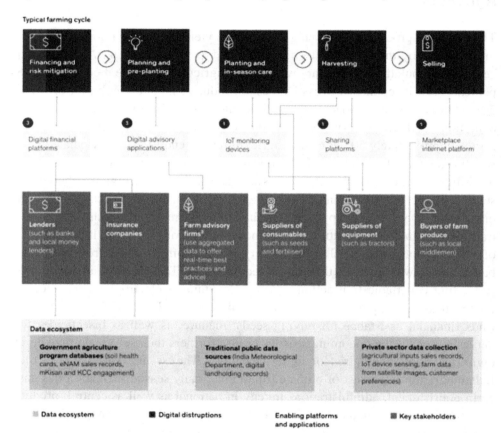

of its GDP on healthcare sector and 3.9 percent in the year 2015 while China spends 4.5 percent of its GDP to 5.3 percent. Every year, India expends $63 per capita on healthcare sector while China with $426 per capita. The availability of doctors and nurses and even midwives are particularly desperate in rural areas. India requires increasing 6.5 million healthcare professionals to reach the global benchmark for the proportion of medical doctors to patients. Cost is a constraint for patient access to care. In 2017, only 34 percent of Indians had health insurance.

Digital technologies in healthcare provide assistance in supplying on demands by filling the scarcity of healthcare professionals up to 15 percent and enhances excellence and confidence. As a result, more patients are interested in telemedicine (Parimbelli et. al, 2018) systems to recover and controllability by their own. The implementations of these systems enhance the quality of services and fill the gap of doctor's shortage. Telemedicine reduces consultations about 30 percent lesser than with person consultation. By digitizing the patient records regarding health profile, the accessibility of patient history is readymade thus improves the patient care as well as reduces time of waiting for doctor. Therefore, digitization needs improved versions of management approaches to attain value. At present digital platforms, permit patients to compare various doctors' assessments in online depending upon the physical training and responses of multiple patients.

Retail

In India, 80 percent of retailers have their own proprietorships and work in generic providence. With these type of businesses, they do not have essential records required for bank loans. Thus, potential growth and productivity with tools are limited. Digital solutions can rearrange these situations such as E-commerce, which enables retailers for enlargement. Retailers who search for fast growth in E-commerce, there is no all-time strategy to follow but the approach changes depending on each retailers scope, scales, locality and product-line. Digital technologies made purchasing and retailing process in an extreme availability range with the increasing usage of mobile phones and implementation of government policies Digital Applications which India provides are financing, digital marketing, stock inventory control, buying and selling operations through E-commerce, digital-payments. These applications made India's retailing production into a streamline. Minor merchants utilize online services and platforms to measure their business activities in low scales. Small merchants do not utilize advanced e-commerce services whereas major merchants use these services called third-party platforms to work for its consumers with highly responsive websites. Croma (Ulas, 2019) one of the major merchant, practices e-commerce platforms as an addition to its own website along with physical equipment.

Logistics

In India, the logistics sector is experiencing an extraordinary revolution, activated by inventions in IT and digitization. In spite of this, the Indian logistics sector, treated as the pillar of a healthy budget even though it is disjointed as well as disorganized. India spends 14-15 percent of its GDP and mainly focuses on manufacturing. For the year 2020, logistics market in India will grow up to USD 307 billion depending upon the study by ACCII (Associated Chambers of Commerce and Industry of India) (Kauf, 2019). Characteristics of digitization in logistics are described below. Collaboration through digitization prospective, logistics trade has enhanced in efficiency as well as reliability. This generates superior requirements for inter-organizational data interchange and information mixing and design for maintaining computer-generated logistics collections. The virtual service providers collect numerous enterprises that permit involvement for the accessibility of logistics services. A classic digital operational model deals with implementation of digital abilities such as authority, procedures, information and presentation administration, and information technology. Connectivity is one of the characteristic that acts a mediator between digital resources and network of systems for connecting one another. Digitization is a flexible and open system where the components and their attributes change every time and influences through events of a system. Integration refers to the capacity of a system to link, incorporate, monetize and part of a device in the digital economy. In information technology, logistics systems incorporation is the procedure of connecting organized systems and software applications substantially.

Figure 4. Digital Logistics environment (Kayikci, 2018)

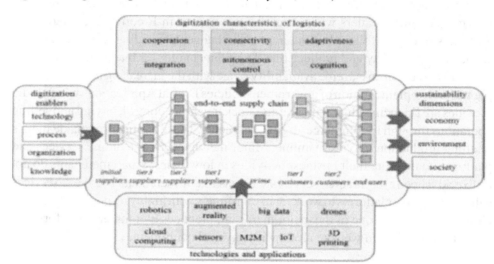

FACTORS ACCELERATING DIGITAL TRANSFORMATION

Revolution of Technology and Transformation

Innovation is a vital element in the improvement of financial resources. Providence of countries enhancement depends upon technology accomplishments and transformations. Businesspersons, as well as programmers who work in digital platforms, must rise. Digital technologies permit SMEs to progress in market intelligence and right to use global markets at low-cost.

Modification of Business Applications With Low-Cost Internet, Electronic Trade And Collective Broadcasting

The Internet provides a platform for millions of daily online businesses and public services that make an essential contribution to individual financial prudence.

Globalization

It is a term that defines the emerging interdependence of the global economy, values, and inhabitants. It is a process where people, companies and various national governments are interacted and integrated. Another aspect of globalization is traditional globalization. With the enlargement of digital technologies (Hart, 2010) in traditional globalization, creates stores and distributes several traditional items digitally. Digital compression technologies are used for distributing music symbols, pictures and words with low-cost.

Artificial Intelligence

AI has immense potential to enhance human life. It reduces the involvement of humans in high-risk areas such as defence. AI technologies can be applied in various sectors to solve the various problems resides in our country such as education, healthcare, Defense and transport. Artificial Intelligence generates healthcare systems more dynamic. Various examples of AI applications in the healthcare industry are existed for making the digitization process faster with fast outcomes. As India has great capacity it can stand at the top of developed nations with AI revolution. Ethics and Morality are working to form the backbone of humanity, which takes AI as a reliable servant, and suitable for mastering humanity.

Internet of Things (IoT)

India is not far from its journey towards the digital future. In the year 2017, four percent of India's GDP was credited to the direct consumption of digital technologies such as mobility, cloud, Internet of Things (IoT), and artificial intelligence (AI). This enhances the digital transformation in several companies. IoT is a simple network which interconnects things and which are embedded with specific devices like sensors, network connectivity, software and some electronics which are meant to perform a definite action as per the requirement. The sensors sense the change in a physical quantity and the data is interpreted to the cloud and the software processes it and the then it decides to perform a particular task.

Blockchain

The Digital India Blockchain Conference 2019 is an industry-focused event, done in Bangalore on 11 May 2019, which connected various industry leaders, business decision-makers, tech innovators and investors. Here highlighted the leading developments in blockchain in India. Blockchain technology is deliberately affecting conventional implementation in India. With respect to this, it's a future view where it moves into public dictionary and adopts to several sectors such as financial services companies, healthcare supply, expenditures, insurance, supply chain and additional sectors, as well as state-owned and central governments.

Cloud Computing

Improved implementation of cloud might support India to deliver on-demand, smarter-citizen centric facilities, besides renovating the nation into a hothouse of modernization. As the nation struggles to speed up its digital transformation journey, cloud is evolving as an acute structure nationwide similar to H2O, power, gas, roads and transport systems. Data-driven facilities are attractive as an ultimate and existential to the world and industries. Hybrid-cloud platforms are developing to be dynamic intentional drivers for improving modernization, effectiveness and production.

CONCLUSION

The basic idea behind the digital transformation is to redesign the organizational structure of a business by implementing digital technologies. This will make the business to achieve various benefits like productivity enhancement, innovation and the reduced cost of the product. In the present paper a comprehensive review is done to understand the impact of digitalization on different sectors in India. It is clearly evident that the concept of digitalization which brings digital transformation is a future research trend. This topic will be very much essential for upcoming generations for a better and comfortable living. The development of better digital technologies will boost the digital transformation in the country. Talking the benefits of digital transformation is the one side of it but, the challenges that have to be faced and the specific demands of digital transformation are to be addressed. Digital transformation is more of a continuous process which requires adjustments in its existing processes, products and its services to meet the needs of the society. Finally it can be concluded that more areas in India are to be digitally transformed and an in-depth study of various digitalization processes are to be clearly understood and a better and effective method should be proposed. This leads to a better society and a better world where things will be cheaper and more effective.

REFERENCES

Arora, S. (2017). *Digital India: Driving the Next Wave of Innovation*. Retrieved from https://snmpcenter.com/digital-india/

Brynjolfsson, A. (2014). *McAfee, The Second Machine Age: Work Progress, and Prosperity in a Time of Brilliant Technologies*. New York: W.W. Norton & Company.

Hart, J. (2010). *Globalization and Digitalization*. Academic Press.

Henriette, E., Feki, M., & Boughzala, I. (2015). The shape of digital transformation: a systematic literature review. *MCIS 2015 Proceedings*, 431-443.

Kaka, N., Madgavkar, A., Kshirsagar, A., Gupta, R., Manyika, J., Bahl, K., & Gupta, S. (2019). *McKinsey Global Institute, Digital India: Technology to transform a connected nation*. Retrieved from https://www.mckinsey.com/business-functions/mckinsey-digital/our-insights/digital-india-technology-to-transform-a-connected-nation

Kauf, S. (2019). Smart logistics as a basis for the development of the smart city. *Transportation Research Procedia*, *39*, 143–149. doi:10.1016/j.trpro.2019.06.016

Kayikci, Y. (2018). Sustainability impact of digitization in logistics. Procedia manufacturing, 21, 782-789.Impact of digitization in logistics. *Procedia Manufacturing*, *21*, 782–789. doi:10.1016/j.promfg.2018.02.184

Matt, C., Hess, T., & Benlian, A. (2015). Digital transformation strategies. *Business & Information Systems Engineering*, *57*(5), 339–343. doi:10.100712599-015-0401-5

OECD. (2019). *Digital Opportunities for Better Agricultural Policies*. Paris: OECD Publishing; doi:10.1787/571a0812-

Parimbelli, E., Bottalico, B., Losiouk, E., Tomasi, M., Santosuosso, A., Lanzola, G., & Bellazzi, R. (2018). Trusting telemedicine: A discussion on risks, safety, legal implications and liability of involved stakeholders. *International Journal of Medical Informatics*, *112*, 90–98. doi:10.1016/j.ijmedinf.2018.01.012 PMID:29500027

Statista. (2019). *Retail e-commerce sales worldwide from 2014 to 2021 (in billion U.S. dollars)*. Retrieved from https://www.statista.com/statistics/379046/worldwide-retail-e-commerce-sales

Ulas, D. (2019). Digital Transformation Process and SMEs. *Procedia Computer Science*, 158, 662-671.Process and SMEs. *Procedia Computer Science*, *158*, 662–671. doi:10.1016/j.procs.2019.09.101

Chapter 2
A Case Study on Data Vulnerabilities in Software Development Lifecycle Model

Syed Muzamil Basha
https://orcid.org/0000-0002-1169-3151
Sri Krishna College of Engineering and Technology, India

Ravi Kumar Poluru
https://orcid.org/0000-0001-8591-5266
Vellore Institute of Technology, India

J. Janet
Sri Krishna College of Engineering and Technology, India

S. Balakrishnan
https://orcid.org/0000-0002-6145-7923
Sri Krishna College of Engineering and Technology, India

D. Dharunya Santhosh
Sri Krishna College of Engineering and Technology, India

A. Kousalya
Sri Krishna College of Engineering and Technology, India

ABSTRACT

Software security has become a very critical part of our lives. A software developer who has a fundamental understanding of software security can have an advantage in the workplace. In the massive Equifax breach that occurred in 2017 that exposed data of roughly 140 million people, attackers exploited a vulnerability in Apache Struts, CVE-2017-5638, which allows remote attackers to execute arbitrary commands when specially crafting user-controlled data in HTTP headers. Sensitive data exposure issues are essential to know to protect customer data. It is fascinating to understand how attackers can exploit application vulnerabilities to perform malicious activities. The authors also want the reader to be aware of the fact that we should always be thinking about how our applications handle user-controlled data so that we can put guards in place to minimize security issues in the development of new applications.

DOI: 10.4018/978-1-7998-2367-4.ch002

INTRODUCTION

In developing software, developers, project managers, and other stakeholders go through a process called the system development life cycle. This process starts with the most essential step, requirements gathering. In the requirements gathering step, stakeholders define and agree on what the system needs to do. This is also where security requirements with the help of the stride method, able to analyze the flow of data and assemble the set of assets that must be secured in a given system. According to the National Institute of Standards and Technology (NIST), the system development life cycle is the overall process of developing, implementing,and retiring information systems through a multi-step process from initiation, analysis, design, implementation, maintenance, and disposal. In the beginning, we perform a requirements gathering, and we want to involve security as early as possible in the project.

The goal, in general, is to be able to answer the following:

Q1: What critical assets and services do we need the system to protect (Gunjal, B, 2019) ?

Q2: How should we define user roles?

Q3: What kinds of privileges to they each have?

Q4: What is the attack surface of the system?

During requirements gathering, what are the critical assets and services that need to be protected? Are there any user roles with different privileges? Also, determine where data can be entered or extracted. Next, we want to create a threat model.To do that, we want first to create a data flow diagram. This involves determining our trust boundaries.We use the STRIDE (Sangchoolie et al., 2018) mnemonic to determine a list of possible threats and some vulnerabilities to the system. The STRIDE mnemonic stands for: S - spoofing, T - tampering, R - repudiation, I -information leakage, D - Denial of Service, and E - Elevation of Privilege.

Three objectives of security: confidentiality, integrity, and availability. **Confidentiality** is preserving authorized restrictions on access and disclosure. To meet the objective of confidentiality, encrypt the data as it flows from one system to another. Example, use access control lists to allow only certain users access, to certain types of data (Wang, Y et al., 2018). **Data integrity** is the property that data meet with an expectation of quality and that the data can be relied on. We could meet the objective of integrity using a message authentication code to verify that what we downloaded off the internet was what we expected. An example of that is using the HMac algorithm (McBride, et al., 2018). Last, our third security objective is **availability**. It's because the definition of that is ensuring timely and reliable access to and use of information. An example of the threat to availability is a Distributed denial-of-service (DDoS) attack (Baker & Şimşek, 2018). Then, a flood of requests come at a short time interval, and your system no longer has the ability to keep up with serving those requests.

In this chapter, we made a deep discussion on concepts in threat modeling and cryptography. That helps in creating threat models and think critically about the threat models created by other people. Also, a basic understanding of applied cryptography, such as encryption and secure hashing — discussion on issues with improperly handling user-controlled data. At the very least, it is fascinating to understand how attackers can exploit application vulnerabilities to perform malicious activities. However, on a much more critical level, it helps those of us who work on creating and maintaining application code to protect the users who use our applications. Description on the three most common types of injection problems: SQL injection, Cross-site Scripting, and Command injection.Discussion on issues with application authentication and session management.

METHODOLOGY

Threat modeling is a process with three main goals.

1. To understand the system that is being proposed. Specifically, we want to be able to understand what assets we're trying to protect, how data flows through that system and any trust boundaries that exist.
2. To find potential threats due to those system vulnerabilities that may exist in the proposed system design.
3. To prioritize those vulnerabilities so that we can go ahead and fix the most important ones in a timely manner.
4. To document our security requirements based on the model created Figure .1 is an example of Initial System Design.

From looking at the example system, we can answer the following questions:

Figure 1. Traditional System Model

Q1: what critical assets and services do we need a system to protect?

First, we need to protect financial data that's stored in the database. Next, we want to be able to protect the requests and responses between the clients and server, and the server and the database. We also want to protect the server resources.

Q2: How should we define user roles?

What kinds of privileges do they each have? The initial description is what came out of the stakeholder meeting is described in Table .1.

Table 1. Role and Privileges of Different levels of users

Role	Privileges
Regular User	• Read only from the database
Financial administrator	• Read from and write to database
System administrator	• Modify Server resources • Initiate database backups

Q3: what's the attack surface of the system?

For example, what are the points at which data can be entered or extracted by an unauthorized user? The stakeholders would like customers in external networks to be able to access the server. The initial design calls for the server to allow UI and API access via HTTP. From first glance, the attack surface would be via the UI, via the API, and both over HTTP.

Figure 2. Dataflow in System Model

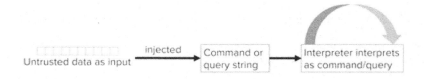

In Figure .2, we can see, the client is making requests to the bank web server. From there, the bank web server sends SQL queries to the bank database. The bank database responds back by sending over data to the bank web server. Then the bank web server processes this data and sends it as a response back to the client. Now that we've answered those general security requirements questions, we can proceed with creating a threat model of the Initial System Design as in Table .2.

The idea of trust boundaries in our threat models as in Figure .3:

Table 2. Description of STRIDE Model

S	Spoofing	A malicious user pretend to be a different user.
T	Tampering	A malicious user modify data used by the system.
R	Repudiation	A malicious user deny that they performed an action to change the system's state.
I	Information Leakage	A malicious user extract information that should be kept secret.
D	Denial of Service	A malicious user exhaust system resources such that the system is no longer functioning as intended.
E	Elevation of privilege	A malicious user increase their ability to work with the system resources.

Figure 3. Data Flow within the nodes of the network

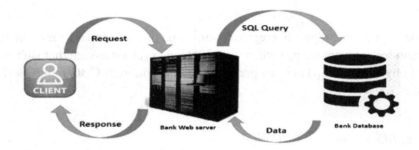

Q1: Do I trust the data moving between the two nodes?
Q2: Is there a different level of trust that I place on either of these two nodes?

The general outline of applied cryptography is introduced with a concept tree that fits all the different ideas together and will help the readers to apply the understandings in terms of applied cryptography. Now, the goal here is to give enough understanding of applied cryptography. This gives the ability to differentiate between kinds of algorithms and know which kind of algorithm to use in a given instance as shown in Figure 4.

Block ciphers are basically an algorithm, meant to take a plaintext message and get out the ciphertext output.So for example, a block cipher (Kondo et al., 2018) of a 128 bits or 256 bits size as shown in Figure .5.

Figure 4. The concept Tree of applied cryptography

Figure 5. organization of Block cipher

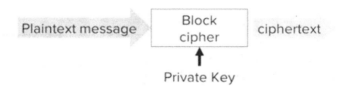

If the original message has a regular pattern and this can leak information. Block cipher modes are what we use when we need to encrypt a message that isn't evenly divisible by block size. Then we perform the encryption in CBC mode as shown in Figure .6.

Figure 6. Block Cipher in CBC Mode

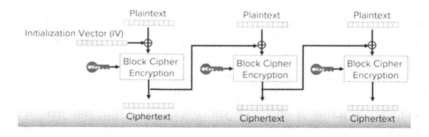

CTR mode requires the use of something called a nonce. A nonce is a number that we use only once, and it adds randomization to the resulting ciphertext. (Ferguson, 2013, pp. 54-79) suggested the encryption algorithm called AES with a 256-bit block size in CBC mode with a random IV.

In symmetric key encryption, both the sender and the receiver have to have the same key. We have the sender and the receiver both using the same private key to either encrypt a message or decrypt a message. An example of this symmetric key algorithm is AES, or also known as advanced encryption standard. The receiver also gives it as input, the same private key that the center has used to encrypt this message. And when the receiver runs this decryption algorithm process, the output is a plaintext message that the sender intended to send the receiver.

Asymmetric cryptography is that concept that leads us to have the ability to agree on a shared secret key. That shared secret key is then used to perform symmetric key encryption. An example of this key exchange protocol is Diffie-Hellman (Smith et al., 2018).Public and private keys are generated using a special algorithm, a key generation algorithm. The relationship between the public and the private key is that there is only one private key to one public key; it's a one to one relationship. Moreover, they use the private to decrypt the message, and the outcome's the plain text message that the sender intended to send to the receiver as shown in Figure .7.

Figure 7. Generation of public and private keys in Encrypting the data

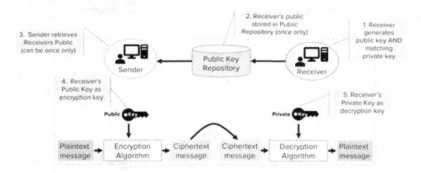

Next, to define hash functions and explain the properties of cryptographic hash functions. Hash functions are used for mapping data to other data, and we can map an arbitrarily long piece of data to data with a fixed size length. Cryptographic hash functions have the following properties.

1. The first property is that the same message always results in the same hash.
2. The next property is that we can't get the message back from a hash unless we try to generate all possible messages.
3. The third property is that two different messages should not result in the same hash value. So, in other words, no hash collision.
4. Another property is that it should be relatively fast.
5. The last property is that if we generate a message and a hash, then modifying that message even just a little bit slightly and then generate another hash from that slightly modified message, we should not see any relationship between the old and the new hash.

Figure 8. Operations of MAC at sender and receiver side

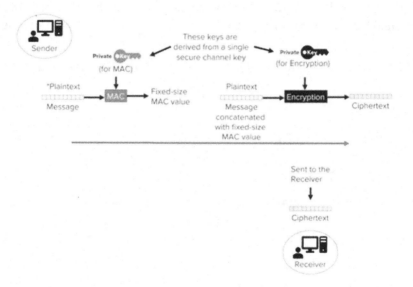

An example of this is the SHA-256 hash function.So, to make a note that the private key for the MAC operation and the private key for the encryption operation, these two keys are derived using an algorithm from a single secure channel key as shown in Figure .8.Now, on the receiver side what they do is they take the ciphertexts that they've received, and they decrypt that ciphertext using the same private key that the sender used and they get as the output the plain text plus the fixed size MAC value. They take this fixed size MAC value, and they put it through as input into a MAC verification algorithm and also as input into the MAC verification algorithm, they give it the private key for the map. The resulting output of that operation is a yes or no question that basically says, "Was it tampered with?

The replay attack is demonstrated as shown in the Figure .9.

Figure 9. Operations of MAC at sender and receiver side

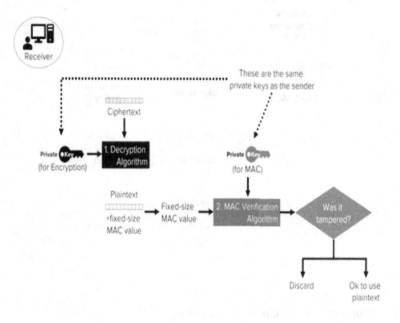

(Shostack, 2014, pp. 102-145) able to explain how cryptography addresses issues with spoofing, tampering, and information disclosure. We will also be able to connect the concepts of cryptographic hash functions, message authentication codes, and encryption to the STRIDE method, and how these cryptography concepts apply to threat models. So one threat that can happen with systems is a man-in-the-middle attack when two or more parties in that system need to authenticate.

ISSUES WITH IMPROPERLY HANDLING USER-CONTROLLED DATA

Discussion on issues with improperly handling user-controlled data. It helps in creating and maintaining application code to protect the users who use our applications. To discuss and describe the three most common types of injection problems, SQL injection, Cross-site scripting, and Command injection. The general idea behind

Figure 10. Working principle of SQL Injection Attack

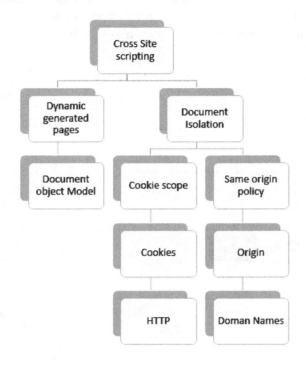

Figure 11. Concept tree on Cross site scripting

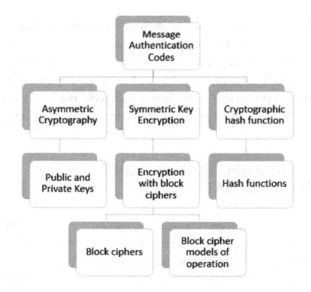

injection attacks is that there are some untrusted data as input that gets added to or embedded into a command or query string as shown in Figure .10.

This string is then sent to an interpreter in this interpreter interprets that string as a commander query. In other words, there is a mismatch between how the developer sees this string coming into the interpreter and how the interpreter sees the string. Specifically, the string being fed into the interpreter is considered by the interpreter as 100% a command or query.

To Identify how HTTP and Document Isolation Play a Role in Cross-site Scripting:

HTTP allows us to be able to view documents on the internet. HTTP is a protocol that sent over another protocol called TCP. HTTP is a way for us to fetch resources (web pages, pictures, scripts) HTTP is a client-server protocol which means that the communication is started on the client-side, HTTP is actually a human-readable protocol. Now it's possible for a JavaScript program which is embedded in that document to read or write cookies related to that document. This is done using the (Document Object Model) DOM.

Another way that document isolation happens or cookie isolation effectively is also something called Origin. Same Origin Policy is a policy that basically isolates JavaScript such that, only the document that has that JavaScript can be accessed by the JavaScript. Origin is something called a tuple, which is a set of three pieces of data. Basically, which are the protocol, the domain, and the port, we can roughly think of the origin in terms of inter-process communication.DOM, which is also known as the Document Object Model and dynamically generating pages. Remember that HTTP is a protocol for fetching resources or documents. In the early days, documents were static. The DOM is a way for us to think about a document as an object. It's a form of an abstraction that allows us to manipulate the document that's fetched from the server. This means that the document has properties and methods like objects have properties and methods in the object-oriented sense of the word. Two important properties that documents have been one its origin into its cookies. This is important to know because it helps us to understand the difference between reflected and stored cross-site scripting versus DOM-based cross-site scripting. The idea here is for an attacker to be able to obtain a session cookie to impersonate a user.

Q1: What about using the Same Origin Policy?
Q2: Why can't Same Origin Policy help us here?

This is because cross-site scripting bypasses Same Origin Policy. The reason why is because the malicious script is in the same document object as the cookie that the attacker wants to steal.In other words, the malicious script is injected into the document object. The document that the vulnerable client is viewing. The tactic that an attacker would take is to use a malicious script and inject that in the document of the vulnerable client. Now, this is the reason why it's important to set the HTTP only cookie header. That's because as we saw before, the HTTP only cookie header says that, the cookie is disallowed to be accessed by JavaScript on the client-side. Cross-site scripting has three different ways. One way could be something called reflected cross-site Scripting. If your web application is vulnerable to reflected cross-site scripting, it means that a malicious script can be injected into a URL parameter, for example. The URL parameter is then used by the server to create the page with the injected script in it then, and right away sent it back to the client. If your web application is vulnerable to sort cross-site scripting, this means that an attacker could inject malicious script, for example, using post-data, and have your vulnerable application store that information in a backend database. Storing this data on a backend database is just taking advantage of normal operations on your web application. When a client wants to fetch a particular document which embeds data from that database. The server generates that document with that injected script, then the client fetches that information and renders it on their browser.

In the third case, if your web application is vulnerable to DOM based cross-site scripting, the way this works is when the DOM environment of the document is modified. Say a URL is used to generate data that modifies the DOM, then you can have malicious data or malicious script injected when that DOM is modified.what reflected cross-site scripting is. Given as example, let say, a malicious user tricks a victim into clicking on the link to vulnerable web application. That link include a malicious script in the link parameter. For example here we see this particular link to a vulnerable application, and the one user input is JavaScript here. This web application is vulnerable to reflected cross-site scripting. And a malicious user says, I want to take advantage of this. And they go in, they encode the script in the URL, and then they get someone, a vulnerable user, to click on this link. For example, through means of phishing. Now this victim then clicks on the link, and the victims client forms a GET request to the vulnerable web application. The vulnerable web application responds back with a document that has the malicious script embedded within it. When the client receives that response from the server, the victim's browser runs that malicious script during the regular rendering of that fetched document.DOM was intended to be manipulated for normal use to make the document more dynamic?

How to Prevent Cross-Site Scripting Vulnerabilities

These prescriptions are given out by OWASP, and they're tried and tested, so these are really good rules to follow. First, we're going to talk about why we would use OWASP (Open Web Application Security Project) so-called positive prevention model, in order to prevent cross-site scripting vulnerabilities in our web applications.

The cross-site scripting rule from OWASP's cross-site scripting rule cheat sheet.

Rule 0: Do not insert untrusted data except in the slots. This is because we want to simplify being to able to prevent cross-site scripting.

1. you should never put untrusted data directly in between script tags.
2. You should never put your untrusted data directly inside an HTML comment.
3. You should never put untrusted data directly into an attribute name.
4. And you should never put untrusted data directly in a tag name.
5. And last, you should never put untrusted data directly in CSS.

Rule 1: use your secure encoding library to HTML escape before inserting untrusted data into HTML element content. **Rule 2:** you want to attribute escape before inserting untrusted data into HTML common attributes. So again, you would use your secure encoding library to encode the untrusted data before you use it as an HTML attribute. **Rule 3:** you want to JavaScript escape before inserting untrusted data into JavaScript data values.

The rules for DOM based cross-site scripting prevention. The first one is a JavaScript Execution Context, and the JavaScript Execution Context is basically a way that the JavaScript runtime uses to track the JavaScript code as it's executing. The JavaScript code is tracked using a call stack. **Rule 1:** HTML escape then JavaScript escape before inserting untrusted data into HTML of your DOM. So before adding an element into the HTML of DOM, first HTML escape then JavaScript escape your untrusted data using your secure encoding library, **Rule 2:** Before modifying an HTML attribute and adding untrusted data there, use your secure library encoder and JavaScript escape that untrusted data. In other words, JavaScript escape before inserting untrusted data into HTML attribute subcontexts within the execution context. **Rule 3:** Avoid including untrusted data within your JavaScript code, because it is difficult to cover all of your edge cases even when you JavaScript encode that untrusted data. **Rule 4:** DOM rule number four. When inserting untrusted data into a CSS attribute, JavaScript escape it using your secure encoding library. Furthermore, you want to URL escape before JavaScript escaping when inserting untrusted data into the URL CSS method. **Rule 5:** Using your secure encoding library, first URL escape and then JavaScript escape the untrusted data before using it in a URL attribute. **Rule 6:** DOM rule number six. You can use the "textContent" property to place untrusted data into the DOM.

Command injection:It happens when a Web application takes some user controlled data and usesthat user controlled data as input into a command. So, it becomes part of a command that is thenpassed on to a shell or an OS command call. A malicious attacker can manipulate the user controlled data to then run their own OS command. Since the OS command calls through the web application is done under the same privileges as a web application process, then the malicious attacker has effectively gain those same privileges. So, for example, if a Web application is vulnerable to a command injection, then through that vulnerability, a malicious attacker can then create a backdoor to eventually perform data exfiltration.

Issues with Application Authentication And Session Management

Authentication is a major component of a secure web application. It ensures that only those users who are properly identified and allowed to use the application are able to access application resources. Session management is the other side of the same coin, since that authenticated state of user requests need to be properly handled and run as one session. When HTTP was first developed, it wasn't built with the ability to keep application session state. In subsequent versions of HTTP, a mechanism was introduced in order to keep application state. Understanding this mechanism is critical to understanding how authentication and session management work in web applications. The basic or core HTTP protocol is stateless. So that means that the relationship between the current and any previous requests from a specific client are unrelated and independent.But then how is it that we can add state? The answer is to extend the HTTP header capabilities to use cookies. So cookies is an HTTP header and cookies allow for a session. Now, without communication encryption, HTTP request and HTTP responses between a client and a server can be read over the network by an eavesdropper. So this also means that an attacker can hijack a client's session. The attacker then is able to obtain the session ID that is sent from the client to the server. Last, the attacker creates a connection between itself and the server, and uses the same session ID as a victim client, effectively hijacking the victim's victim client session.In HSTS (HTTP strict transport security), the first time the client communicates with a server, the server tells the client to automatically communicate with it using HTTPS. So the browser then remembers to always use HTTPS for any future connections.

One of the ideas of REST (Representational State Transfer) is that each request from the client, the server needs to have all of the information needed in order to understand that particular request. The next main idea of REST is that requests are performed on a resource like a piece of data. For example, a file or the concept like a session. As long as the resource can be uniquely identified using an identifier. For example, using a URL. We can think of a session as first with a login page, you would be forming a new session. So REST example would be to add this request of GET/ session/login. So when we think about authentication and session management, we might be tempted to create our own authentication session management subsystem. But we want to avoid doing that because logic and security issues could exist in our own authentication and session management subsystem. It takes time for these to be found and fixed. But with current existing web application frameworks, they had been previously tested and tried on production, and previous bugs have been fixed. These are convenient to use because web application frameworks will already have the plumbing for authenticating users and creating and destroying sessions. So for example, with the language of Ruby, Ruby on Rails as a web application framework, and it has something called the has_secure_password functionality, which adds methods to your user model to set an authenticate against the password.

Secure Methods For Authentication And session Management In Web Applications

The idea is that we want to make it harder for an attacker to be able to perform user ID or password enumeration. Then we are going to mention quickly about using logs to log authentication errors. And this will eventually help you if you have to deal with a security incident. The idea or the name of the game is during authentication, when there is an authentication error, they get harder for an attacker to guess why. If this authentication error is communicated to the user incorrectly, these error messages could be used by an attacker to perform username or a password enumeration against your system. Timing attacks are basically attacks where an attacker will determine on average how long it takes for the system to respond when a user is authenticated correctly versus when a user is authenticated incorrectly. If there is a significant average discrepancy in the timing of those two, then they can guess what authentication is correct and incorrect and can use that information for username or password enumeration against your system. But however, it's good to know that some web application frameworks take this into account. They help with making it such that the system responds roughly about the same amount of time when a correct authenticated user is correctly authenticated. First is when a user is not authenticated correctly because of a password issue. A couple of guidelines for how to handle error messages during authentication. The idea is to create very generic error responses during authentication. This holds true for HTTP or HTML error responses. And error message sent back as response of an authentication failure should not give information about the status of the account or whether the username or password was incorrect.

For error messages relating to an incorrect user ID or an incorrect password, you can say something along the lines of login failed, incorrect user ID, or incorrect password. This sort of error message makes it such that an attacker won't be able to determine a valid user ID during an enumeration attempt. Last but not least, we want to log password failures to our logging system, and you want to include the timestamp and the username on that account. You also want to log all account lockouts, and you want to include in your log your timestamp and the username on that account. So you want to log this on the backend, and of course, you don't want to give this as feedback to the user. This is just for you for your system to log, and this will help in the future. If an incident were to occur, the incident response team can have this extra information for them to conduct for their investigations.

We want to handle error messages during authentication in such a way that we send back to the generic error message. And you want to do this in order to make it harder for an attacker to perform user ID or password enumeration. You also want to log authentication errors or account lockouts in your logging system in the server back end, and this is to help the incident response investigators in the future. Because HTTP is stateless, in order to create the notion of a state we need to use some sort of mechanism to remember a previous request as being a portion of a much larger session. State management can also be achieved using HTTP authentication, for example. Now there are several things that you want to keep in mind when you are writing your web application, and specifically, when you need to create a secure session life cycle. What you want to do is to create strong tokens. What this means, effectively, is from the very beginning, make sure to create tokens. So these tokens are what you are giving to the web browser from the web server. Make sure to create these tokens that are difficult to guess. You want these sessions' tokens to be as random as possible. We want to make sure that attackers can't brute force through session token values to guess any existing sessions. This is because if attackers are able to guess existing session tokens, they can take over the session associated to those session tokens. Another thing that we want to keep in mind is to make sure that the transportation of these session tokens from the web server to a browser is always using an encrypted channel. So HTTPS should be used between the browser and the server. If your web application happens to allow multiple logins from more than one place, your system won't be able to tell whether that is because an attacker has used a session token, or it's because a user happens to be logged in more than once. So preventing logins from more than one place removes that ambiguity.

Another thing that you want to make sure to keep in mind is to have a look at your cookie scope, both the cookie domain scope and path scope. You want to set cookie scope to be as restrictive as possible. Remember that cookie domain scope can be such that, if you specify a cookie scope, and the cookie scope is set to the parent domain of the web application. Any web applications in the sub domains of that parent domain will then be able to receive the cookie from the user's browser if the user happens to access it. For example, if you had food.com as your cookie scope, and that is the parent domain of your web application, and your web application happens to live in webapp.food.com. Then testapp.food.com will also be able to receive the cookies that you have set for webapp.food.com, if a user happens to browse to testapp.food.com. Thinking about expiring these sessions, you want to make sure that your web application has a proper logout functionality, and it's working as expected.

The Relationship Between Authentication, Session Management, And Access Control

Access control can be defined using three components. First, there's the principle. A principle is a user or a processor machine. The second component is the action that is allowed by that principle. The third component is the resource to be acted upon by that principle. Basically, we want to define how we can control which principle is allowed to access which resources. Access control only makes sense if you know what you're protecting. There are several kinds of access control models. One among them is called role-based access control and that's where users are assigned to functional roles like for example: administrator or regular user or guest. These different functional roles have different sets of privileges. Now, there are other kinds. One that I can mention here is discretionary access control and that's where owners of resources grant access to other users to access their resources. If those owners of those resources don't explicitly grant access to those resources, access is automatically denied. Another access control model is called identity-based access control. That's where a user is allowed access to a resource only if they appear in a certain whitelist of allowed users for that particular resource. There are several more that aren't mentioned here, but you can find the others online. We focus on role-based access control, authentication validates the principles identity and initiates this creation of the session. Recall that session management keeps track of the state while the application is in use. During this session, access control acts as a gatekeeper to application resources.

Moving on to the two broad privilege attack types. The first kind is called vertical privilege attack. These are attacks where an attacker attempts to gain more abilities to be able to modify or act upon a resource. For example, when an attacker starts out as a user with regular user privileges, then escalates their privileges to be able to gain administrator user privileges. In contrast, horizontal privilege attacks are when an attacker is able to access more than the resources to which he or she has been given access. For example, if initially I am user one and it was intended that I could only access or act upon file one, but it turns out that because of a flaw in the web application I can also act upon file two, which I as user one I'm not supposed to access because I don't own it and user two owns it.

The session management threat called session fixation. Specifically, we will explain what session fixation is, and how to prevent these vulnerabilities. When a web application trusts a session ID that is given to it. For example, an attacker can trick a victim client into using a particular session ID using some methods, where for example, one method could be that because the web application inherently is designed to take in the session ID through a URL, it causes that web application to be vulnerable to session fixation attacks. Then what an attacker can do is to create a phishing email, which contains the web applications URL, where a session ID is set in that URL.

This phishing email can be sent to the victim client, and then the victim client can go and click on this URL, and then is forced to use that particular session ID. Another method could be that an attacker sends a victim client to a specially crafted login page that the attacker controls, and then uses a hidden form field to give the victim client a particular session ID.

Another way could be that if the web application is vulnerable to cross-site scripting, the attacker can generate a phishing email which contains the vulnerable web applications URL, in addition to a malicious script that is injected there. In this malicious script, the client then runs it and is forced to use a specific session ID.

Issues with Sensitive Data Exposure

These issues are important to know so that you can help protect your customer's data. In 2015, nearly 10 gigabytes of customer data stored by ashleymadison.com was leaked on the so-called dark web. This data included names, addresses, and phone numbers attached to Ashley Madison member profiles, and included credit card data and transaction information. Sensitive data exposure issues are important to know so that you can help protect your customer's data. Fundamentally, we want to be able to categorize the data that our application handles so that we can take appropriate measures to protect them. Some data might not be as sensitive as other kinds of data, such as credit card information. It is important to be able to think critically about the kinds of sensitive data that your web application will need to process and protect. The specific issues that we're going to discuss in this module include first, using Personally Identifiable Information (PII), to basically create the session ID. The second issue is when the web application is not encrypting sensitive information using standards. A third issue is improperly storing passwords. The last issue that we're going to discuss is using HTTP for sensitive client-server exchanges instead of the more secure HTTPS.

There is a general strategy list that comes from OWASP. The first strategy that you can use, and this is basically the fundamental strategy that you would want to employ when you're trying to protect sensitive data usage in your web application, is to know the types of data that you'll be transmitting or storing, and what levels of sensitivity those kinds of data have. Once you know this information, then you know how to build a security requirements list for your web application, such that you have a plan, or you can generate a plan to handle them safely. Which leads us to the second general strategy, is to basically build into your software requirements.

The security requirements for handling the sensitive data, that you are going to be using in your web application. Another general strategy is to pay attention to how the kinds of data can be cached, and where and know how to disable caching of your sensitive data. For example, your sensitive data that your web application handles could be cached at a proxy, or it could be cached on the browser side. So understanding where these points are will help you to generate strategies in order to then go about handling caching of the sensitive data that you'll be handling. Another general strategy, is to know how to use cryptography even in a basic sense and to understand what the minimum current requirements or current standards are. The last general strategy that you can use is, to not store sensitive data unless you really need to do it.

CONCLUSION

In this chapter, we made a deep discussion on the concepts of threat modeling and cryptography. The issues with improperly handling user-controlled data, application authentication and session management, sensitive data exposureand mitigating these issues. Exploited two different vulnerabilities in a web application that was designed to be vulnerable called WebGoat and Burp. In Future, The experiments on the two web applications are been carried out to have hands-on experiences on different types of attacks.

REFERENCES

Baker, W. T. (2018). *U.S. Patent Application No. 10/055,791*. US Patent Office.

Gunjal, B. (2019). Knowledge management: Why do we need it for corporates. *Malaysian Journal of Library & Information Science*.

Kondo, K., Sasaki, Y., Todo, Y., & Iwata, T. (2018). On the design rationale of SIMON block cipher: Integral attacks and impossible differential attacks against SIMON variants. *IEICE Transactions on Fundamentals of Electronics, Communications and Computer Science, 101*(1), 88–98. doi:10.1587/transfun.E101.A.88

McBride, T., Ekstrom, M., Lusty, L., Sexton, J., & Townsend, A. (2018). *Data Integrity: Identifying and Protecting Assets Against Ransomware and Other Destructive Events*. National Institute of Standards and Technology.

Sangchoolie, B., Folkesson, P., & Vinter, J. (2018, September). A study of the interplay between safety and security using model-implemented fault injection. In *2018 14th European Dependable Computing Conference (EDCC)* (pp. 41-48). IEEE. 10.1109/EDCC.2018.00018

Schneier, B., Kohno, T., & Ferguson, N. (2013). *Cryptography engineering: design principles and practical applications*. Wiley.

Shostack, A. (2014). *Threat modeling: Designing for security*. John Wiley & Sons.

Şimşek, M., & Şentürk, A. (2018). Fast and lightweight detection and filtering method for low-rate TCP targeted distributed denial of service (LDDoS) attacks. *International Journal of Communication Systems, 31*(18), e3823. doi:10.1002/dac.3823

Smith, N. M., DeLeeuw, W. C., & Willis, T. G. (2018). *U.S. Patent No. 9,860,057*. Washington, DC: U.S. Patent and Trademark Office.

Wang, Y., & Kogan, A. (2018). Designing confidentiality-preserving Blockchain-based transaction processing systems. *International Journal of Accounting Information Systems, 30*, 1–18. doi:10.1016/j.accinf.2018.06.001

Chapter 3
Digital Transformation
of Diplomacy:
The Way Forward for Small Island States

Sam Goundar
ⓘD https://orcid.org/0000-0001-6465-1097
The University of the South Pacific, Fiji

Bettylyn Chandra
The University of the South Pacific, Fiji

Akashdeep Bhardwaj
ⓘD https://orcid.org/0000-0001-7361-

0465
University of Petroleum and Energy Studies, India

Fatemeh Saber
University of Malaya, Malaysia

Subhash Appana
The University of the South Pacific, Suva, Fiji

ABSTRACT

This chapter seeks to examine the digital transformation (digitalisation) of diplomacy and how such digital transformations can be used to positively influence and improve a country's foreign services. The chapter further explores how the country's diplomats and their Foreign Service counterparts at Ministry of Foreign Affairs (MFA) can utilize the tools provided by digitalisation to advance the country's interests. Given the critical intelligence data, diplomatic protocols, and confidential information exchanged at the diplomatic level between countries, it is equally important to evaluate and assess the cyber security measures that are being taken to secure the digital network of the diplomatic missions. Scholarly research was initially conducted to position the field of research amongst pertinent literature to ascertain the use of digital tools in diplomacy and present key deliberations that exist.

DOI: 10.4018/978-1-7998-2367-4.ch003

INTRODUCTION

In this age of information and communication technology, soft power has progressed by the influences of digital technology on the conceptualization, practice and institutions of diplomacy. The social web is key together with instant messaging and online platforms provided by mobile communications where diplomacy of state-to-state relations is encompassing of state to civil society relations.

Norwegian Ambassadors use Skype to engage with university students in public diplomacy, whilst Palestinians use Facebook to engage with Israelis and Kenya uses Twitter for consular aid (Manor, 2017. However, at the same time users of these platforms should be wary that information technology and systems could threaten the privacy of individuals.

In the international fora of state relationships, diplomacy is the art of carrying out negotiations, forging alliances, deliberate on treaties and making agreements based on face-to-face forums. Today, diplomacy is the cornerstone governing foreign policy settings and is taking new shape and substance in the fast evolving age of digitalization. The internet has allowed for the real time communication and exchange of information across global platforms where the conduct of foreign policy meetings can be held in virtual environments like Skype.

Figure 1. Social Media Fact Sheet of Foreign Ministries. Source: Diplo Foundation (2019)

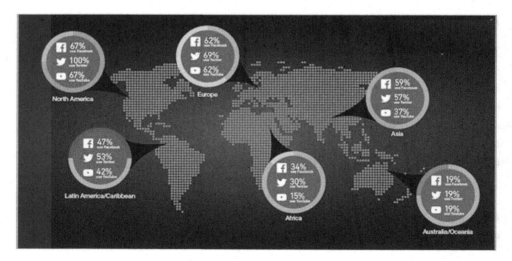

In the process, the internet has typically amplified the array of actors and their interests in making international policy decisions and shifting from states to be inclusive of non-state actors like intergovernmental organizations. Tools of the internet like social media platforms and blogs have exposed foreign policy makers to global viewers and at the same permitted governments to reach their intended audiences instantaneously.

The merging of the internet and mobile technology for example, permits even the least developed countries privy to access business prospects directly across state borders and create much needed economic opportunities.

For the stateless like the Kurds it has created mobilization with a 'virtual state' embedded in social media; for the practitioners and academics of climate change the internet has provided a platform to network and debate for a global common good.

This paper examines the way in which the digitalization of diplomacy can be used to positively affect the diplomacy of small island states like Fiji in the global arena. Scholarly research is initially conducted to position the subject amongst pertinent literature to ascertain the use of digital tools in diplomacy and present key deliberations that exist. In-depth interviews with key personnel like Deputy Secretary Policy, Foreign Service Desk officers, and Deputy Secretary of MFA will provide the qualitative analysis on Fiji's perspective. The advantages of using the digital tools for diplomacy, the impact of internet on international relations will be explored, challenges like violations to the communication protocol examined to provide guidance proposed to manage these platforms.

Figure 2. Global Use of Social Networks by Foreign Ministries. Source: Diplo Foundation (2019)

According to the Diplo Foundation (2019), the number of active users on social networks has increased exponentially over the past few years. If we take Facebook and Twitter, for instance, the number of monthly users surpasses the one billion mark in 2016. Diplomats have long realised that in public diplomacy, they need to be where the audience is. Five years ago, many of today's top e-diplomacy practitioners were recognising the importance of social media, and started engaging with non-state actors directly on social networks. From experimenting with platforms to integrating e-tools, some foreign ministries today are advanced and active users of social networks with their own fair share of followers. The figures above illustrate the pace at which foreign ministries were quick to jump on social media; integrate into institutions' online presence; which were the most popular platforms over time; and what the level of engagement with citizens was.

The conclusion reached is important as it provides a holistic overview, based on the digitalization of diplomacy that offers an invaluable perspective for the practitioners in MFA and its diplomatic missions abroad. In this way, digital tools can be used by diplomats and staff to reach out to new audiences, diaspora, tackle its geographic isolation and overcome the constraints of traditional diplomacy. Timely cyber security threat assessments needs to be carried out at each of the country's distributed diplomatic missions network abroad and its connectivity to the country's Ministry of Foreign Affairs centralised network system.

LITERATURE REVIEW

Diplomacy altered considerably during the 20th century where direct communication with the government of one country and the population of another was banned by the international community and could be regarded as breach of sovereignty. It seems that changes in diplomacy hinges on some form of 'technology' revolution. Traditional diplomacy evolved to public diplomacy with the use of radio in 1917 when both Russia and Germany used radio to broadcast directly to populations of neighboring states advocating revolutionist propaganda. At this point, the monologue became public diplomacy.

The main tools of public diplomacy became radio, cultural exchange of people and ideas as when the first astronauts landed on the moon it was the Voice of America radio that broadcast to millions on earth the words of Neil Armstrong, (Public Diplomacy, 2019).

The debate among scholars today continue about a new form of public diplomacy. At the turn of the 21st century, public diplomacy has evolved to encompass the digitalization of diplomacy. The public platform is now a dialogue between state actors and non-state actors with the use of digital tools. How an MFA can successfully utilize these digital tools and benefit as purported by the term 'digitalization of diplomacy' depends on its overarching ability to incorporate the MFA and its missions abroad; the diplomats themselves; the audiences of diplomacy and the procedures and guidelines for these institutions in using the digital platforms.

Figure 3. Facts and Statistics of Social Media Usage by Foreign Ministries. Source: Diplo Foundation (2019)

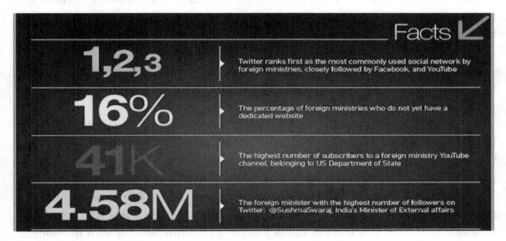

This paper supports the view by Manor (2017), who aptly produced a matrix conceptualizing the digitalization of diplomacy the term coined to encompass an evolving digital landscape and to focus on four dimensions of diplomacy mainly:

1. Institutions of diplomacy;
2. Practitioners of diplomacy;
3. The audiences of diplomacy; and
4. the conduct of diplomacy

Pitted in the matrix relative to these dimensions, are four fields of influence mainly:

1. conceptual;
2. behavioral;
3. procedural; and
4. the normative (values, beliefs), (Manor, 2017).

These prescriptive means can be utilized to assess institutional capacity and implement new technologies that lead to normative, behavioral, procedural changes in the MFAs with the outcomes of more effective diplomacy. Within these constructs, (four dimensions and four fields) we can bring a logical explanation to the intersection between digital technology and diplomacy.

The matrix offers a systematic classification of domains through which the influence of digitization can be investigated. As Manor, (2017) further states that the processes of digitization is inclusive of diplomats, missions and MFAs which overtime, these processes influences the manner in which diplomats and their audiences behave to achieve their objectives . As such, the impact of digital technology on diplomacy can be identified according to the particular field resulting in the outcome ie the related dimension.

Digital technology has given rise to online opinionated public platforms where individuals want to be heard and share political views, their opinions of local and global events implying a caring society.

Once a diplomat shares his views on social media like President Trump on Twitter, he becomes more transparent in relation to his work with personal self-exposure resulting in professional transparency. Thus, for better or for worse the attention given by online audience to tweets made by Trump illustrates the political power of Twitter (OUPBlog, 2019). According to Duncombe (2019), Twitter perhaps tested the traditional way in which diplomats and political leaders practiced statecraft diplomacy. Twitter was used as the negotiating medium dealing with the nuclear deal between Iran and US and its allies in the nuclear deal.

In a way digital technology has enabled the adoption of new norms, values and beliefs (Duncombe, 2019), where diplomats and political leaders use twitter through social media platforms to conduct important diplomatic communication with their counterparts. The adoption of these new norms, values and beliefs gives way to behavioral change and the impact occurs in the practice of diplomacy. The shift from traditional face-to-face diplomacy to social media negotiations has resulted in the conceptual change that is transformational diplomacy.

Further, the use of Twitter communication as a share and care online platform by Iran and US diplomats from 2013, given the severing of diplomatic ties since 1980, has seen threatening encounters between the two nations kept at bay. For example in January 2016, two US Navy patrol boats wandered into Iranian territorial waters threatening its sovereignty, was detained by Iranian authorities. However, within 24 hours the patrol boats were released.

Diplo Foundation (2019), reports on how instrumental was the sustained use of Twitter and its role in affecting diplomacy. Ongoing studies from Diplo Foundation found that 50% of foreign ministries globally use twitter, 48% Facebook and 37% YouTube. Prevalent is the use of social media platforms in North and Latin America, Europe and Asia. This has made the diplomats and state leaders more transparent in the way they conduct their international relationships and project their states' interests abroad. Tweets' by Trump hours before the Hanoi Meet with Kim Jong Un projected his message to entice North Korea to denuclearize and thrive with new economic possibilities (Lahiri, 2019). What could not be said face to face was said on this platform to set the mood of the meet and prepare Kim of what to expect.

The Internet has a profound effect on diplomacy according to Kurbalija, (2017). The effects are on the two cornerstones of diplomacy: information and communication. Diplomats deal with, collect, and manage information. Diplomats communicate in person, via diplomatic notes, and at international conferences. It remains to be seen how profound these changes will be in the short- and long-term perspective. The Internet has changed and continues to change the environment in which diplomats operate (sovereignty, interdependence, geo-strategy). The Internet also brings new topics to diplomatic agendas (Internet governance, cybersecurity) and it changes the practice of diplomacy by introducing new tools (Wikipedia, social media, tele-conferencing).

Diplomats have to adjust to these changes. A century ago, they were mainly negotiating peace agreements and borders. Today, and increasingly in the future, they will have to negotiate – for example – how the interests of their citizens will be protected in cyberspace. They will also have to learn how to interact via social media spaces. Diplomatic cables and notes verbal are no longer sufficient for effectively performing diplomatic tasks (Kurbalija, 2017).

According to (Holmes, 2013), e-Diplomacy as a form of public diplomacy has generated significant attention and criticism, with views ranging from technology allowing "people around the world to obtain ever more information through horizontal peer-to-peer networks rather than through the old vertical process by which information flowed down from the traditional sources of media authority" to claiming that efforts in public diplomacy often are understood as little more than top down dissemination of (counter)-propaganda. From a public diplomacy perspective then the goal of utilizing ICTs, or e-Diplomacy strategies, is the production, dissemination, and maintenance of knowledge that helps to further state interests. The advent of these technologies has fundamentally changed the ways state can both engage and inform foreign audiences. One need not look far for examples of this type of information penetration. In 2009, President Obama released a YouTube video message to Persian-speaking peoples of the world to mark the occasion of the Nowruz holiday. While the Iranian government did not necessarily appreciate the gesture, everyday Iranians did; according to Politico, the video had more views in Tehran than San Francisco (Holmes, 2013).

The Internet revolution has affected all aspects of life, including International relations. Diplomacy as a tool of foreign policy has also been transformed by this revolution. A paper by (Adesina, 2017) examines the concept of digital diplomacy, focusing on the use of digital media in the field of diplomacy and how countries are utilizing these tools in the pursuit of their foreign policies. It examines the opportunities and challenges these media offer for diplomatic activities, and argues that countries cannot afford to be left behind in this era of digital diplomacy as they can greatly benefit from these emerging diplomatic trends. Digital diplomacy and Internet activities as a whole can greatly assist in projecting a state's foreign policy positions to domestic and foreign audiences.

Contemporary diplomacy is subject to the same pressures of globalization as many other communication industries. However, insights from different areas of Media and Communication Studies have only been partly explored in the context of diplomacy. An article by (Pamment, 2016) aims to investigate the ways in which contemporary diplomatic advocacy campaigns cope with fundamental problems such as media repertoires, co-created content, collective intelligence, digital convergence and stakeholder management. The article contends that co-creation and co-option of shared values through transmedia engagement techniques perform a disciplining role.

PROBLEM STATEMENT

Although digitalization of diplomacy has given substance to MFAs where they can maximize their potential role in projecting public diplomacy, reaching out to their diaspora or crisis communication; this paper ascertains that traditional diplomacy of foreign affairs will always remain the basis of face-to-face state relationships in reaching deliberations on state-to-state interests. In recent days, Trump has floated the idea of a third North Korea meeting. Given all the digital tools available, the biggest superpower still feels the need to seek face-to-face state diplomacy (Landler, 2019).

Further, it will look at how digital technology is fast shaping international relations between states and non-state actors. Digital diplomacy through social media platforms and rapid increase in mobile connectivity has allowed nontraditional engagement between citizens and government, which in turn can influence decision making for governments. Similarly, world leaders use social media tools to engage directly with audience they wish to influence.

Digital technology is being used by states globally to advance foreign policy. What is the impact of the internet on international developments? How effective is the use of ICT in digital diplomacy such as promoting global economic growth? Are practitioners and diplomats satisfied with the use of the digital tools including social media platforms?

RESEARCH METHODOLOGY

The primary source of data was taken from four person interviews that spoke on the four dimensions as stated by the Manor's (2017) Matrix. In this way, the authors was able to give perspective to what would be an otherwise muddled study of how digitalization could impact small island states. The interviews discussed their perspectives around the four dimensions of diplomacy and how they influenced each other in the context of the country's MFA.

These individuals have served as diplomats, are major policy writers for the country's engagements globally and have travelled to United Nations meetings; and engaged on advisory panels to the state leader and various government Ministers on issues such as the Cotonou Agreement with the European Union and Climate Change including the lead up to COP 23 and COP 24.

Academic literature provided the secondary source. Notably this paper will base its findings on research and analysis previously conducted in terms of the matrix provided by Manor (2017), with the findings of previous researchers.

During the presearch phase, key words and databases were selected based on a combination of (a) strategies used in prior literature reviews and (b) test searches with candidate key words, filters, and databases. Some of the prior literature reviews focused on specific e-Diplomacy, Digital Diplomacy and Digital Transformation of Diplomacy, whereas others investigated certain aspects of digital diplomacy usage or content regardless of the social media platform. The present study integrates a combination of both social media platform-specific and general search phrases to explore an array of studies involving single or multiple types of social media and other web-based platforms. The key words used were e-Diplomacy, Digital Diplomacy and Digital Transformation of Diplomacy. Each of these search phrases has been used in at least one prior literature review. Many of the prior digital diplomacy literature reviews and published papers were grounded in a particular field of study and in our case, digital diplomacy.

Findings/Analysis

The analysis of the findings are aligned according to (Manor 2017) as referenced in Table 1 below based on the in-depth interviews with local diplomats and MFA staff.

Table 1. Digitalization of Diplomacy. Note. This table has been reproduced from (Manor, 2017)

Dimension of Diplomacy	Normative (norms, values, beliefs)	Behavioral	Procedural	Conceptual
Audiences of Diplomacy	Connected publics are volatile and unpredictable (Haynal, 2011)	Digital publics constitute networks of selective exposure (Hayden, 2012)	Peer to peer diplomacy (Attias, 2012)	Diplomacy as engaging with connected publics (Melissen, 2005)
Institutes of diplomacy	Digital Diplomacy as managing organizational culture of MFA's (Bjola, 2017)	Networked diplomacy (Slaughter, 2009) Digital Diplomacy and Digital Containment (Bjola, Pamment, 2016)	Selfie diplomacy (Manor, 2017; Segev, 2016)	MFAs as service providers (Manor, 2017
Practitioners of Diplomacy	Diplomats must conceptualize and imagine digital diplomacy before it can be practiced (Manor, 2017)	Twiplomacy study (Manor, 2017	Digital diplomacy as transmedia engagement (Pamment, 2016)	From club mentality to network mentality (Heine, 2013)
Practice of Diplomacy	Lack of online engagement with social media users	Digital diplomacy as crisis communication	Digital diaspora diplomacy (Rana, 2013)	Digital diplomacy as change management (Bjola; Holmes 2015)

Previous research have ascertained that ***online audiences can be unpredictable in their reactions*** for example to online Tweets from state leaders and diplomats and rather incredulous of the information Twitted. Public connected via social media to foreign diplomatic missions and it services are often volatile and unpredictable (Haynal, 2011). The advent of new web technologies included in the "Web 2.0," such as Facebook, Twitter, and so forth, have spurred much attention in how states are able to disseminate information of their choosing to particular constituencies and groups abroad. Thus the e-Diplomacy professionals, referenced above, working in state departments and foreign ministries are ultimately engaged in the practice of politics through engagement with foreign others, understood as a form of "public diplomacy."

According to (Baba, 2019), Fiji diplomats should be trained to use social media tools like Twitter and avoid unnecessary ridicule from their audiences, where the diplomat could waste enormous time in counter tweets. She felt that as the MFAs in the Oceania region and in particular, the country of study is only about 19% engaged with Twitter, Facebook or YouTube; the time is appropriate to provide guidance to use digital platforms. e-Diplomacy as a form of public diplomacy has generated significant attention and criticism, with views ranging from technology allowing "people around the world to obtain ever more information through horizontal peer-to-peer networks rather than through the old vertical process by which information flowed down from the traditional sources of media authority" to claiming that efforts in public diplomacy often are understood as little more than top down dissemination of (counter)-propaganda

As such, MFA headquarters (HQ) would be able to collate data and provide the target audience for a particular social media platform. For example in the United Kingdom, the diaspora communicate widely through Facebook. MFA should now develop necessary policies to be in place for use of digital platforms and at the same time allow missions to collaborate with their counterparts and international organizations to find best practices in reaching out to their audiences and maximize their diplomatic roles.

For **institutions of diplomacy**, similar sentiments were echoed by Emberson (2019), who could not envisage his busy Director's role as head of the Multilateral Bureau without being connected, as argued by (Slaughter, 2009). Emberson (2019) felt that traditional diplomacy could only get better with constant networking in order to be heard and remain relevant in the enormous global fora.

However, the success of digitalization in a MFA could bring about counter trends. For example, diplomatic engagement that depend on minimal shared considerations and reciprocal candidness to work could be destroyed. Nevertheless, when emotions dominate the discourse opinions formed online can be taken out of context when facts are sidelined. As such, the MFA could miss the intended diplomatic audience and would waste time regurgitating its emotive stance with its sympathizers. For example, Trump had an agenda to use Twitter to provoke the masses with situations that would incite anger and then would punctuate it with 'Sad' (Popper, 2017).

Importantly as researched by (Bjola, 2017) and (Pemmant, 2016), regarding behavior and the need to be aware of preemptive measures to combat disinformation and as purported by (Emberson, 2019) the need to curb threats of cyberattacks. With the country, being the hub of the Pacific and a key regional partner in security and defense partner of New Zealand and Australia an attack on the country could escalate to these nations.

MFAs are now conceptualized as service providers. The growing use of MFAs as service providers with consular aide like online visa applications; trade and economic business application portals amongst others as seen in the current Fiji MFA website. Similarly, embassy websites the world over contain pertinent information such as 'advice for travelers', which can receive over million visits per month; country branding including culture and languages; and trade and investments portals.

Adesina (2017) released a public interest statement indicating, "Digital diplomacy is usually conceptualized as a form of public diplomacy. It involves the use of digital technologies and social media platforms such as Twitter, Facebook, and Weibo by states to enter into communication with foreign publics usually in a non-costly manner. In her paper, Adesina (2017) examines the concept of digital diplomacy, focusing on the use of digital media in the field of diplomacy and how countries are utilizing these tools in the pursuit of their foreign policies. It examines the opportunities and challenges these media offer for diplomatic activities, and argues that countries cannot afford to be left behind in this era of digital diplomacy as they can greatly benefit from these emerging diplomatic trends.

One major factor that has affected diplomacy in this modern age is the revolution in ICTs. Digital diplomacy does not actually replace the traditional face-to-face diplomacy. Traditional and digital diplomacy co-exist and complement, rather than compete with, each other. Digital diplomacy and Internet activities as a whole can greatly assist in projecting a state's foreign policy positions to domestic and foreign audiences (Adesina, 2017).

For **practitioners of diplomacy**, Nayasi (2019) emphasized the need to move away from the traditional exclusive club of diplomats to be inclusive of non-state actors. A case in example, in climate change discussions; recent Cotonou trade discussions happened between the country's MFA and the civil society. The objective is to generate awareness and at the same ntime collaborate to put an inclusive agenda to the EU on the Contonou Agreement, which will impact trade providers in the country and its sugar industry. Nayasi (2019) feels in order for diplomats to make right decisions together with state leaders; civil society should be included relative to the negotiations.

The **practice of diplomacy,** according to Cokanasiga (2019), was about the importance of missions to engage with their diaspora using the right medium like Facebook in UK to provide necessary real time information like any terrorist attacks in the vicinity; communicate on natural disasters amongst others. However, at the same time the MFA and its missions should be mindful of guidelines and procedures to follow when issuing emergency notifications. On the other hand, Cokanasiga (2019) felt that digital platforms could only be used to enhance traditional face-to-face diplomacy and that human interaction and warmth or otherwise can never be replaced by bots or social media platforms to make decisions on the global fora.

Early initiatives on data diplomacy have started developing. For example, the British Foreign and Commonwealth Office plans to establish a Data Director and to strengthen the use of data mining, as announced in its recently published report, Future FCO. Other diplomatic services are exploring data diplomacy from a multidisciplinary approach, taking into considering the skills that diplomats need to harness the benefits of data. As part of this research, a first roundtable, held in

Geneva, brought together diplomats and practitioners from international organisations to address (big) data in diplomatic reporting, humanitarian affairs, public diplomacy, development, and the sustainable development goals (Kurbalija, 2019).

CONCLUSION

On receiving the first telegraph note in 1860, British Prime Minister, Lord Palmerston was reported to exclaim, "My God, this is the end to diplomacy!" (Diplo Foundation, 2018). Internet and digital technology has advance the way diplomats and state leaders interact on the international platform, where economic benefits and trade agreements can be formalized. However, traditional face-to-face diplomacy remains the cornerstone of foreign policy settings where information and communication are cornerstones to diplomacy and its state relations.

At this time, smart collaborative efforts with other MFAs from developing countries for in-house training on digital use and digital essentials like Twitter and Facebook will ensure that the target audience is reached and message contents understood. Other tools like Viber have come in handy in UN corridors and are crucial in keeping various groups informed when attending various meeting platforms on timings, urgent updates to the representative speaker who is about to speak and cannot be interrupted otherwise.

The country of this research can be proactive with policies and guidelines in encouraging their diplomats to be abreast with the rest of the world and be relevant on the digital wave.

REFERENCES

Adesina, O. S. (2017). Foreign policy in an era of digital diplomacy. *Cogent Social Sciences*, *3*(1), 1297175. doi:10.1080/23311886.2017.1297175

Bjola, C. (2017). Trends and counter-trends in digital diplomacy. *The Soft Power*, *30*, 126–129.

Digdipblog.files.wordpress.com. (2019). Available at: https://digdipblog.files.wordpress.com/2017/08/the-digitalization-of-diplomacy-working-paper-number-1.pdf.

Diplo Foundation. (2018). *Digital Diplomacy, E-diplomacy, Cyber diplomacy*. https://www.diplomacy.edu/e-diplomacy

Diplo Foundation. (2019). *Social Media Fact Sheets of Foreign Ministries – Diplo Foundation*. https://www.diplomacy.edu/blog/infographic-social-media-factsheet-foreign-ministries

Duncombe, C. (2019). *Twitter and transformative diplomacy: social media and Iran–US relations*. Available at: https://academic.oup.com/ia/article/93/3/545/3077244

Haynal, G. (2011). Corporate diplomacy in the information age: Catching up to the dispersal of power. *Diplomacy in the digital age: Essays in honour of Ambassador Allan Gotlieb*, 209-224.

Holmes, M. (2013). *What is e-Diplomacy?* In 7th European Consortium for Political Research General Conference, Bordeaux.

Kurbalija, J. (2017). Diplomacy in a Globalizing World. In Diplomacy in a globalizing world. Oxford University Press.

Lahiri, T. (2019). *Trump spent the hours before meeting Kim Jong Un tweeting about "Da Nang Dick" and Michael Cohen*. https://qz.com/1560926/trump-tweets-about-da-nang-dick-michael-cohen-in-hanoi/

Landler, M. (2019, April 11). *Trump Says He's Open to Third North Korea Meeting, and 'Smaller Deals' Are Possible*. https://www.nytimes.com/2019/04/11/us/politics/trump-north-korea-summit.html

Manor, I. (2017). *The Digitalization of Diplomacy: Toward Clarification of a Fractured Terminology*. Working Paper. Exploring Digital Diplomacy.

OUPblog. (2019). *How Twitter enhances conventional practices of diplomacy*. Available at: https://blog.oup.com/2017/10/twitter-diplomacy-practices-foreign-policy/

Pamment, J. (2016). Digital diplomacy as transmedia engagement: Aligning theories of participatory culture with international advocacy campaigns. *New Media & Society*, *18*(9), 2046–2062. doi:10.1177/1461444815577792

Popper, B. (2017, June 26). *New study explains why Trump's 'Sad' tweets are so effective*. https://www.theverge.com/2017/6/26/15872904/trump-tweet-psychology-sad-moral-emotional-words

Public Diplomacy. (2019). *Public Diplomacy Alumni Association. Diplo Foundation*. Available online at http://www.publicdiplomacy.org/1.htm

Slaughter, A. M. (2009). *A new world order*. Princeton University Press.

Chapter 4
Information Security Policies and Procedures Guidance for Agencies

Dasari Kalyani

ⓘD https://orcid.org/0000-0001-8197-3733

VNR Vignana Jyothi Institute of Engineering and Technology, India

ABSTRACT

In today's digital e-commerce and m-commerce world, the information itself acts as an asset and exists in the form of hardware, software, procedure, or a person. So the security of these information systems and management is a big challenging issue for small and large-scale agencies. So this chapter discusses the major role and responsibility of the organization's management in identifying the need for information security policy in today's world of changing security principles and controls. It focuses on various policy types suitable for all kinds of security models and procedures with the background details such as security policy making, functionality, and its impact on an agency culture. Information security policies are helpful to identify and assess risk levels with the available set of technological security tools. The chapter describes the management strategies to write a good policy and selection of the right policy public announcement. The agencies must also ensure that the designed policies are properly implemented and ensure compliance through frequent intermediate revisions.

DOI: 10.4018/978-1-7998-2367-4.ch004

INTRODUCTION

For the past few years, it has been proven how digital communication information systems are vulnerable to various attacks. The information systems or information itself is a critical asset to business profitability or loss. In many cases, the more sophisticated attacks silently penetrate through critical information systems and explore to exploit valuable assets of the organization that consists of either secret or sensitive information.

What is Information System

An information system can be considered as a group of interrelated components which are able to retrieve, process, store and distribute relevant sensitive information securely in support of decision making or controlling the entire organization. It consists of not only the data in it but also refers to users and methods whether automated or manual methods organized to collect, process, transmit and disseminate data that is responsible for. From the 1960s and mid-1970s majority of information systems were manual systems later on these are mainly computerized and software-intensive systems known as mainframe-based, client-server based and web-based information systems.

Formally, the Information System (IS) is known as a product or component, a protocol for cryptographic system (or) a small card for wireless network access, a disk controller on personal computer (or) an operating system and a communication system on a network (or) an organization's staff (or) the internet with maximum number of computers (or) an application system such as payroll system, financial system and so on. In simple terms, an information system is composed of either data, hardware units, software, procedures and/or people with major data management functionalities like data input, data storage, data processing, data control, and output results.

Why is Information Security

The information is considered as a critical and sensitive corporate asset. So the security of this kind of assets is also crucial. The security of information systems(assets) is one of the success factors for business matters. It is important that the information systems remain secure and that the data contained in them do not fall into the hands of those who are not allowed to have access to it. Any misuse of sensitive or critical information systems by internal employees or an external entity, however, lead to very serious challenges to organizational agencies such as loss in terms of productivity, revenue or any legal liabilities and other workplace issues. so in today's digital world, the agencies or organizations need to have effective corrective measures to enforce their suitable and apt usage of policies to minimize their loss tendency as well as the increase of productivity by knowledgeable workers.

WHAT IS INFORMATION SECURITY

The main objective or purpose of information security and its management is to sustain the protection of the integrity, availability and the confidentiality of transmitted data and the availability of classified or identified information systems (Cleveland, 2004). Any organization or agency's effort towards securing their information systems must be successful if and only if it works in conjunction with the firm or organization's own information security policy structure management. There are certain security principles based on which every policy underlies.

Security Principles

The Organization for Economic Cooperation and Development known ad OECD issued a chain of recommended principle guidelines document(manual) purposeful for the phenomenal incident of legal issues, laws, policies, technical measures, organizational executive support, and employee awareness programs to be executed (Lebek, et.al., 2013). These guidelines include:

a. Accountability: Every user is held responsible for every specific action that is involved with the security of information systems.

b. Awareness: To enable the information security confidence within the organization, it is very essential to have knowledge of security practices, procedures, and measures to be imparted to the employees of it.

c. Ethics: The methodologies that are been initiated for securing the information systems must respect each individual privacy, humanitarian rights, and statutory interests of peers.

d. Proportionality and Integration: All accessible security measures must be integrated to have a defensive layer over the information systems based on its value and the risk factor involved due information openness.

e. Authorization and Timeliness: The authorized users only should access specific information together timely and coordinated if any security infringement.

f. Re-evaluate: Security tools or any other security mechanisms, technological tools must revalue frequently and recurrently to make sure that an organization's demands are being met.

g.   Limited Access and Separation of duty: Individuals are identified with a specific job or duty assigned to the one with limited access to complete the job that they are responsible for.

h.   Auditing: To ensure the compliance with established procedures and associate results are time-to-time monitored perfectly.

i.   Redundant and Risk-less: To address the continued and uninterrupted access through redundant information systems while monitoring the risk factor as well as reduce or eliminate completely as much as possible.

According to University of Nebraska-Lincoln, there are few best practices to be implemented on to mitigate various security related issues. They are, timely data classification, ensure all stakeholders follow firm's policies and standards, regular audit trails and monitor and change of management procedures.Top of Form

j.   Bottom of Form

k.

IT Infrastructure Security Tools

In case of any organization or agency has been failed to secure critical assets of the organization known as the information assets is due to several reasons but not just due to lack of sufficient security tools for the past twenty years. There is an abundant number of security tools available in the market (Kovacich, Gerald, 1998) to meet the needs of the modern enterprise challenges. They are available under mandatory and optional categories.

i)   Network access controls: these policies mainly focus on Identifying authorized entities and grant role-based access to information assets. This is best suitable to address the needs of ever-growing and increasing IT infrastructure complex issues of organizations. The policies defined for network access restricts the unauthorized misuse to enterprise resources.

ii)   Data loss protection: These tools guarantees the protection of sensitive data transmission in and out of the organization either accidentally or maliciously. These tools completely scan for specific data patterns which reveal the sensitive information during its transmission. it has the complete track record of internal or external threat agent activity or unusual behavior.

iii)   Firewalls: Firewalls protect the information against unauthorized access or log in by filtering the network traffic flow as per the rules or pattern matching set by the network administrator. Inclusion of Intrusion prevention or intrusion detection system with the firewalls is an added advantage of anomaly detection and mitigation of threats proactively by doing deepest analysis on network traffic.

iv)   Endpoint protection: These are essential to protect information exists on laptops, servers, desktops or any other endpoint device and removable media against the virus, worms. these tools enable centrally managed devices are continuously monitored for both anomaly detection and prevention.

Information Security Policy – History

The scope of documented security policy always should be broad, faithful, and unambiguous. It must be translated accurately and technologically convenient and flexible to implement. The cost of policymaking and its implementation can't be much higher than that of information asset that is being secured or protected. A policy should be very clear not just like a quantitative documentary manual .it is recommended to be as specific as possible and useable and well defined to be understood by all stakeholders. The organization's ever-challenging real-world goal is indirectly reflected through its policy definition itself. A policy should reflect not only the standards to enforce or strengthen the security level of information systems resource assets repository within the organization (Doherty, 2009) but also the state liable penalties against its misuse. Finally, every policy should seek a proper balance between the ease of user access and privacy as well as security. At last, it is very important to incorporate that, all policies are approved, monitored and supported by the C-level officers, otherwise, even the best well-defined policy would fail.

ORGANIZATIONAL POLICY STRUCTURE

The Role of Security Policy in Organizations

In today' digital world, entire communication is digital. So just the installation of well-known locks or any other data or any other protection mechanisms we incorporate is not sufficient for securing the information assets of an agency. It is recommended to have strong information security policymaking, senior management support and approval is vital to succeed and strengthen the security levels. The agency culture is playing a critical and important role in the policy development process.

Organizational Policy Development

Policies, Procedures, Standards, and Guidelines

Organizations use security related policies and standard procedures to contour the rules indeed the methodology to deal with sensitive or critical data related problems that generally arise. An Organization's defined strategic plan and designed policies and procedures(Chris Hare, 2001) as in Figure 1. are mainly used to mould employees and make them to understand the importance of information security and also the organization's views and values on specific security issues, and what will be a consequence of, if they failed to adhere to it. In general, the policies are instructional statements in respect of how an organization desirous to conduct oneself whereas procedures designate preciesly how to implement a piece of business policy or perform the initiated policy step by step without any conflicts. These are high-level statements in the form of organizational policies provide guidance (Doherty et.at., 2009) to workers who must make present and future decision. A policy can be strictly not only to secure information systems but also be used to identify endangered risks and to transfer identified risks to third party or mitigate those risks.

Figure 1. Security Policy, Standards, and Procedures

All kinds of organizations can have their own policy to execute physical security and to prevent unauthorized resource access attacks either within or external to the office premises. Any policy that is been defined is applicable not only to internal employees of the organization even to the general public users who must be followed strictly, without any discrepancy and deviation. For example, if an organization wants to provide an authorized entry into the premises then one of its strategic plan (Ismail et.at., 2017) can be stated as "The public can have accessibility only up to the public reception point; but beyond that point only authorized employees are allowed" while the procedure is given with a detailed step-by-step instructional guidelines given to stakeholders with the details showing how to dispense with an entity, the one who is trying to cross the reception point and trying to enter into the restricted office premises having no authorized access cards.

Policy: The policy statement shall be defined as "All the employees must identify themselves with a two-factor identification process. i.e., they may use identity card with biometric fingerprint scan while they enter or exit.

Procedure: In compliance with the above-stated policy, now the procedure shall be documented well in the following way.

1) Any stakeholder or the requestor who is trying to make way towards the office premises passing through the reception point must undergo the first security guard checkpoint.

2) All the staff workforce employees, authorized stakeholders or the requestors must display an issued respective authorized identity card to the guard at security check point for their identity check validation and its approval.

3) The security guard ensures and confirms that the requestor is an authorized one after a thorough check of identity card, photo, name of an employee and the signature of cards issuing authority . In case of any discrepancy that requestor may be directed to senior officer or human resources department.

4) The security identity-check of the requestor is followed by a fingerprint scan to ensure and confirm authenticated access to an assigned individual role.

5) Any unidentified or unauthorized persons must be strictly restricted from entry and guided to vacate the premises by the security guard.

Figure 2. Security Policy Key Elements

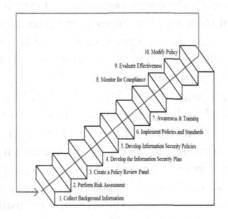

The key elements of Policies shown in Figure 2. are stated below.

- Set the tone of the organization's management
- Establish key roles and responsibilities of employees
- Classification of sensitive key resource systems
- Guidelines for authorized access to critical assets
- Provide guidelines for decision support
- Exhibit the scope and horizon of authority levels
- Extent the basis of guidelines and procedures for stakeholders
- Signify accountability from top executives to lower-level employees

Standards and Guidelines: A standard can be used to enumerate the technological needs in order to comply with the specific task which has been defined in the form of policy and structured in the form of procedures. i.e., Standards - are the derived statements from a policy which is defined at the top level. The standards define specific, measurable requirements which can provide specific technical specifications in turn for subsequent verification of policy compliance. Unlike policies, the guidelines are only suggestions to fulfil but are not mandatory. i.e., the guidelines are optional but recommended specifications.

POLICY MANAGEMENT HIERARCHY

Essentially, there is a five-layer hierarchical structure which is required to confirm by the organizations as a part of policy management(Goel et.al., 2010). These layers as mentioned in Figure 3. are exemplified as follows.

The First layer states, Exhibit & Legislation: The decisions that are taken at this phase have an influence on the entire organization nevertheless of its functional unit size. The impact of strategic plan ranges from revenue and proceeds to export-controlled material. In case, the legislation entrenched by the government, which often successively leads to the creation of a different set of policies that may or may not be authorized to accept in an organization.

The Second layer presents, Policy: This references to a stratagem which has been initiated and evolved further by the stakeholders of an organization and finally endorsed (approved) by a chief level senior management committee with the detailed description about its importance to the organization throughout the lifetime.

The Third layer announces, Standards: These are typically extracted from the defined policies at the second layer. A standard defines a specific, measurable and detailed statement which can be used subsequently to justify the defined policy compliance during its implementation. The standards are mandatory to adopt by the agency. These standards define what must be done while hiding the details of how it is to be done.

Now the Fourth layer publishes, Procedures: These are detailed instructional step-by-step documents provided to explain what the end-user or any other stakeholder must fallow, to implement the organizational policies and standards to the maximum extent.

The Fifth layer expounds Guidelines: This will identify proper guided material that an organization would like to see its stakeholders or members do for securing intended information systems. These are generally known as optional recommendations.

Figure 3. Secure Policy Development Hierarchy

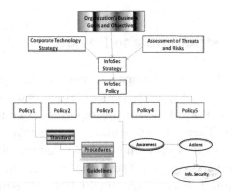

Based on the organizational dimensionality, there may be a thin additional layer, that exists in between the standards layer (Third) and the procedures layer (Fourth). This layer mainly convey practices, which can be linked to a set of processes and practices that define why and how procedures and guidelines can be implemented in compliance with the pre-established policies of an organization. An example, which shows all strategic decision-making phases in an organization to secure information systems are as follows.

- Business goals and objectives: "we shall embrace and expand the use of electronic commerce and related technologies in order to achieve cost reduction and business efficiency to serve our worldwide customers".
- Corporate technology strategy: "we will increase the reach of our core business applications to our customers through the use the internet and the WWW".

- The management works together with CSO and CIO to find the most possible way a hacker or virus will take to get into the system. This could be the result of having performed an assessment of the threats and the resulting risks.
- Strategy saying: "we will use cost-effective security measures to protect our organization assets".
- Security policy: "All users will be authenticated whether or not working remotely. This will be applicable to full-time employees in permanent service of the organization as well as those sourced from contractors".
- Standard: Could be "Remote access users will use dual-factor authentication using authentication tokens".
- Procedure: "Users are to contact the remote access security administrator to receive their authentication token after they have been approved for such access".

Policy Creation, Distribution and Review

Before the implication of policy and management of security policy, it is entailed to ensure that, the classification of systems' possess critical and sensitive information is mandatory. This classification is based on the importance of information being held, its usage and sensitivity. There are also a chain of roles take part in the real-world security policy formation. It is very important to examine while developing and implementing agency related policies. These roles are very important because they impart distinct responsibilities (Kovacich, Gerald, 1998) to resolve the dissimilarities that arise during the requirements and while satisfying different components of the policy. The defined roles are stated as follows:

1. Originator or Owner knew to be a person who initiates and creates the information systems security requirements.
2. An authorizer is well known to be an entity which manages the accessibility of the information system.
3. Custodian is the one who governs the identity of entities' accesses to the sensitive information and carries out granting of authorized access based on security requirements.
4. User is the one who essentially accesses and uses the intended information to complete an assigned job liability.

Information Security Standards

The standard defined in terms of much detailed statement of known policy specifying what must be done in compliance with the chosen organizational policy. The standards have the same requirements for compliance as that of policies. Standards are considered as informal documentation or part of organizational culture, as in de facto standards. The standards should be scrutinized, ratified and broadcasted by an authorized group. These documents specify the use of specific technologies such as operating system, applications, server tools, router configurations, etc. in a uniform way throughout the organization.

Defining standards is an easy job because the implementation of such defined standards must be validated recurrently to ensure and maintain compliance with the identified policies (Manik Dey, 2007). i.e., the lifetime or review period of a standard is at least five years. It is to make emphatic that, the standard is significant to accomplish, though the cost of implementation and its conservation maintenance is generally high. Consequently, only a very few organizations literally create standards unless characteristically required, due to their high application and maintenance costs. These standards are informal in other words these are part of organizational industry culture as in de facto standards. The designed standards of an organization should be announced, scrutinized and ratified by a committee to make it formal document or a de jure standards.

Information Security Procedures

The procedures that are defined to secure information systems should be as distinctive as the industrial organization. There is no predominantly accepted standard perspective to write a procedure. Writing the procedure(s) is generally considered as one of the most laborious parts, as it requires providing extended details to the respective identified policy and standard. So procedure development often requires the involvement of many supplementary people than writing consistent documents. Finally, the development of procedure incorporate the establishment of a team of specialists means the people who really involved in doing the job while preparing the procedural steps, which in turn are supervised by the manager. The complete document of the agency's procedure should reflect the actual rules or commands to be imparted among the stakeholders are given, if any altercation of those commands and the expected outcome results are also stated. There are several ways of writing the procedures in compliance with the specified policy of an organization, while the other documentories like policies are written to fetch the management's decision in the form of strategic plan stating the rules to be inculcated among the stakeholders in a distinct mode. The defined procedure describes how the actual work would get to be executed.

Example Statements:

A Policy statement - "Access to network resource will be granted through a unique user ID and password".

A Standards statement – "Passwords will be 8 characters long".

A Guidelines, Procedures and practices – "Passwords should include one non-alphanumeric character which is not found in the dictionary".

Information Security Guidelines

Information systems guidelines is an essential fundamental element of sound security practice. Guidelines are easier to write and execute. This guidelines document holds the actual details of the policy in the form of inoperative recommendations with regard to management. Guidelines would like to state the details like how it should be implemented and what standards and procedures should supervene by the stakeholders and employees of the organization. They describe how an employee must perform their responsibilities while having the previlige to elect what guidelines to be considered in compliance with the policy(Michael Alexander, 1996). For example, an agency's guidelines document may possess spyware removal information, malware cleanup, data conversion, etc. As a part of spreading security awareness among the employees of an organization and any other entities concerned with it, guidelines are published via manuals stored on the company intranet or distributed in the form of a booklet. Though the guidelines are separate yet linked with the documents of general policies designed and developed by top-level management committee members.

TYPES OF POLICY

All organizational strategic plan based policies are considerably classified into four major broad varieties. They are senior management statement of policy, regulatory policy, advisory policy, and informative policy. As the policies are treated as key and foremost documentation of an entire organization. It is significant to define and design specific distinct policies (Micki Krause, & Tipton Harold)which are appropriate and applicable to the entire organization, while the individual departments may comply with designed policies with an independent implementation structure.

Senior Management Statement Policy

This type is known to be the first step in the design of the policy. Generally, senior management statement of policy is a high-level, executive and general statement in compliance with the business strategic plan. The senior management i.e., The senior officers or senior managers have ultimate and functional responsibility. This type of policy consists of three key elements (Peltier & Thomas, 1999). First - The organization's business model information systems - To acknowledge the importance of networking and other computing resources. Second - Authorization of lower-level statements - which are in the implementable form such as standards, procedures and guidelines management. Third - A statement of support - for enterprise business systems information security all through the whole lifetime.

Regulatory Policy

The regulatory policy ensures and follows standard procedures or the best practices of operation suitable for a specific agency or industry. These are the policies must perform owing to compliance, regulation or any other legal issues so as to prevalent in the organization's operating environment applies to both internal and external. This type of regulatory policy is made up of a series of valid legitimate detailed base practices which outline in fact what must be done when it must be done? Who does it? giving confidence that it is subsequently following the accepted agency's policy (Ifinedo, 2014) and also can provide insights to why it is important to do it?. Regulatory policies are typically very specific and detailed to the agency in which the firm operates on.

Regulatory policies are specific and detailed statements must be implemented by the industry where the business organization operates. It is also owing to the regulation of any other legal requirements as prevalent in the industry's internal or external operating environment. This type of policy often has some conditional constraints regarding their usage approach in a context where people need to make instantaneous decisions based on certain facts. In general, a policy which is proficient to inscribe all feasible end outcomes may result into an immensely complex, burdensome to apply, and very intractable to enforce kind of policies.

Advisory Policy

Advisory policy contributes to strong recommendations but may not be mandated. These are the statements reflecting the consequences of not following the defined policy by a certain group. These are often written in very robust terms about the action to be taken or a method to be followed in a certain state. Normally, it is aimed at well informed chief level individuals with details and facts which allow them to make decisions with regard to the situation, and the consequences of not adhering to the policy and how to act. As the advisory policies are much simple and easy to adhere, the enforcement of this policy is not applied with much effort. Most policies come under this broad advisory policy category. However, the policy will state the alternate course of action or impact of not backing the advice and forecasted ramification are revealed within this advisory policy. While the specific impacts associated with not following the business conduct policy or guidelines such as the omission of the required information to make critical decisions, unaccounted deadlines, non-observance of risks and auditor evaluation reports finally may result in termination of the job.

So this kind of advisory policies' accuracy and validity often can have a remarkable impact on the organization. As the advisory policies are designed by keeping some kind of limitations or prohibitions, these policies should be defined and evaluated by experienced and expert individuals. These advisory policies can be extended up to a negligible level by providing a minimal opportunity for the individuals while maintaining a document with all exceptional cases in the policy.

Informative Policy

The informative type policy exists simply as an informative document which communicates particulars to the determined reader. The reader or audience could be a certain internal or external entity who was envisioned in executing the policy. As an advisory policy, the informative policy does not impose any kind punishment or penalty as a sequel to an individual entity for not adhering to the policy. Though the informative policies carry well-built information regarding the specific conditional situations, these are less important compared with senior management statement policy, advisory or regulatory policies. So these informational policies are made available as references to another kind of policies to initiate more details about the organizational policy. It is very important to distribute informative policies which contain sensitive details to a limited extent to avoid risks to the organization.

CONCLUSION

The importance of information security in an organization or an agency lies with knowing its importance, the level of understanding and awareness is very crucial in nature. The senior management, the top-level governing team held major prime responsibility to motivate and set out the long-term direction to be engineered by the whole organization. If the stakeholders do not understand the necessary information systems security of or failure to adhere to the strategic plan while the engineer may lead the whole organization in destruction, increasing downtime and thus loss of productivity. So the security solution should be carefully designed by chief level team members to achieve cost-effectiveness and return-of-investment adding business values, apart from yielding regulations. The security of Information systems and its management based on some standards is a continuous process but not a product or technology to be installed and executed forever. The structure of information security management comprises policies, standards, and procedures, guidelines, and standards. The overall strategic plan or information security objectives tend to change with the latest market trends and requirements of an organization. The contemporary methodologies' compliance check should be reviewed and updated to equivalent requirements. This gap analysis finding will ensure the long term benefits to the organization by protecting its resources in the most effective manner. Finally, we conclude that the success of an Information Security systems Management Standards (ISMS) lies in the supreme composite of well-designed Policies, Procedures, Compliances, Standards, Processes, guidelines, Products, and Technology.

REFERENCES

Alexander. (1996). *The Underground Guide to Computer Security.* Addison Wesley Publishing Company.

Dey, M. (2007). *Information security management - A Practical Approach.* Windhoek: AFRICON.

Doherty, N. F., Anastasakis, L., & Fulford, H. (2009, December). The information security policy unpacked: A critical study of the content of university policies. *International Journal of Information Management, 29*(6), 449–457. doi:10.1016/j.ijinfomgt.2009.05.003

Ernst & Young, L.L.P. (2004). *Information Security Survey.* Technical report. Author.

Goel, S., & Chengalur, I. N. (2010, December). Metrics for characterizing the form of security policies. *The Journal of Strategic Information Systems, 19*(4), 281–295. doi:10.1016/j.jsis.2010.10.002

Hare, C. (2001). Information Security policies, procedures, and standards: Establishing an essential code of conduct. CRC Press LLC.

Ifinedo, P. (2014, January). Information systems security policy compliance: An empirical study of the effects of socialisation influence and cognition. *Information & Management, 51*(1), 69–79. doi:10.1016/j.im.2013.10.001

Ismail, W. B. W., Widyarto, S., Ahmad, R. A. T. R., & Ghani, K. A. (2017). A generic framework for information security policy development. *4th International Conference on Electrical Engineering, Computer Science and Informatics (EECSI)*, 1-6. 10.1109/EECSI.2017.8239132

Kovacich, G. (1998). *Information Systems Security Officer's Guide*. Butterworth-Heinemann.

Lebek, B., Uffen, J., Breitner, M. H., Neumann, M., & Hohler, B. (2013). Employees' information security awareness and behavior: A literature review. *Proceedings of the Annual Hawaii International Conference on System Sciences*, 2978-2987. 10.1109/HICSS.2013.192

Peltier, T. (1999). *Information Security Policies, A Practitioner's Guide*. Academic Press.

Soomro, Z. A., Shah, M. H., & Ahmed, J. (2016). Information security management needs more holistic approach: A literature Review. *International Journal of Information Management, 36*(2), 215–225. doi:10.1016/j.ijinfomgt.2015.11.009

Specification for Information Security Management Systems. (1999). *Information security management, part 2*. Technical Report BS 7799–2.

Cryptography Security Services:
Network Security, Attacks, and Mechanisms

Pooja Kaplesh
Chandigarh University, India

ABSTRACT

This chapter gives an overview about the need for computer security and different types of network securities. Different types of attacks like active and passive are discussed that can harm system resources. This chapter also provides the basics of the cryptography system and basic terms used in cryptography. Security services provided by cryptography are also discussed such as data integrity, privacy/confidentiality, user authentication, message authentication, authorization, digital signatures, validation, access control, and non-repudiation along with their mechanisms.

INTRODUCTION

Modern age is the age of data or information. We deal with various types of data, daily. This data is stored in the database and can be used for communication purpose. And we need to implement security at each step to secure this data. Thousands of millions of data travel over the network for accomplishing successful transmission of data, sent across the world. This data needs an assurance that the data sent should not be altered or accessed by any unauthorized party. And the area that deals with this security issues of data is Cryptography.

Cryptography is a science which is useful for designing and developing the cryptographic systems or frameworks. These systems are called cryptosystems, which contains various methods for encryption and decryption purpose. It is the area where we study theoretically and practically about the techniques which generally provide a secure communication over the network. *Cryptography* means to provide privacy and protect data from unauthorized access. Cryptography is a subdomain of cryptology. Because cryptography refers to the cryptographic techniques such as encryption and decryption but *cryptology* covers the study of both cryptography and cryptanalysis. The word cryptology made up of two Greek words: KRYPTOS (means hidden) and LOGOS(means word). *Cryptanalysis* is the process of getting the plaintext from the cipher text without being in control of the key or the system (called code breaking). Prof. D. Chandrasekhar Rao (2018) has discussed basic areas or levels at which we need security:

- **Computer Security**: It is a part of information security that provides data security, hardware, software, and firmware security using a collection of designed tools.
- **Network Security:** It is an activity designed to secure the integrity and usability of your network i.e. protect data during transmission over a network using different software and hardware technologies.
- **Internet or web Security**: Activity to secure data while transmitting through a number of interconnected networks. It means to provide complete security against threats, malware and viruses for all devices.

NEED OF NETWORK SECURITY

Millions of important information is exchanged daily on internet in today's world. This information can be misused by attackers. With Internet advancements, Computer networks become bigger and network security has turned out to be critical. Software should be secured against outside attacks also. By increasing network security, the chances of privacy spoofing, identity or information theft could be decreased. Security is important for the following reasons (Sandeep,2010):

1) To secure the information from unwanted modification by unauthorized users
2) To secure the secret information so that third person cannot access it.
3) To make information to be delivered to intended destination properly without any loss

4) To keep record of acknowledgments or responses received by any user for a message so that user cannot deny later on that he has not received such messages.
5) To restrict a user to send information to another user with name of a third one.

Another level of security is Computer security which means to secure your computer system from any harm or unwanted damages caused due to network. Such damages could be caused due to the viruses and spywares that may even delete all the information from your system drive or may create hardware problems too. Therefore the network should be secured from such type of harmful software. The persons who intentionally install these software on the network are called Hackers. Sandeep (2010) has presented in his paper that to save information from attackers or hackers, need of computer security is must as:-

1) It needs a complete protection from viruses infected files.
2) To provide proper protection from malwares like worms and bombs.
3) It needs a proper protection from Trojan Horses as they are very harmful for your computer.
4) Three goals of network security: Confidentiality, Integrity and Availability (CIA) model(will be discussed later on in this chapter)

TYPES OF NETWORK SECURITY

COMODO creating trust online (2019) showed in his work that security is required at various levels as discussed below:

1) Antimalware and Antivirus Software
2) Application level Security
3) Behavioral Analytics
4) Email Security
5) Data Loss Prevention
6) Firewalls
7) Intrusion Prevention System
8) Mobile Device Security
9) Virtual Private Network (VPN)
10) Web or internet Security
11) Wireless System Security
12) Endpoint Protection or Security
13) Network Access Control (NAC)

Antimalware and antivirus Programs

Virus is a specific term and Malware is a broader term that includes viruses, worms, Trojans, spywares and ransomware. Malware programs are very dangerous because they can harm a network and are not able to identify easily for days or weeks. It is very important to secure your information against malicious activities. Antivirus and antimalware (also known as malware removal tools) software help you to protect your system against viruses and other malicious activities. These software scan for malware programs and frequently track information in order to detect any malicious activity or malware, delete it and then fix damage. Anti-malware and antivirus both falls under the category of cyber security.

Application level Security

Application security is the process of keeping apps more secure by finding, fixing, preventing vulnerabilities and enhancing the security of apps. It means use of software, hardware, and processes to secure applications from malicious activities. Millions of applications are designed nowadays but none of them is designed perfectly so it's very important to secure these apps. It is feasible for any application to contain vulnerabilities which are useful for attackers to make entry into the network. Therefore application level security contains the procedures to close door for these vulnerabilities.

Behavioral Analytics

Behavior analytics means to detect abnormal network behavior i.e. patterns of data (data that is not according to rules or standards) transmitted through a network. The analytics tools are used to detect the anomaly or abnormal behavior and then alert security teams (IT managers) to detect and stop this unusual behavior. These tools study, analyze and then make a report of these abnormal activities that are not following the rules or standards of normal behavior. Among the users of behavior analytics is the National Security Agency, which utilizes the analytics to recognize dangers to its private cloud framework

Data Loss Prevention

It is an approach to make sure that users working in an organization should not send sensitive and useful information outside the network so that it is not accessed by unauthorized users. Data loss prevention (DLP) technologies use a set of network security measures that help a network administrator to control what data users can transfer. It prevents users from uploading and sending any valuable information in an unsafe manner.

Email Security

Email is among the most generally used and required network services. Email portals are viewed as the main risk vector for a security breach. It is considered to be most easy way for attackers to spread malware through spam emails and then forcefully making the user to open the attachments or links to harm the system resources. These attackers utilize social designing strategies and individual data so as to construct refined phishing efforts to mislead recipients and afterward send them to destinations helping up malware. Therefore it's very important to secure Email portals. To block or control incoming and outgoing data, an email security application is used to prevent the loss of sensitive information.

Firewalls

Firewalls act as a barrier between authorized internal networks and unauthorized external networks such as Internet. A set of policies and defined rules are implemented to either block or allow a particular traffic. A firewall may be implemented as a hardware device and software program also. The firewall effectively manages incoming and outgoing traffic on the basis of these predefined rules on your system, analyze links, and then secures all links while connected to internet.

Intrusion Prevention System (IPS)

IPS is a network security or threat prevention system that examines a network flow for various suspicious activities like security threats or policy violations. According to Royal Holloway (2009) "The basic role of an IPS is to identify malicious activity, keep a log information, try to block the malicious activity, and then finally to report it".

Mobile Device Security

Mobile devices security provides full security to data on portable devices and also to the network system that connect various devices. The basic portable devices within a network are tablets, smartphones, and personal computers. These days, 90% of business use mobile devices and the growth in Internet of Things (IoT) devices present new difficulties to arrange security. Subsequently, IT need to adjust its way to deal with security. A network security plan must record for all of the different locations and uses that employees demand of the company network, however you can find a way to improve your cell phone security.

Virtual Private Network (VPN)

VPN is a type of network security that is used to create a secure and encrypted connection over a public network like internet. A VPN uses the shared public system for its working and use various security rules or standards and tunneling protocols to maintain privacy. VPN clients of an organization's network want to access resources on remote system need to connect to a VPN gateway server. Before granting access to internal network resources like printers, file servers, printers and private network, a gateway requires the device to verify its identity. In order to authenticate the identity and communication between network and device a remote VPN basically uses IPsec or Secure Sockets Layer protocols.

Web or internet Security

The process of protecting confidential information that is stored online from unauthorized user access and alteration is called web security. Perfect web security techniques used to control the access of a user to web, denying access to suspicious sites, and also blocking.

Wireless Security

The idea of Wireless security deals with protection of various devices or systems like computers, tablets, mobile devices, laptops and other portable devices along with the network and their connections from attacks, threats and vulnerabilities in wireless system. These networks are not much secure as wired networks and this clear path for hackers to enter. It is in this way important for the wireless security to be solid. Many wireless security protocols are designed to secure wireless networks. Some of them are WEP, WPA, and WPA2.

Endpoint Security

Endpoint Security also called endpoint protection is a network security technique used to provide security to corporate networks when these networks get accessed through remote devices like mobile devices, laptops and wireless devices. For example, Comodo Advanced Endpoint Protection software provides seven layers of security including file reputation, viruscope, auto-sandbox, URL filtering, host intrusion prevention, antivirus software and firewall. All these services are offered as a single service in order to secure them from both identified and unidentified threats.

Network Access Control (NAC)

This is essentially a network management approach that is executed through software or an integrated approach. The basic objective is to create and manage identity and access control, guarantee security policies are used, and removes, prevent and reduce security risks in a network environment. It comprises procedures, protocols, policies, tools and techniques that basically restrict and regulate what a person may or may not access on a network i.e. this system security process encourages to manage access to your system. In order to keep out potential attackers, it is important to identify each user and device. This without a doubt will assist you with enforcing your security strategies. Nonconforming users or devices may be granted only limited access or may be simply blocked.

TYPES OF SECURITY ATTACKS

An attack is a specific technique used to exploit vulnerability. A threat is a danger that can cause harm to your system and its resources. This can create a loss of data confidentiality, data availability and also data integrity. Threats may be intentional or may be unintentional or accidental. Vulnerability is basically weakness in a system that may be subjected by a threat. To reduce overall risk one should reduce system vulnerability and this may also limit the impact of threats on the system. Prof. Dong Xuanand Adam C. Champion (2017) discussed about various attacks and threats in his paper. These are as follow:

Types of Attacks

Active Attacks

In this security attacks, the attacker attempts to read the data during its transmission through channel and then try to alter or modify the information. Active attacks are threat to integrity and availability. Different forms of active attacks are:

- **Masquerade or spoofing:** Itis also called Interruption attack in which unauthorized attacker tries to prevent as authorized person to get access into system resources. **For example,** attacker can steal the bank details like card number and PIN of a bank customer and can get access to customer account by pretending that he/she is an authorized person.

- **Modification:** This type of attack is possible using two ways *replay attack* and *alteration*. In the *replay* attack, attacker obtains a copy or sequence of data or message sent by user and later replays or resent it. **For example**, a person sends a request to bank for receiving a payment. In between attacker get all the bank details of that person by intercepting the message and then sent this request again to receive another payment from bank. While *alteration* of the message involves some modification to the original information and then use it for its own purpose.
- **Repudiation:** It means sender or receiver may deny later on that they have not sent or receive any message. **For example**, when a person buys a product from a manufacturer and pays for it online but later on manufacturer denies that he has not received any payment and asks to pay it again.
- **Denial of Service (DOS)**: DOS attack (threat to unavailability) may slow down or totally interrupt the service of a system. Attacker used to send too many requests to server that the server may crashes (making server unavailable) due to heavy load on system. Attacker may analyze and delete server request to a client make client to trust that server is not working or responding.

Passive Attacks

In passive attack, the attacker goal is just to obtain information but attacker does not modify data or harm system. System continues with its working as normal but attacker may harm the sender or receiver. These threats are threats to confidentiality. Passive attacks are hard to identify as they don't include any modification in the user data or system resources. These types of attacks prevent attacks rather than detection.

- **Eavesdropping or snooping:** Attacker or unauthorized person can intercept data and can use it for its own benefit. **For example**, Listen to telephone conversation, interception of email messages and transferred files. To prevent this, encryption techniques are used.
- **Traffic Analysis:** Even if we use encryption techniques, attacker might still observe pattern of message during its transmission. Attacker can determine location or identity of user exchanging information and then could inspect the frequency and length of message that is exchanged. It is feasible to prevent passive attacks by means of encryption.

CRYPTOGRAPHY SECURITY SERVICES

Open system or layered model provides different types of security services, which ensures appropriate security of data transfers and system resources as defined by ITU-T X.800 recommendation. Network Security provides various services with respect to message and user(entity) also. These security services implement security policies by using various security mechanisms. The various types of X.800 services are discussed in Security services(2013). These are as follow:

Authentication

Authentication is the technique of verifying the identity of a user or message. Various types of authentication processes are discussed in Entity Authentication(2013) paper. These are as follow:

- **Peer Entity or user Authentication:** It is the process of verifying a user or entity before getting access to system resources. For example, if a student wants to access the resources of his institute then student required to be authenticated (by putting credentials)while logging through the institute portal to prove that he is a valid user. It is basically to protect the interests of the university and the student.
- **Data Origin or message Authentication:** Authenticity of a message must be verified by the receiver. This service allows the receiver to verify the identity of sender to make sure that message has come from a valid source.

  Basic Authentication Methods for network security: Strong authentication methods are presented in Network World (2016) document as given below:

  a) **Biometric security:** Biometric is the process of verifying physical traits of a person using a scanning hardware device to verify the identity of a user. This approach is good because two users can not have same physical traits. Some basic biometric authentication methods include face scanning and identification, fingerprint scan and recognition, retinal and iris scans and voice recognition.

  b) **Token Authentication:** Token-based authentication is a security method that is used to verify the identity of a user who wants to log in to a system, server and a network using a security token provided by the server. The service follows the process of validating the security token and afterward it processes the user request. Token could be a card which gives access to a building **for example**, when you go to attend a conference in some other place and you stay in hotel. When you check into a hotel, you need to show your identity proof and then you will get a token(card) which lets you to enter into room.

c) **Multi-Factor Authentication:** This method requires two or more ways to verify the identity of a user. ATM is a good example of this technique as you require a ATM card as a physical token and a security PIN to make a transaction.

d) **Out-of-Band Authentication (OOB):** OOB uses absolutely individual channels, similar to cell phones, to validate transactions that generated on a computer system. Any transaction in which one need to transfer money from one place to another, require more validation to finish a transaction like generation of phone call, text or notification etc. It is much more difficult for a hacker to steal money with two necessary individual channels.

Access Control

Access control is a security service that controls the access to a system or resources. It limits the access that who or what can view or use resources. Users are granted access and certain privileges to resources or information and system. Access control systems use some methods like authentication and authorization of users by identifying required login credentials such as PIN, passwords, biometric credentials, and security tokens to provide limited access to resources. There are two types of access control

- **Logical Access Control**
- **Physical Access Control**
  - **Logical access control:** It includes control limits to resources like connections to computer networks, data or information and system files.
  - **Physical access control:** It means provide limited access to physical resources like rooms, buildings and physical computer assets or resources.

Categories of Access Control

The main categories of access control as discussed in Bhargavi H. Goswami(2012) paper are as follow:

a) **Mandatory access control (MAC):** This type of security access model is used in military applications and government organizations in which access rights are provided by a central authority on the basis of multiple levels of security. The grants or denies access are provided on the basis of user or device information security clearance. For example, Security Enhanced Linux is an example of a mandatory access control that is used on the Linux OS.

b) **Discretionary access control (DAC):** In discretionary access control method, administrators define the policies that who can access the resources or system or what all is allowed to be accessed.

c) **Role-based access control (RBAC):** It is mostly used access control method that limits access to computer resources on the basis of predefined business levels rather than individual identity to users like executive level, engineer level 1. The role-based security structure depends on a complex model of role assignments, permissions and role authorizations implemented using role engineering to provide access to systems. MAC and DAC frameworks are implemented using RBAC systems.

d) **Attribute-based access control (ABAC):** This control service provide access rights on the basis of some rules and policies by using the attributes of users, systems and environmental conditions.

Data Confidentiality

Confidentiality assures that private data remains private i.e. the data sent across the network isn't disclosed to the adversary. Only authorized person get access to the sensitive information and should remain confidential to unauthorized person. **For example**, your bank details like account number, PIN code etc. should not be disclosed to any third person. Confidentiality is maintained using different data encryption techniques. Encryption can be performed using algorithms like symmetric key and the asymmetric key algorithms.

- **Connection Confidentiality:** It means protect data of all users while reading the content of data on a connection.
- **Traffic Flow Confidentiality:** It refers to provide protection to the information that might be derived from observation of traffic flows.
- **Connectionless Confidentiality:** It refers to protect user data in a single data block
- **Selective-Field Confidentiality:** It means confidentiality of only selected fields within the user Data on a connection or in a single data block.

Data Integrity

Data Integrity assuring that an object is not altered illegally. The data received should be exactly same as sent by an authorized user without any modification, insertion and deletion.

- **Connection Integrity with Recovery**: It means provide integrity to user data during its transmission on a connection and detect if there is any modification, insertion, and deletion on content of data then perform recovery on data and convert into actual contents.
- **Connection Integrity without Recovery**: It refers to providing data integrity during transmission and detect for any modification but not providing the recovery upon the data.
- **Selective-Field Connection Integrity**: It provides integrity on selected data only while transferred over a connection and detects whether the selected fields are inserted, modified, deleted, or replayed.
- **Connectionless data Integrity**: This service provides integrity upon the block of data and also prevent if any modification performed but not recover the message.
- **Selective-Field Connectionless Integrity**: It refers to provide for the integrity of selected fields within a single connectionless data block and then determine whether the selected fields have been modified.

Non-Repudiation

This assuring against a party that denying a data or a communication that was initiated by that party. It ensures that someone cannot deny that he has sent a message. It provides proof of the origin of data and the integrity of the data. **For example**, if you sign a legal contract your signature is a nonrepudiation device. You cannot later deny to the terms of the contract that you have not signed that document. Digital signatures ensure this.

- **Non-repudiation, Origin:** It is the proof that the message was sent by the intended user or entity only.
- **Non-repudiation, Destination:** It is the proof that the message was received by the intended person only.

SECURITY MECHANISMS

Security mechanisms are technical tools and techniques that are used to implement security services. The basic objective to implement these mechanisms is to detect, avoid, or recover from a security attack or threat. Various security mechanisms discussed by Shunmugapriya (2018) in his work are as followed:

1) **Encipherment:** Encipherment is a security mechanism that provides security by transforming a data into unreadable format so that a third person cannot read or understand it. It refers to hide data from third or unauthorized person to maintain its privacy or confidentiality. Data is transformed using some mathematical algorithms and encryption keys. Different substitution and transformation algorithms are used to implement encipherment. Some of them are Caesar cipher, Playfair, columnar transposition etc.

2) **Data integrity:** It is the process of maintaining accuracy and consistency of data that is, data should not be modified during its transmission. Various error detection and correction algorithms are used to ensure data integrity. Some of them are CRC(Cyclic Redundancy Checks) for error detection and Hamming code for error correction etc. A checksum value is calculated in both sender and receiver side. If computed value is same in both sides then data is error free otherwise not.

3) **Digital Signatures:** It is a mathematical mechanism that is used to verify the authenticity and integrity of a digital message or document. It is a method that binds a user(or entity) to the digital data. This binding is verified by receiver or by any third person. Digital signature value is calculated from the data and a secret key of the person who sign the document. In real scenario, receiver needs to verify that the message belongs to the sender only and he should not deny that he has not sent this message(non-repudiation).

4) **Authentication Exchange:** It is the process of conform the identity of users. In this, two users (sender and receiver) need to exchange some message credentials in order to prove their identity to each other. This exchange process must be through a secure channel like secure socket layer (SSL) which is best in securing the communication channel.

5) **Traffic Padding:** Traffic padding security mechanisms is used to provide protection against traffic analysis attacks. This technique is used to hide traffic pattern during transmission. The idea is basically to add dummy pattern in between the actual pattern so that unauthorized person (called intruder) won't be able to read and understand the actual traffic pattern or data.

6) **Routing Control:** A routing control mechanism refers to monitoring all outgoing traffic through a communication channel and selects a best path for data transmission. In order to prevent the hacker from analyzing traffic on a particular route or path, its better practice to continuously change different available routes between sender and receiver.

7) **Notarization:** Notarization is a technique of involving a third person (trusted party) to control the communication between two persons. The receiver can take a trusted person to store the sender request information in order to prevent the sender later on denying that this request is not made by him/her.

Table 1. Relationship between security services and mechanisms

Services	Security Mechanisms							
Services	Encipherment	Digital signatures	Access Control	Data Integrity	Authentication Exchange	Traffic Padding	Routing Control	Notarization
Peer entity authentication	Yes	Yes	------	------	Yes	------	------	------
Data origin authentication	Yes	Yes	------	------	------	------	------	------
Access control	------	------	Yes	------	------	------	------	------
Traffic flow confidentiality	Yes	------	------	------	------	Yes	Yes	------
Data Integrity	Yes	Yes	------	Yes	------	------	------	------
Non-Repudiation	------	Yes	------	Yes	------	------	------	Yes
Confidentiality	Yes	------	------	------	------	------	Yes	------
Availability	------	------	------	Yes	Yes	------	------	------

8) **Access control:** This mechanism use methods to prove that a user has access right to the data or resources owned by a system. Locks and login credentials are two analogous mechanisms of access control.

Relationship Between Security Services and Mechanism

In a network or system, usually the security module will provide a number of services to ensure a complete security solution is available. These services may help to assure that a communication is authentic, or to assure that a file transmitted is confidential. A security service makes use of one or more security mechanisms. The following table 1 shows different types of security services use various types of security mechanisms.

CRYPTOGRAPHY AND ITS BASIC TERMS

Cryptography

The art or science containing methods to transform a readable (or intelligible) message into one that is not readable (or unintelligible), and then use methods to retransform that message back to its original message or readable format is called cryptography. Professor Guevara Noubir (2004), Dan Boneh & Victor Shoup (2016) have presented very well in his work, the various terminologies of cryptographic system. These are:

- **Plaintext**: It is the real original message in understandable form
- **Cipher text**: It is converted or transformed message that cannot be understood.
- **Cipher**: Cipher is an algorithm (transposition and/or substitution methods) that converts or transforms plain text into cipher text

- **Key**: Some secret code or information known to the sender and receiver only and used by the cipher or algorithm in conversion process.
- **Encryption or encode (Encipher):** The method to transfer plaintext to cipher text using a cipher or algorithm and a key is called encryption.
- **Decryption or decode (Decipher):** The method to transfer cipher text back into plaintext using a cipher or algorithm and a key is called decryption.
- **Code breaking or Cryptanalysis**: The process of transforming a cipher or unreadable message or tex tback into a readable message without the knowledge of any key is called cryptanalysis.
- **Cryptology**: It is a study of both cryptography and cryptanalysis
- **Symmetric or Secret Key Encryption:** Symmetric key or secret key encryption uses a secret key and the same cipher or cryptographic algorithm to encrypt or decrypt a message e.g. DSA.
- **Asymmetric or public Key Encryption:** Asymmetric key or public key encryption uses two keys(a private key and public key) and the same cipher or cryptographic algorithm to encrypt or decrypt a message like RSA algorithm

As per discussion in Mark Adler & Jean-Loup Gailly (2002) paper, Asymmetric key encryption and decryption methods are expensive compared to symmetric key encryption and decryption. Symmetric key algorithms are better in performance hence preferred for any bulk encryption.

REFERENCES

Adler, M., & Gailly, J.-L. (2002). *An introduction to cryptography*. Available at: https://www.cs.unibo.it/babaoglu/courses/security/resources/documents/intro-to-crypto.pdf

Andress, J. (2011). *The Basics of Information Security. Understanding the Fundamentals of InfoSec in Theory and Practice*. Elsevier.

Authentication, E. (2013). *Network security, security services*. Available at:http://www.abcd.lk/sliit/eBooks/Data%20Communications%20and%20Networking/Chapter%2031.pdf

Boneh, D., & Shoup, V. (2016). *A Graduate Course in Applied Cryptography*. https://toc.cryptobook.us/

Comodo. (2019). *COMODO creating trust online: Network security*. Available at: https://enterprise.comodo.com/blog/what-is-network-security/

Goswami. (2012). *Network Security*. Available at: https://bhg2.files.wordpress. com/2012/08/ch1.pdf

Holloway, R. (2009). *Network Security hierarchy. University of London Kenny Paterson's Lectures for: M*. Sc. in Information Security.

Network Security. (2000). *Cisco systems, Network Security, ISOC NTW 2000.* Available at: http://www.potaroo.net/t4/pdf/security.pdf

Network World. (2016). *Strong authentication methods.* Available at: https://www. networkworld.com/article/2296774/seven-strong-authentication-methods.html

Noubir, P. G. (2004). *Fundamentals of cryptography.* Available at: http://www.ccs. neu.edu/home/noubir/Courses/CSU610/S06/cryptography.pdf

NPTEL. (n.d.). *Network Security, CSE IIT, Kharagpur.* Available at: https://nptel. ac.in/courses/106105080/pdf/M8L1.pdf

Pawar & Anuradha. (2015). Network Security and Types of Attacks in Network. *International Conference on Computer, Communication and Convergence.* 10.1016/j. procs.2015.04.126

Preneel. (2011). *Cryptographic algorithms.* Available at: https://handouts.secappdev. org/handouts/2011/Bart%20Preneel/preneel_cryptographic_algorithms_2011.pdf

Rao, Rath, & Kabat. (2018). *Cryptography And Network Security Lecture Notes.* Veer Surendra Sai University of Technology.

Sandeep. (2010). *Need of network security.* Available at: https://www. indiastudychannel.com/resources/105777-Need-of-Network-Security.aspx

Schneier, B. (1994). *Applied Cryptography.* New York: Publishers, John Kiley & Sons, Inc.

Security services. (2013). http://www.idconline.com/technical_references/pdfs/ data_communications/Security_Services.pdf

Shunmugapriya. (2018). *Security Services and Mechanisms.* Available at https:// eezytutorials.com/Cryptography-And-Network-Security/Security-services-and-mechanisms.php#.XLsqzugzbIU

Stallings, W. (2003). *Cryptography and Network Security. In Principles and Practices.* Prentice Hall.

The OSI Security Architecture. (n.d.). Available at: https://cgi.csc.liv.ac.uk/~alexei/ COMP522_10/COMP522-SecurityArchitecture_07.pdf

Turner, D. M. (2017). *Applying Cryptographic Security Services - a NIST summary*. Available at: https://www.cryptomathic.com/news-events/blog/applying-cryptographic-security-services-a-nist-summary

Vacca, J. R. (2009). *Computer and Information Security Handbook*. Morgan KaufmannSeries in Computer Security.

Xuan & Champion. (2017). *Threats and attacks*. Available at: http://web.cse.ohio-state.edu/~champion.17/4471/4471_lecture_2.pdf

Chapter 6

Analysing Ethical Issues of a Patient Information Systems Using the PAPA Model

Sam Goundar
iD https://orcid.org/0000-0001-6465-1097
The University of the South Pacific, Fiji

Alvish Pillai
The University of the South Pacific, Fiji

Akashdeep Bhardwaj
iD https://orcid.org/0000-0001-7361-0465
University of Petroleum and Energy Studies, India

ABSTRACT

Healthcare is a vital portion of today's medical environment, and it is necessary for medical providers to do their work in an efficient and effective manner. Everyday, hundreds of thousands of patients visit medical amenities stimulating the administration to run smoothly. Almost all hospitals and the health centers in Fiji are now heavily dependent on a patient information system (PATISplus) that helps the employees to manage all the medical and administrative information. In this chapter, the authors analyse the ethical issues of a patient information systems (PATIS) using the PAPA model. This is in terms of privacy, accessibility, accuracy, and property. This chapter reviews current policies within the Ministry of Health and Medical Services in Fiji and also if there is a need of development of standard operating procedures in view of the PAPA model.

DOI: 10.4018/978-1-7998-2367-4.ch006

INTRODUCTION

Hospital information system (HIS) is an element of health informatics that provide a common source of information about a patient's health history. These systems enhance the ability of health care professionals to coordinate care by providing a patient health information and visit history at the place and time that it is needed.

The need to strengthen Fiji's health information system (HIS) has been an ongoing issue for many years as highlighted in several assessment reports [FHSIP/HIMMA 1999; 2005;]. HIS at MoHMS had been receiving support from their partners such as AusAid and JICA during last decade and the data was collected from the sources due to lots of previous work. However policies were developed and information usage got less attention.

Health information system in Fiji is multipart and consolidated with wide data collection. Although the system was able to grab and gather information, it is limited to analysis, corroboration and comment on processes that would convert data into useful decision making information. Fiji's health information through PATISPlus flow at the moment supports information requirements of upper management and is designed to stream data for the annual reporting needs of the Ministry. (Health Information Unit, MoH: 2009).

This research will be conducted at the Colonial War Memorial hospital (CWMH) one of the three largest hospital in the country. It is a referral hospital which also caters for referrals from the pacific neighboring countries. The research will focus on finding out the linkage, if any between the currently used CWMH PATIS system and the PAPA model introduced by Mason which is the four most crucial ethical issues of the information era on 1986 which is Privacy, Accuracy, Property and Accessibility abbreviated to PAPA.

This research will find out if there are any ethical issues in the current patient information systems using the PAPA model. This is to be undertaken to find out if the four concepts of PAPA model (Privacy, Accessibility, Accuracy and Property) are being considered in view of how patient information is collected, analyzed, managed, disseminated and used at the CWMH. In doing this, the study will also attempt to see if there are existing policies and procedures available to guide the use of PATIS ethically within CWMH and if so, what are the gaps and areas of improvement needed to strengthen the system.

The paper is important as results of the study will highlight the strengths and weaknesses of the current PATIS system at CWMH and furthermore, it will inform decision makers of relevant areas of improvement in terms of policies and procedures and also inform or raise awareness to the owners of the information (the patients) on important aspects to consider and be mindful of in terms of their health information, in as far as how they can access it or how it is used by the secondary users.

Now days anyone can access information from phones, desktops, internet etc. while previously the public gets to know things when published in the papers or announced in the radios. But in today's era with the different forums of social medial these information is no longer confidential. Thus it is important that at operational level people are aware of what they are doing and also on the other hand raise awareness to the patients on their rights in terms of information and also in terms of what they can do when they think their rights have been violated when it comes to usage of their personal health information or medical records.

This research will be using quantitative method whereby interviews will be taken by devising a set of questionnaires based on the PAPA model. A desktop review will also be undertaken to see what is there in place taking into account the use of PAPA model. The contribution will be giving guidance to the internal uses and also the patients on ways of improvement once the gaps have been identified.

PATIS user access is provided by the Ministry's Information Technology department with access restricted to users for their domains. PATIS reports is used to improve reporting systems on services such as number of patients and to quantify medicine usage. Additionally, privacy is ensured through user passwords and usernames and selective access is provided to senior managers for editing of information on PATIS.

The massive use of computer science and information technology in the business world and other institutions has brought many ethical issues and concern. In 1986, Dr. Richard Mason wrote a seminal article in which he categorized information ethics issues into four categories, which are Privacy, Accuracy, Property and Accessibility abbreviated to PAPA. Mason's PAPA model focused on the individual impairment which could arise from the unethical or misuse of information and information technology. Using this framework, the group hope to analyze and evaluate the PATIS used at CWMH and reach the conclusion on any ethical issues that have or may have emerged due to the unethical use of information technology.

Problem Statement

Privacy, accessibility and accuracy issues surrounding the use of PATIS can lead to dissemination or spread of confidential patient information. Inaccurate reporting can be a result of inaccurate data entry and providing administrator access to components of PATIS can also be cause for concern. Through utilization of the PAPA model as the methodology, the group intends to identify existence of ethical and/or social issues with PATIS within CWMH.

LITERATURE REVIEW

Today's society today has become progressively rooted in the digital information era therefor ethics in information system continues to be an important and widely discussed issues in academics and organisations whether it be private, public or non-profit organisation. The world of technology has dramatically evolve in the decades. The use of data in every organisations be it a private, service or non-government organisation data is now a major ingredient for decision making.

Almazan et al 2017 developed a model for the evaluation of the success of the IS for small and medium enterprises (SME) to determine the influence of the IS in the organizational results. To reach this goal, the Partial Least Squares (PLS) statistical technique was used through a survey in Mexico. In concluding, the study highlighted that the users that achieved greater satisfaction are motivated toward a greater use of the IS, where a greater satisfaction and use lead to better results at the organizational level. In other words, the organizations with greater technological infrastructure, development methodologies, and competence of their programmers improve the results of the quality of the system, contributing to the individual and organizational development of the company.

According to Laudon et.al 2018, data growth technology and analytics have created openings for organisations to use big data to advance operations and decision making. With the many benefits that technology has brought about in view of big data it has also provide big challenges to the business in view of ethical and social issues. *"Digital technology creates new opportunities for invading your privacy and using information that could cause you harm"*, Laudon & Laudon, (2018).

The implementation of HRIS in the public sector offers its own set of challenges. Troshani et al 2011 argued that HRIS are becoming increasingly important in helping modern organizations manage their human assets effectively, therefore the study focused on isolating factors that influence the organizational; adoption of HRIS in public sector organizations. In conclusion, the study emphasised on the need for champions in the public sector organizations to demonstrate HRIS benefits before their adoption can succeed. In addition, various organizational factors, including management commitment and human capability, the authors also found that broader environmental factors including regulatory compliance can have a deep impact on the success of HRIS adoption by creating urgency in adoption intentions.

On the other hand, Alam et al 2016 explored factors influencing the management decisions to adopt human resource information system in the hospital industry of Bangladesh. Thirteen factors under four dimensions were investigated to explore their influence on HRIS adoption decisions in hospitals. The results identified 5 most critical factors i.e. IT infrastructure, top management support, IT capabilities of staff, perceived cost, and competitive pressure as influential factors towards adoption. In implementing and analysing ethical issues relating to PATISPlus at the hospitals, the 5 critical factors identified above is extremely useful.

According to Marshall (1999) viewed technology as part of material culture and ethical issue because failure to progress on broad social agreement on right applications of modern technology might possibly lead to collapse in social cohesion and the rise of communal conflict. Belle Woodward (2011) states that in 1986, Mason introduced four broad categories of ethical issues of the information age: that is privacy, accuracy, property and access which is now known as PAPA.

They further elaborated that Mason's concern for privacy was that an individual should be able to decide what personal information to hold private, what information to share and be confident that shared information would be kept safe. As for accuracy this focused on discussion on who was responsible for the accuracy and authenticity of information and what retribution was due to those injured by erroneous data.

Zafar (2015) identified that by design, HRIS hold confidential and sensitive information therefore, one needs to ensure the security of these systems from unintentional mistakes that may compromise such information. Current systems design and training procedures of HRIS unintentionally help reinforce unsecure behaviours that result in non-malicious security breaches. Measures to improve security through design and training may occur by breaking the use/impact cycle that individuals have habitually formed. Using strong contexts and cues allow trainers to interrupt individuals' habits. Then, they have the opportunity to enforce the repetition of the desired behaviour.

Haux (2005) concluded that modern information processing methodology and information and communication technology has strongly influenced our societies, including their health care. Health information systems have to be developed and explored that enhance opportunities for global access to health services and medical knowledge. New opportunities for the systematic processing of data, information and knowledge in medicine and health care may considerably contribute to the progress of medicine and health sciences as well as to the progress of informatics in general.

Heeks (2005) on the other hand attempted to develop a better conceptual foundation for, and practical; guidance on, health information systems failure and success. The design-reality gap model was piloted to demonstrate its value as a tool for risk assessment and mitigation on HIS projects. It was found that the design-reality gap model can be used to address the problem of HIS failure, both as a post hoc evaluative tool and as a pre hoc risk assessment and mitigation tool. It also validates a set of methods, techniques, roles and competencies needed to support the dynamic improvisations that are found to underpin cases of HIS success.

It was further stated by Belle Woodward (2011) that Mason's discussion of property addressed intellectual property rights, including those not necessarily protected by law and he also makes reference to the physical property such as the

" conduits through which information passes" and the final one in view of PAPA framework is access which dealt with the right or authority to obtain information.

Peslak (2016) validates the PAPA issues and finds all the topics are currently viewed as important ethical issues. The study also finds that overall there are high levels of concern with all four issues but finds that privacy is viewed as most important followed by accessibility and accuracy which are viewed equally and property which is viewed lowest, but still very important. A demographic analysis reveals that gender plays a significant role in determining recognition of privacy and accuracy as important ethical issues.

Electronic patient records and sensor networks for in-home patient monitoring are at the current forefront of new technologies. Meingast (2006) identified that the face of health care is changing as new technologies are being incorporated into the existing infratructure. While there are benefits to technologies, associated privacy and security issues need to be analyzed to make these systems socially acceptable. It was suggested that issues of data access, storage and analysis are not unique to the medical arena. These problems have been looked at in a numbers of areas, from financial services to internet shopping and technical solutions exist which can be applied to health care to increase privacy and security in a multi-user setting.

Kuhn & Giuse (2001) identified both proven benefits and critical issues of hospital information systems evolving towards health information systems. Reports on HIS successes and failures were analyzed, and core challenges were identified. It was found that there are several more problems than reports on successes suggest. Among today's core problems are integration, human-computer interaction, socio-technical issues, and support of processes..

Winter et al 2010, introduced hospital information systems, which are the most complex of instances of institutional information systems, and trans institutional information systems. It mentions that Health Information Systems are dealing with processing data, information, and knowledge in health care environments. Especially with regards to chronic diseases, it becomes more and more important to organize health care in a patient-centric way, such that all participating in or outpatient care institutions cooperate very closely.

Ward (2004) highlighted the clinical information system is becoming more common in intensive care units. These systems have the ability to record, store and retrieve large amounts of clinical patient data with great ease. Unfortunately, there is not much information available about the accuracy of the data coming from these systems. The study concluded that there are still some hurdles that must be overcome before these systems can truly reach their potential for research and quality assurance. Limiting the human role is important especially since most of these data entry and whose work demands are every increasing.

Ayatollahi et al 2009, presents the ED staff perspectives about the accessibility and confidentiality of information in the Emergency Department in Northern Ireland. The results showed that the ED staff had role-based access to the current information systems, and these systems met only a small part of their information needs. Although the ED staff believed that improving the accessibility of information could be helpful in emergency care services, there were concerns about the confidentiality of information. It was concluded that to design a system, the accessibility and confidentiality of information should be addressed in parallel. A balance between these two is needed, as the failure of each of these may negatively influence the use of the system.

Denley & Smith (1998) described a practical approach to managing the confidentiality of patient information in large-scale clinical information systems in the acute hospital. Control over access to the individual patient is required, with this access only be granted when the members of staff's rights match a patient's current clinical contact.

The Patient Information Management System (PIMS) is used in Indian health services to track the patient information and their history. PIMS is divided into three modules: Admission/Discharge/Transfer (ADT), Scheduling, and Sensitive Patient Tracking. The PIMS ADT delivers instructions to extensive collection of customers in India Health Service amenities in day-to-day use of the ADT Module of the PIMS software. The ADT module of the PIMS platform delivers widespread software to organizational purposes interrelated to patient admission, discharge, transfer, census, incomplete chart tracking, and day surgery. The data collected and sustained by the ADT software is accessible online to wide-ranging users in the medicinal capability to support in daily tasks and better competence, lessening form-filling and decreasing errors. The ADT software offers for effectual and correct gathering, preservation, and end result of data, therefore increasing health care facility's ability to run worth attention to its patients. ADT includes the following:

- Bed Control
- Day Surgery
- Incomplete Chart
- ADT Reports
- ADT Supervisor

Accessibility of Data

The systems have restrictions on the accessibility of the data and only specific members are given the full access, others use data for which they have been contracted permission. Information is given to those personnel who need to know and before release of any kind of information the caller's identification and job purpose is verified with the supervisor. Limited basis of information use is authorized.

Confidentiality

Sensitivity of electronic and hardcopy data is always kept in consideration and protected where hardcopy storage containing confidentiality information is locked in room or cabinet. All information is protected from the public view at all times and any use of storage device is formatted. Patient confidentiality is always maintained with the use of PIMS system.

Anderson (2007) investigated the present status of information technology in health care, the perceived benefits and barriers by primary care physicians by carrying out literature analysis and survey data from primary care physicians on adoption of information technology. It was found that there could be major barriers to the implementation of information technology and its practice. These barriers include lack of access to capital by health care providers, complex systems and lack of data standards that permit exchange of clinical data, privacy concerns and legal barriers. Overcoming these barriers will require subsidies and performance incentives by payers and government; certification and standardization of vendor applications that permit clinical data exchange; removal of legal barriers and greater security of medical data.

Fessler & Gremy (2001) in its opinion paper introduced the concept of ethics and to argue on its importance for health information systems. In conclusion, it stated that any technology sets a relationship between human beings and their environment, physical and human. No technology can be seen as merely instrumental. This is especially relevant when dealing with large automatic information systems, developed to contribute to the management and integration of large organizations, such as hospitals. In such a context, the environment is mainly made up of humans. In evaluating such information systems, human factors preside over merely technical factors. A perfect hand-and software system can be an absolute failure in everyday use.

Backups

Backups of the system and files are made on regular basis and stored in a secured environment away from the system. Strategic plans are discussed well in advance during occurrence of natural disasters, loss of processing and system recovery mechanisms.

Developers

Developers are always mindful of data confidentiality, availability and integrity when developing system and strictly follow programming standards and conventions. Any software changes need to be given a reason and programmers initials with change date. All software remains the property of the government and not the developer. Duties policies and procedures are fully observed. (OIT: 2009)

According to a research done by the World Health Organisation (WHO) the acceptance and usage of patient information systems in nearby states is high. World Bank income group, and globally – showed that electronic information systems are progressively approved in medical environments; though it is commonly used in the high income countries such as Brazil, China and India are introducing the electronic system.

Electronic systems contribute widely in service quality and cost effective for instant, patient health problems are easy tracked and treated overtime particularly for chronic diseases. Patient data analysis provides for new insight and better understanding of the health systems.

Electronic Health System (EHS) is designed in such a way that it can facilitate data exchange and dissimilar the disease definitions. Criterions need to be realistic to the data and the systems to permit and enable interchange data among many sources. The implementation of ideals is continuing thriving in nearby Member States with principles for medical construction, data, interoperability, language, and messaging. These are vital groundwork for the application of patient information systems since they enable perfect communication. Most countries have moved ahead to establish legal works in protection of the patient data. (WHO: 2012)

Basically Fiji and India have the similar patient information system. Both of the systems enhance the easy accessibility for patient information such as the personal, illness and other relevant details. Systems function is common and security issue for the information is vital. Purpose for Fiji, India and WHO research indicates that collective patient records is beneficial at the national level for preparation, strategy design, program management, observing and assessment, and disease investigation. Attentive illness grade styles, forms and reaction to involvements, means can be recovered.

Ethical issues has been a major disucssion around the use of health information or patient information sytems. In view of privacy and security the In additions to concerns about privacy and secuirty the vital ethical issues in the use of health information technology has spin around the principles of providing safe and effective care and avoiding harm, Berner (2008). Berne, (2008) further stated that in other terms information technology can be well thought out like other interreferences in that one needs to balance the benefits using these systems with the potentianl risks to the patient. Furthermore like any other systems in place the legal issues around regulations on the use of these systems and monintoring the effects to ensreu that these systems are used properly and safety

Automated health information technology systems have the prospective to provide primary care physicians with tools to manage patient care and work in multidisciplinary teams, Cathy Schoen (2012). The spread of health information technology capacity in the United States and Canda has provided opportunites for global learning as physicians become informative of the health information sytems.

Health information system in Fiji is multipart and consolidated with wide data collection. Although the system was able to grab and gather information, it is limited to analysis, corroboration and comment on processes that would convert data into useful decision making information. Fiji's health information through PATISPlus flow at the moment supports information requirements of upper management and is designed to stream data for the annual reporting needs of the Ministry. (Health Information Unit, MoH: 2009).

The Ministry of Health PATIS User Manual (2008) stated that having unique patient identifier number are many, but the most significant is ensuring that the data belongs to the right/patient and the records for individual patients can be linked across multiple sites.

A patient information system **(PATISPlus)** is a home grown computer system developed with DFAT to provide support for Fiji's Health Sector. PATIS was first implemented at the Waiyevo Hospital in 2001 and have regularly evolved to make it a user friendly and suitable system for Fiji use. The staff initially used it for handling bills and hospital catalog. It had eleven modules, namely Person Master Index, Admission Transfer and Discharge, A&E/GOPD, SOPD, Public Health, Dental, Pharmacy, Microbiology, Disease Index and Radiology.

PATIS has changed since then, and hospital information systems now include the combination of all medical, monetary and managerial presentations. In 2012, the PATIS application has been upgraded from windows based to web based. Now it is known as PATISPlus and has twelve modules: Person Master Index, Admission Transfer and Discharge, A&E/GOPD, SOPD, Pregnancy and Pregnancy and births, Pharmacy, Surgery, Appointments, Radiology, Site Administration, Enquiry and Reports. The Person Master Index (PMI) is used by all other modules to uniquely identify the client and record the incidences of services in the appropriate module.

These systems contain information about patients' health status and treatment provided at any health service in Fiji and indicates any disease pattern with service utilization. It also helps in decision making at all levels of management and short term and long term service planning. PATISPlus use has many advantages such as:

§ Gives a unique patient identifier number referred to as National Health Number (NHN) during their first registration on a particular PATISPlus database. Details will be automatically transmitted to all PATISPlus installations ensuring patient to use only one number for services at any health facilities in Fiji. National Health number is in nine digit format.

§ It creates an electronic copy of patient data relevant for future care.

§ Data is available at all facilities with PATISPlus access and allows continuity care.

§ Plans and evaluation of clinical services in PATISPlus facilities is according to the data.

The National Health Number ensures that the data belongs to the right patient and the records for each patient can be linked to several sites for their safety and care quality. The system also generates pre-programmed labels to prevent errors in identification. It keeps a record of personal details, admission/transfer/discharge, general outpatient, pregnancy and birth details, death details and specialist services. All new and updated data including deletion in PATISPlus is based on real time whereas the old PATIS the data was transferred from each hospital to the Central Office database on scheduled times daily between the hours of 9.00 and 11.00pm.

Statement of Problem - Research Questions

The research questions are as follows:

1. To find out the ethical issues around the use of PATIS system at the Ministry of Health and Medical Services using PAPA Model; and
2. Identify the positive and negative ethical issues around the use of PATIS using the PAPA model.

METHODOLOGY

To successfully carry out this research the following methods were undertaken:

1. Desktop review (what is there); and
2. Interview (based on questionnaires).

A quantitative, cross-sectional study will be carried out. The techniques to collect data will include:

1. Development of a questionnaire based on the PAPA model.
2. Distribution of questionnaires to selected nurses at three busiest wards in the selected unit/division within the Colonial War Memorial Hospital (CWMH).
3. Distribution of questionnaires to selected patients who would be randomly selected during a 3 days visit at the CWMH.

Plan for Data Collection and Management

Written approval was obtained from:

1. Permanent Secretary for Health & Medical Services;
2. Management of CWMH; and
3. The Ethical Committee within the Ministry.
    ◦   Questionnaires were distributed as identified above
    ◦   Hard copies of data obtained during the study period were securely stored under lock and key with the team leader. Electronic copies of data were securely stored with password protection accessible only by the team leader.

Plan for Data Processing and Analysis

1. Data was recorded into Microsoft Excel and analysed with the use of MS Excel
2. Categorical variables from this study were summarized as percentages and frequencies while continuous variables were summarized by mean and standard deviation.
3. Data is presented using tables, bar graphs and pie charts.

Ethical Considerations

1. Adequate level of confidentiality of the data is assured.
2. No staff/user name or any private information regarding the staff/users will be divulged during the research.
3. Additionally, no personal staff/patient details will be recorded.
4. All data collected will be securely stored in a locked cupboard with the researcher and the softcopies will be password protected.
5. Personal details of staff/patients will be de-identified by simply removing names from records and labelled as '1 or A', etc.

RESULTS AND FINDINGS

Health Professionals - Colonial War Memorial Hospital

Figure 1 illustrates that of the 70 health professional participants, majority were nurses (43%), attributed to the large number of nurses at the facility. Pharmacists accounted for 15 of the 70 participants whereas other participants included recorders and radiology and laboratory staff.

Figure 1. Health Professionals at the Hospital (n = 70)

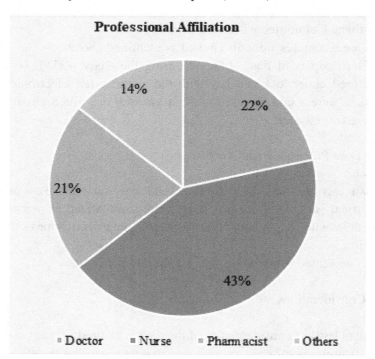

Figure 2 identified some of the reasons why the health professionals used PATISPlus. 30% of the respondents indicated entering patient information as the major use while pharmacy use accounted for 21% of the respondents use. 16% of the participants indicated that it is used for reporting purposes.

Figure 3: Each of the participants had multiple responses for advantages of the system. Majority of the response was that PATISPlus is easy to use, followed by ease of follow-up for patients, access other health records and recording purposes.

Figure 2. Why are you using PATISPlus?

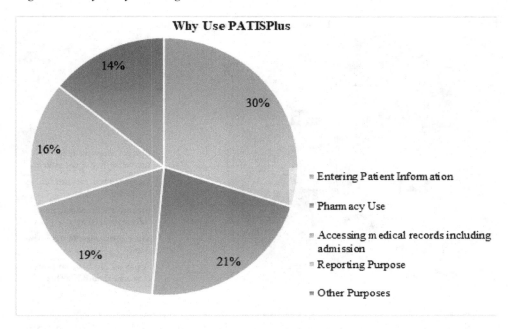

Figure 3. Advantages of using PATISPlus

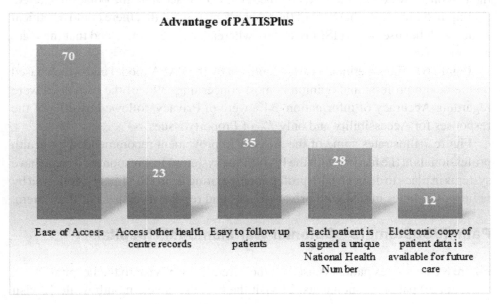

Figure 4. Disadvantages of using PATISPlus

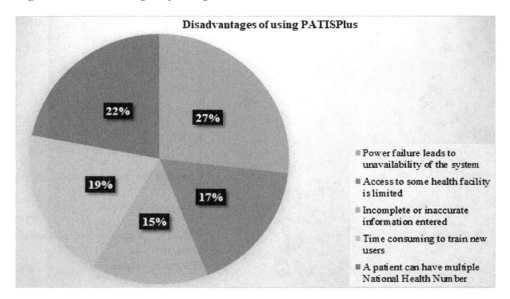

Figure 4 represents the diasadvatges highlighted by the health professionals. 27% of the responses were that during power failures, the system is unavailable, followed by 22% of the responses indicating patients end up having multiple NHN's. 15% of the responses were that there can be incomplete or inaccurate information entered.

Figure 5 illustrates that 81% of the respondents agreed that there could be ethical issues with the use of PATISPlus system whereas only 13% indicated that there are no ethical issues.

Figure 6 defines 4 ethical issues identified by the PAPA model and which based on the health professional opinion is most concerning. 39% of the responses were regarding Accuracy of information, 34% were of Privacy, followed by 20% of the responses for Accessibility and only 7% of Property issues.

Figure 7 illustrates some of the areas of improvement recommended by health professionals at the facility with the PATISPlus system. Most responses were to have systems in place to detect health professionals exiting from the Ministry, followed by review of policies in line with privacy issues and regular awareness of the system.

Patient/Customers - Colonial War Memorial Hospital

Figure 8 categorises patients based on their frequency of visit to the hospital. From a total of 50 patient respondents, 21 visit the hospital once a month while 12 visit once a week followed by 11 every 3 months and 6 every 6 months.

Figure 5. Ethical issues of PATISPlus

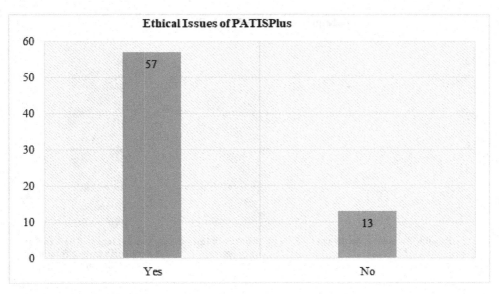

Figure 6. Issues with the Use of PATISPlus

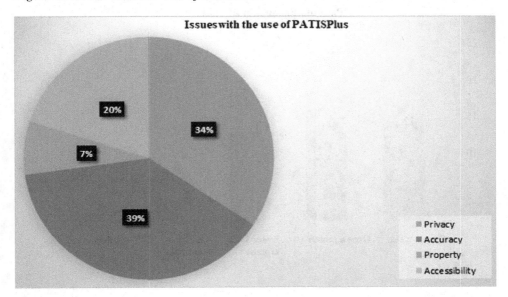

Figure 7. Areas of improvement for PATISPlus

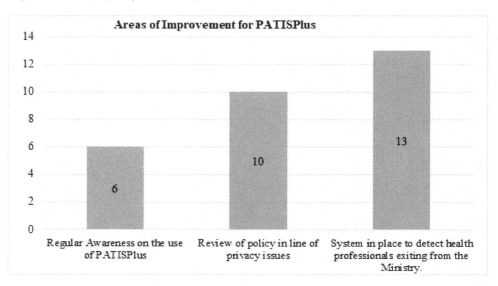

Figure 8. Patients frequency of visits

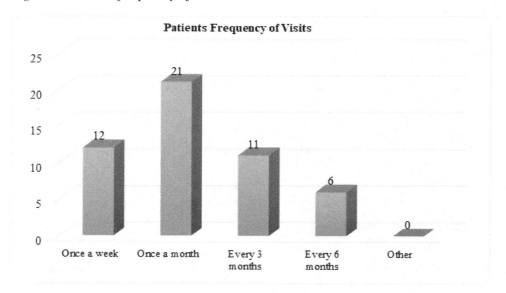

Figure 9. Patients awareness of PATISPlus

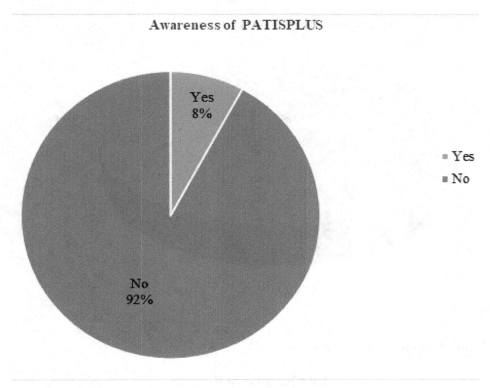

Figure 9 indicates that majority of the patient participants are not aware of a PATISPlus system at the facility, while only 8% indicated yes, they are aware.

Figure 10 highlights that 84% of the patients are aware that their medical records are also kept electornically, whereas 16% of the patients did not know if the records were kept manually.

Figure 11 illustrates that of the 50 participants, 66% feel safe that the medical records are kept safe while 33% do not feel safe about the existence of electronic medical records.

Figure 12 illustrates that 38% of the responses regarding ethical issues had to do with Privacy, followed by 27% to do with Accuracy, 23% for Accessibility and 12% for Property.

Figure 10. Patients awareness of their electronic records

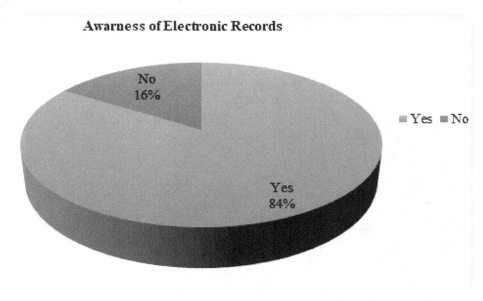

Figure 11. Safe keeping of records

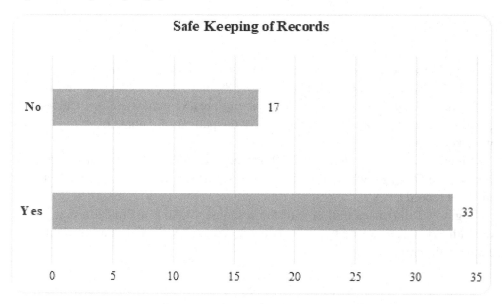

Figure 12. Ethical issues related to the PAPA mode

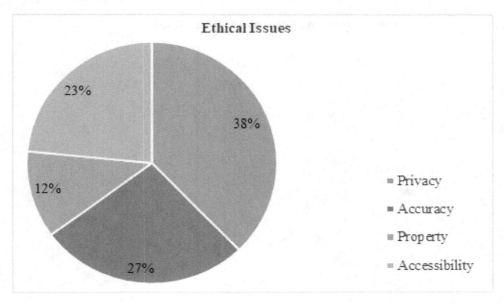

Figure 13. Purpose of using PATISPlus

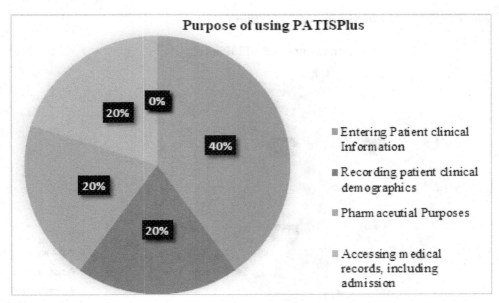

Figure 14. Ethical issues with PATISPlus (Management)

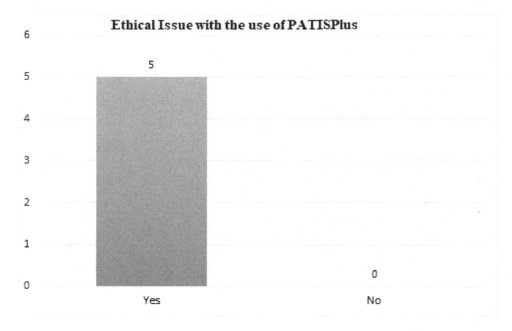

Figure 15. Issues with the use of PATISPlus (Management)

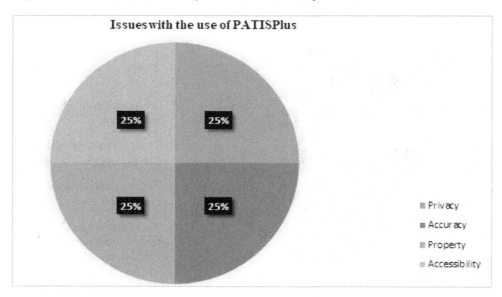

Figure 16. Improvments to PATISPlus (Management)

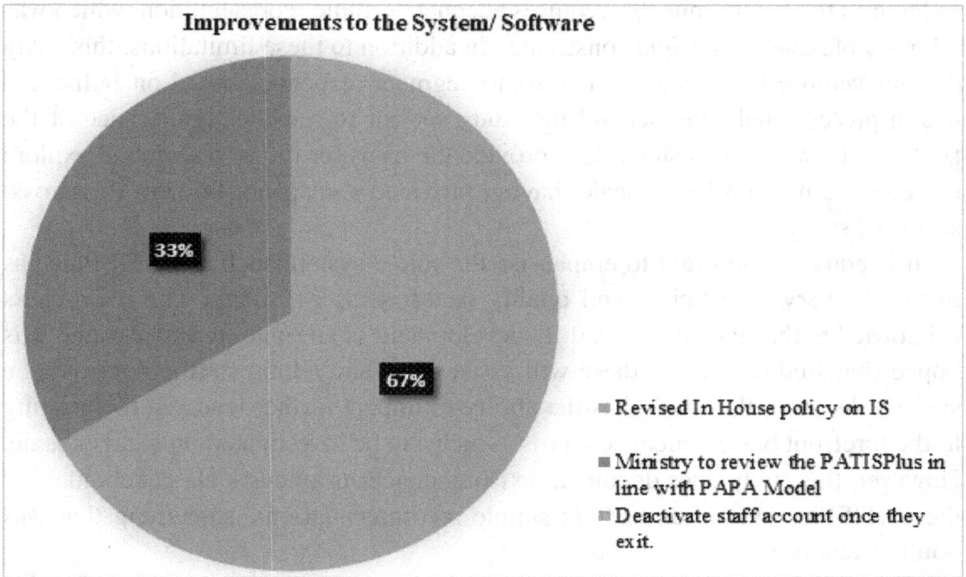

Improvements to the System/ Software

Management - Colonial War Memorial Hospital

Figure 13 illustrates the various purpose for which the management use PATISPlus. 40% of the management utilize it for entering patient information, while 20% use it for reporting, pharmacy and other purposes.

Figure 14 highlights that all 5 management staff agree that there may be some degree of ethical issues with the use of PATISPlus system.

Figure 15 indicates that all of the 4 major PAPA model issues are of concern to the management staff in equal proportions.

Figure 16 illustrates that 67% of the respondents recommend a revised in-house policy on information systems, while the Ministry needs to review PATISPlus based on the 4 factors.

DISCUSSION

The study titled 'Analysing Ethical Issues of a Patient Information Systems Using the PAPA Model,' carried out at a local hospital identified several ethical concerns amongst uses, managements and customers of the PATISPlus system.

It is important to identify that exploring such ethical concerns in an organization as large as the health ministry requires adequate sample representation, which was not possible due to multiple constraints. In addition to these limitations, this study did not venture into detailed analysis to segment responses based on individual health professionals, neither did the study set out to test the significance of the findings. However, this study does provide the basis for future research to explore these concerns on a larger scale, having provided a snapshot through this cross-sectional study.

It is equally important to emphasise the role a system such as PATISPlus has in the delivery of efficient and quality health services in Fiji. The researchers acknowledge that the system and its development is an ongoing process and it is hoped that studies such as these will assist users and administrators improve the system. As such, this study has the ability to impact further research by bringing to the forefront basic ethical concerns, which can be investigated on a larger scale. However, this study does document existing concerns amongst all stakeholders of the PATISPlus system and offers simple recommendations, something that was non-existent prior to this research.

As highlighted in Figure 1, majority of the health professionals involved in this study included nurses, hence a possibility of some responses skewed towards their use and understanding of the system. Pharmacists and doctors also account for a large volume of usage of the PATISPlus system. Similarly, management from the facility were also distributed questionnaires for response.

Attributing to the larger nursing participation, 30% of the respondents indicated that PATISPlus is mostly used for entering patient information while pharmacy use accounts for the second most type of use. It was also indicated that the system is utilized for reporting purposes as well.

The health professionals listed multiple advantages of the system, including ease of access. However, in responding to the PAPA model, 20% of the responses were ethical issues identified due to accessibility. One of the disadvantages mentioned included the system may have incomplete or inaccurate information recorded. This accounted for 15% of the total responses. Similarly, based solely on the PAPA model, 39% of the responses were concerns regarding accuracy of information when participants were queried on the ethical issues. Moreover, health professionals also identified that access of the system to some peripheral health facilities is a disadvantage. On the other hand, the respondents from management highlighted that all of the 4 ethical issues mentioned require equal attention.

There was an overwhelming 81% of the participants who indicated that they have ethical issues with the PATISPlus system while only 19% indicated otherwise. From the viewpoint of health professionals who are the primary users of the system, this is an alarming concern. When queried on which specific ethical issues concerned them, as highlighted earlier, these including (in order of most to least concerning), accuracy, privacy, accessibility and property. In comparison, the patient participants had indicated that their most concerning ethical issues were (in order of most to least), privacy, accuracy, accessibility and property. Such statistics indicate that accuracy and privacy are the highest ethical concerns among the participants of this small-scale study. Similarly, all of the 5 (100%) of the participants from management indicated having ethical issues with the PATISPlus system.

Additionally, the health professionals who participated in this study did have some recommendations and these included to have policies in line with addressing the ethical issues, particularly privacy and also increasing awareness of the PATISPlus system. These recommendations could also be put forward to the Ministry for improvement and are also in line with recommendations identified through literature reviews. The management team highlighted the importance of recommendations such as having in-house policies on all information systems and for PATISPlus to be reviewed taking into consideration the ethical issues identified.

On the other hand, the study also included 50 patients as part of the study. Most of these patients were frequent visitors to the hospital, particularly on a monthly basis. The study did not evaluate the purpose of these visits as it did not offer any significance to the findings. When asked if the participants were aware of the PATISPlus system, 92% of the respondents indicated No, while only 8% had some knowledge of this system. Additionally, the participants' were also asked if they were aware of the existence of electronic records of their health information. 84% of the respondents indicated Yes, they are aware of electronic medical records and 66% of the participants then went on to highlight that they are concerned about the safe keeping of these records. As alluded to earlier, most of the patient participants identified privacy as their primary ethical concern followed by accuracy.

CONCLUSION

The study investigated and subsequently highlighted ethical issues with the PATISPlus system using the PAPA model. It was found that privacy and accuracy issues are most concerning to the stakeholders inclusive of health professionals, patients and management. Additionally, although not most concerning, issues with accessibility and property remain as common ethical concerns for the participants as well. The findings indicate similarity with findings from similar hospital based research with privacy and accuracy being primary ethical concerns amongst stakeholders. Having identified these ethical issues, the Ministry and relevant institutions can build on this study and put in measures to control or address these issues. As with any information system, improvements can be made to improve service delivery and more importantly, protect the information and data. This study has offers practical solutions to this end.

RECOMMENDATIONS

It is recommended that:

§   Further research be carried out on a larger scale to have a clearer picture of the ethical issues and concerns regarding PATISPlus and its usability. In doing so, a larger sample size involving multiple facilities should be included as part of the study.

§   Data analysis could include information based on different health professionals and not merely a summary of the views and opinions of all health professionals as participants.

§   The Ministry and relevant stakeholders to investigate potential sources of ethical issues (privacy, accuracy, accessibility & property) highlighted in this study and find solutions to overcome these issues.

§   Efforts should be put in place to improve accessibility of this system to all health facilities

§   Awareness of the existence of such a system be provided to all stakeholders, which could bring to light recommendations from stakeholders for systems improvement.

§   Data accuracy and protection systems to be made a core part of the PATISPlus system so as to ensure accuracy and protection.

§   Regulations or legislation should be drafted to protect information and data with strict penalties for any breaches.

REFERENCES

Alam, M. G. R., Masum, A. K. M., Beh, L.-S., & Hong, C. S. (2016). Critical Factors Influencing Decision to Adopt Human Resource Information System (HRIS) in Hospitals. *PLoS One*, *11*(8), e0160366. doi:10.1371/journal.pone.0160366 PubMed

Almazán, D. A., Tovar, Y. S., & José, M. (2017). Medina Quintero, Influence of information systems on organizational results. *Contaduría y Administración*, *62*(2), 321–338. doi:10.1016/j.cya.2017.03.001

Anderson, J. G. (2007). Social, ethical and legal barriers to e-health. *International Journal of Medical Informatics, 76*(5-6), 480–483. PubMed

Ayatollahi, H., Bath, P. A., & Goodacre, S. (2009). Accessibility versus confidentiality of information in the emergency department. *Emergency Medicine Journal, 26*(12), 857–860. doi:10.1136/emj.2008.070557 PubMed

Belle Woodward, N. M. (2011, August). Expansion and validation of the PAPA Framework. *Information Systems Education Journal, 9*(3). https://isedj.org/2011-9/N3/ISEDJv9n3p28.pdf

Berne, E. S. (2008). Ethical and Legal Issues in the Use of Health Information Technology to Improve Patient Safety. HEC FORUMSpringer Netherlands. doi:10.100710730-008-9074-5

Cathy Schoen, R. O. (2012). A Survey Of Primary Care Doctors In Ten Countries Shows Progress In Use Of Health Information Technology, Less In Other Areas. *Health Affairs, 31*(12). https://www.healthaffairs.org/doi/full/10.1377/hlthaff.2012.0884 PubMed

Fessler, J. M., & Grémy, F. (2001). Opinion Paper: Ethical Problems in Health Information Systems. *Methods of Information in Medicine, 40*(04), 359–361. doi:10.1055/s-0038-1634432 PubMed

Haux, R. (2006). Health information systems–past, present, future. *International Journal of Medical Informatics, 75*(3-4), 268–281. doi:10.1016/j.ijmedinf.2005.08.002 PubMed

Health Information Unit. Ministry of Health. (2009). Health metric network. In Fiji Health Information System: Review and Assessment. Ministry of Health, Suva.

Heeks, R. (2006). Health information systems: Failure, success and improvisation. *International Journal of Medical Informatics, 75*(2), 125–137. doi:10.1016/j.ijmedinf.2005.07.024 PubMed

Kuhn, K. A., & Giuse, D. A. (2001). From hospital information systems to health information systems. *Methods of Information in Medicine, 40*(04), 275–287. doi:10.1055/s-0038-1634170 PubMed

Laudon, K. C., & Laudon, J. P. (2018). *Management Information Systems - Managing the Digital Firm* (15th ed.). Pearson.

Marshall, K. P. (1999). Has Technology Introduced New Ethical Problems? *Journal of Business Ethics, 19*(1), 81–90. doi:10.1023/A:1006154023743

Meingast, M., Roosta, T., & Sastry, S. (2006, August). Security and privacy issues with health care information technology. In 2006 International Conference of the IEEE Engineering in Medicine and Biology Society (pp. 5453-5458). IEEE. doi:10.1109/IEMBS.2006.260060

Ministry of Health. (2008). *PATIS User Training Manual*. Suva: Author.

Ministry of Health. (2014). *PATISPlus User Manual, PMI, Appointments, ATD, and SOPD modules. In-service manual*. Author.

Office of Information Technology (OIT) Division of Information Resource Management. (2009). *Resource and Patient Management System, Patient Information Management System (PIMS), Admission/Discharge/Transfer, Version 5.3 Patch 1009*. Albuquerque, NM: Author.

Peslak, A. R. (2006). PAPA revisited: A current empirical study of the Mason framework. *Journal of Computer Information Systems, 46*(3), 117–123.

Straub, D. W. Jr, & Collins, R. W. (1990). Key information liability issues facing managers: Software piracy, proprietary databases, and individual rights to privacy. *Management Information Systems Quarterly, 14*(2), 143–156. doi:10.2307/248772

Troshani, I., Jerram, C., & Hill, S. R. (2010). Exploring the Public Sector Adoption of HRIS. *Industrial Management & Data Systems, 111*(3), 470–488. doi:10.1108/02635571111118314

Ward, N. S. (2004). The accuracy of clinical information systems. *Journal of Critical Care, 19*(4), 221–225. doi:10.1016/j.jcrc.2004.09.005 PubMed

Winter, A., Haux, R., Ammenwerth, E., Brigl, B., Hellrung, N., & Jahn, F. (2010). Health information systems. In Health Information Systems (pp. 33–42). London: Springer; doi:10.1007/978-1-84996-441-8_4.

World Health Organization. (2012). *Management of patient information, Trends and challenges in Member States, Global Observatory for eHealth series*. Author.

Zafar, H., Randolph, A. B., & Martin, N. (2017). *Toward a More Secure HRIS: The Role of HCI and Unconscious Behavior*. Academic Press.

APPENDIX 1

Questionnaires for Health Professionals - Colonial War Memorial Hospital

1. Please identify your professional affiliation at the hospital.
   - Doctor
   - Nurse
   - Pharmacist
   - Other, please specify _____

2. How often do you use the PATISPlus software/system?
   - Daily
   - Few times a week
   - Never
   - Other, please specify _____

3. Please indicate the purpose for which you access or utilize the PATISPlus software/system.
   - Entering patient clinical information
   - Recording patient demographics
   - Pharmaceutical purposes
   - Accessing medical records, including admission details
   - Reporting purposes
   - Others, please specify _____

4. In your opinion, what are the advantages (if any) of using PATISPlus? Please list.

   _____

   _____

   _____

5. In your opinion, what are the disadvantages (if any) of using PATISPlus? Please list.

   _____

   _____

   _____

6. What are some of the challenges of using PATISPlus? Please list.

   _____

   _____

   _____

7. Do you think there are ethical issues with the use of PATISPlus?
    ◦   Yes (Please go to Question 8)
    ◦   No
8. Identify which of the following issue(s) concerns you as a health care professional with the use of PATISPlus. (Tick as many)
    ◦   Privacy
    ◦   Accuracy
    ◦   Property
    ◦   Accessibility
9. In your opinion, what are some areas of improvement you would suggest to the PATISPlus system/software?

_____

_____

_____

_____

APPENDIX 2

Questionnaires for Patient/Customers - Colonial War Memorial Hospital

1. How long have you been visiting this hospital as a patient?
    ◦   Less than 1 year
    ◦   Between 1 – 5 years
    ◦   More than 5 years
2. Are you aware of the PATISPlus software/system?
    ◦   Yes
    ◦   No
3. Are you aware that your medical records are also kept electronically?
    ◦   Yes
    ◦   No
4. Do you feel safe that your medical records are kept electronically?
    ◦   Yes
    ◦   No (please go to Question 5)
5. What concerns (if any) would you have with maintaining your medical information/records electronically? (Tick as many)
    ◦   Privacy
    ◦   Accuracy
    ◦   Property
    ◦   Accessibility

APPENDIX 3

Questionnaires for Management - Colonial War Memorial Hospital

1. How often do you use the PATISPlus software/system?
   - Daily
   - Few times a week
   - Never
   - Other, please specify _____

2. Please indicate the purpose for which you access or utilize the PATISPlus software/system.
   - Entering patient clinical information
   - Recording patient demographics
   - Pharmaceutical purposes
   - Accessing medical records, including admission details
   - Reporting purposes
   - Others, please specify _____
     _____

3. In your opinion, what are the advantages (if any) of using PATISPlus? Please list.

   _____

   _____

4. In your opinion, what are the disadvantages (if any) of using PATISPlus? Please list.

   _____

   _____

5. What are some of the challenges of using PATISPlus? Please list.

   _____

   _____

6. Do you think there are ethical issues with the use of PATISPlus?
   - Yes (Please go to Question 7)
   - No

7. Identify which of the following issue(s) concerns you as a health care professional with the use of PATISPlus. (Tick as many)
    ◦ Privacy
    ◦ Accuracy
    ◦ Property
    ◦ Accessibility
8. Are records available through PATISPlus utilized for any other purposes other than medical/diagnostic/reporting?
    ◦ Yes
    ◦ No
9. If answered yes to Question 8, please identify what other purpose is this information utilized for?

_____

_____

10. Are patients/customers made aware of the use of information from PATISPlus for the purposes identified in Question 9?
    ◦ Yes
    ◦ No
11. In your opinion, what are some areas of improvement you would suggest to the PATISPlus system/software?

_____

_____

Chapter 7
Blockchain Technology and Its Applications

Lavanya Lingareddy
Sree Vidyanikethan Engineering College, India

Parthiban Krishnamoorthy
Sree Vidyanikethan Engineering College, India

ABSTRACT

Like other new generation information technologies such as IoT, big data, AI, and cloud, cryptocurrency and blockchain became buzz words in both industry and academia due to their advantageous features. With the features like decentralization, transparency, immutability, blockchain technology became more famous and is emerging in almost all fields like banking, education, healthcare, government, and real estate. Blockchain technology was introduced in the year 1991. It came into existence after this technology was created for bitcoin, a digital cryptocurrency by Santoshi Nakamoto in the year 2008. Since then, the blockchain is evolving rapidly. Even though blockchain usage is in high demand in all the sectors and it has received attention from many international organizations, most of the people lag in knowledge of blockchain technology and Cryptocurrency and how exactly they work. This chapter explores more in detail what blockchain technology is, how it works, and its applications.

DOI: 10.4018/978-1-7998-2367-4.ch007

INTRODUCTION

In the current era of technology blockchain technology became very familiar, especially it is now the backbone technology of digital cryptocurrency. Initially blockchain technology was described by Stuart Haber and W.ScottStornetta in the year 1991 as cryptographically secured links of blocks. Later it was first conceptualized in 2008 by a person Satoshi nakamoto as a core component of the cryptocurrency bitcoin.

A blockchain originally 'Block' 'Chain', is an increasing chain of blocks which are linked with each other using cryptography. It is an open distributed ledger which can record every transaction between two parties in a permanent and effective way. It is typically managed by peer to peer network, to make it use as distributed ledger (Berryhill, J et al., 2018). As the data is distributed to all blocks the data once recorded cannot be modified or stolen without doing modifications to the subsequent blocks.

Bitcoin is one of the most popular cryptocurrencies which uses blockchain technology. Bitcoin is a cryptocurrency technology with the blockchain technology came to light for the first time. Bitcoin is used to exchange the digital assets securely without any third party like banks online was proposed in 2008 first and later it was implanted in2009.

With the key feature like decentralization, Transparency, Immutability, persistency etc., blockchain technology can decrease the cost and increase the efficiency. As it allows transactions to be finished without any intermediates such as banks, Blockchain can be used in various financial services such as digital assets, remittance and online payment. The later sections of this chapter will explain in detail about what is blockchain technology, how it works and its applications (Berryhill, J et al., 2018).

WHAT IS BLOCKCHAIN?

There is a lot of stuff on blockchain from various sources, such as blogs, Wikipedia, conference proceedings, forum posts, book sand journal articles.There is no particular definition for "what is blockchain?". It may vary from person to person and source to source, depending on how they analyze the concept. In simple terms Blockchain is "chain of Blocks". Some people may say "public distributed decentralized ledger". According to the sources of Wikipedia". A blockchain is a decentralized, distributed and public digital ledger that is used to record transactions across many computers so that any involved record cannot be altered retroactively, without the alteration of all subsequent blocks" (He, P et al., 2017).

A blockchain is continuous linked list of blocks and each block is called a record, which will keep track of the transaction data, unique hash value, and previous hash value to link with the previous record. Since there is no central node to maintain

Figure 1. Sample Blockchain Structure

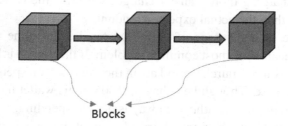

Blocks

the records and data is distributed to all the nodes, data protection will be more. If the intruders try to attack or hack the network then they must modify all the copies of data in the blocks, so it is less possible to compute the hash values which will consume huge computation power and attack the blockchain network. Hence it is highly suggestable in financial services.

The blockchain allows transactions which is also known as digital information to be recorded and distributed, but can't be modified (Junyao Wang, R, 2019). The topic little difficult to bind our heads around without looking at the technology in close. Hence it is important to know why it is actually useful? so let's have a glance at why the earliest application of blockchain technology came to existence. We can simply represent a block chain as shown in the fig.1.

A blockchain system is categorized into mainly 3 types: i) public blockchain, ii) Private Blockchain, iii) Consortium Blockchain. In the Public blockchain system all the blocks are visible to everyone and also, they could take part in the consensus process. While as for private blockchain only the nodes which are confined to the specific organization can participate in the consensus process. Since the private blockchain network is fully controlled by the particular organization we can treat it as a centralized network. Whereas the third one consortium blockchain is constructed partially decentralized by several organizations since only few or portion of the nodes would be participated in the consensus process.

The consensus process in blockchain is the process of validation of the blocks to add certain blocks to the existing blockchain. This process is often called as Proof of Work (POW) in the blockchain process. In order to perform this, miner who will involve in the validation process use some consensus algorithms (Pilkington, M, 2016).

Why Block Chain?

To know about the importance of blockchain we need have glance at what makes it so important. So, let's look into the current issues of banking sector.

Issue-1: If we want to transfer the amount from one account to another account then banks are charging more transfer charges with this the receiver will receive less money than the actual expected amount.

Issue-2: Because of high usage of digital currencies in online websites double spending became the most common problem. If the person is having 100$ and he spent 80$ on one purchase and again the same person spent another 50$ on another purchase. Though he is having 100$ in his wallet he spent 130$, this kind of spending in unauthorized way is double spending.

Issue-3: These days Hacking of unauthorized accounts became very much common which may lead to huge loss in financial and banking sectors.

In order to solve the above issues, we need a system or technology which should be able to sustain from the above issues. Then the technology people came up with idea of block chain technology in financial services e-commerce, banking etc., and introduced first digital currency concept called Bitcoin. Later it gave path to so many digital currency technologies like Ethereum, Zcash, Ripple, Dash, etc. With the digital cryptocurrency technic, the amount spent on transfers were very much reduced and also it gave the solution to the double spending by authorizing and checking the wallets before payments or placing the orders. Because of the decentralization concept a greater number of copies of the transactions are available in the nodes, the data loss and hacking also became impossible.

Blockchain not only gave solution to the financial services, it also fills the lights in most important sectors like healthcare, education, Real estate, government etc. so, today's industry also spread their wings in blockchain technology to improve the current system in an efficient and secure manner (Pilkington, M, 2016).

FEATURES OF BLOCKCHAIN

The features of blockchain which makes the block familiar are as follows

Decentralization

Before Cryptocurrencies came into pictures, most of the financial services were centralized. The idea behind the centralization is very simple. The centralized services will use the centralized entity to store all the data and we need to interact solely with that centralized entity to access any information you required.

One best example of a centralization is banks. The banks store all the account details and money transactions of all the customers in the centralized entity.

The best example for centralization is client - server models which we are using in the current days. Even the giant companies like google, Facebook, Yahoo etc also using the centralization concept. If the client requests for some data in the above specified sites (google, yahoo...), it will search for the requested data in the respective server and then delivers the response to the client (Seebacher, S and Schüritz, R, 2017).

In this process of centralization the entire data is stored in the central system or server of the particular company. Due to this reason, it may lead to any of the following situations:

If the server fails?
If the data in the server gets hacked?
If the centralised system shutdowns or gets corrupted due to some reasons?

Any of the above conditions will result in huge data loss, because of centralization all the data will be stored in the single central system, so we can't recover the data also.

In order to avoid these circumstances cryptocurrencies are using the feature of decentralization, with which data will be distributed all the nodes in the network and the transactions will also record in all the nodes. Hence, if one system fails then we can recover the details from other nodes in the network. Data hacking also less possible, as multiple copies exist in the network, if the intruder tries to attack the network, he needs to change or hack all the copies of nodes which is highly impossible in term of computation cost and time (Seebacher, S and Schüritz, R, 2017).

Transparency

Transparency is also one of the most important and little ambiguous feature of blockchain. Why I state this concept is ambiguous means one the one side we are saying that blockchain is the most secured technology and on the other hand we are saying that it is transparent, this may create little ambiguous to the readers. Now we will wash out this ambiguity by looking in to the actual working of this process.

Again we will consider the cryptocurrency technology to explain this feature. For example if A wants to send some amount to B. Here we will generate two keys to transfer the amount, one public key and a private key will be there, Public key is the one which will be visible to all the users in the network in simple terms public key is like E-mail ID which can be sharable (Seebacher, S and Schüritz, R, 2017). Private Key is one which is given to the user on the network and cannot be sharable, in simple terms it's like password. Hence, if A wants to transfer amount to B then A will make use of his private key and then B will authenticate the transaction by means of public key of A which is shared in the network. Once the transactions get completed all the nodes in the network will get the copy of the transaction. Hence if the change has to done by unauthorised person then the copy in all the nodes also should get modify.

With the feature of transparency one can avoid double spending of digital currency online, because if a person wants to buy something in online the transaction of the particular purchase will be authenticated and verified by means of public and private keys then only the person will be able to buy the product. Hence because of the authentication process he can't purchase another item if the amount is not sufficient in the wallet.

Immutability

This is one of the most important characteristic of block chain which makes it most popular. In the context of blockchain immutability means, the network is highly secured and can't be utilised or tampered by unauthorized users. It gains this feature because of implementing the hashing technic. In general, hashing means taking an input string of any length and giving out an output of a fixed length. In the context of cryptocurrencies like bitcoin, the transactions which are performed by the user are taken as an input and a hashing algorithm is applied to the input which gives an output of fixed length new hash value. The hashing algorithm is different for different technics. Bitcoin uses SHA-256, for Ethereum Ethash algorithm is used (Saberi, S et al., 2019). As Blockchain is nothing but links of blocks, each block in the Bitcoin stores the previous hash value in order to link with the next block.

The hashing cryptographic functions have different features, if one has to go into the inner details of hashing functions they must go through the corresponding materials on the websites or textbooks. The most interesting feature of the hashing technique "Avalanche effect", which gives more security to the crypto currency technique.

The avalanche effect! What it means?

With this feature the hash function will gets modified drastically if an unauthorised one tries to do small modification to hash. Because of this feature intruders can be less able to attack the network since the small modification may lead to the huge effect in the hash and without hash it is not simple to attack the network.

Proof Of Work

Proof of work is a technic to validate transactions in a blockchain network by solving a complex mathematical puzzle. Proof of work is a method in which miners compete against each other to solve the mathematical puzzle (Saberi, S et al., 2019). Miners are the people or users who try to solve the puzzle as early as possible. The first miner who solves the puzzle is rewarded. The puzzle is solved by determining a nonce that generates a hash value and an output lesser than a given target. Miners verify the transactions within a block and add the block to the blockchain when confirmed.

In blockchain the target is adjusted every 2016 blocks, approximately for every 14 days. The average time of block formation is 10 minutes. The difficulty of the puzzle increases or decreases depending on the time it takes to mine the blocks.

Mining

Mining is a process in which some people involve and tries to verify the transactions and the verified block will be added to the chain list. In blockchain, when miners use their resources to validate a new transaction and record them on the public ledger, they are given a reward. The miners will spend effort, time, money etc. to verify the transaction. As a reward, the miner who solves the puzzle will get 12.5 bitcoins. The block reward is halved every 210,000 blocks (approximately every 4 years).

HOW BLOCKCHAIN WORKS

Again we need to go back to "what is blockchain?" Simply a blockchain is group of linked record called blocks or it is public distributed ledger. Now we will come back to the concept of how a blockchain works?, what does a block contain in the blockchain? Etc. The generalized structure of block chain is shown in the figure-1. It is seen clearly that blocks are there and each block is linked with the next block. Now we will see what actually a block contains and how it is linked with the next block.

Each and every block in the block chain consists of 4 parts, in which one part will store the transaction data like how much is transferred from whom to whom. The other part of the will store the nonce, which takes the input as transaction data in the block and gives it to hashing algorithm and generates the unique hash value. The hash value which is generated by the nonce is stored in the third field of the block called hash field. In the fourth field of the block contains the previous hash value in order to link with the previous block. The first block in chain contains null value, as it does not contain any previous block. Hence, the first block in the blockchain is called the genesis block. The structure of the block is as shown in the figure-2.

Because of this structure of blockchain each and every block data is transparent and will be visible to all the nodes in the network. Suppose if know the Id any company then you can be able to see all the transactions of that company (Zibin Zheng and ShaoanXie, R, 2017). There is no centralized database or server in the blockchain system to process the transactions. The transactions of the blocks will be verified and authenticated by miners as explained in the mining.

Figure 2. Structure of block in blockchain

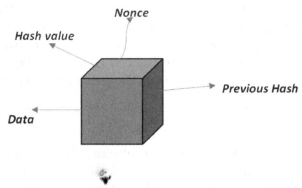

Applications of Blockchain

Blockchain is one of the most important technologies in the world. Almost all the fields in the current world are adopting this technology because of their beneficial features or characteristics.

Blockchain in Healthcare

Some of the primary concerns in health care industry are exact maintenance of medical record and patient record. Medical field has improved in the past decades in terms of vertical innovation, but it still lags in terms of horizontal innovation. Vertical innovation in the sense the medicines which they improved for certain diseases and horizontal innovation in the sense of technology. Though the medical field is moving towards the technology it is surprising that there is no unique patients ID yet, no proper maintenance of medical records, data interoperability, etc. Blockchain shows the way to all these problems in medical industry.

The features of blockchain such as hash function, cryptographic algorithms make easier the work and helps in identification of the patient record. As the blockchain is decentralized network, with the use of this technology in medical field will makes the pharmacists and technicians work easier. Patients can also be able to recognize whether the drug provided is prescribed by physicians (Zibin Zheng and ShaoanXie, R, 2017). The reports of the patients can be securely accessed by the doctors, nurses, lab technicians, and other healthcare practitioners to serve the patient better. With the data integrating facility the patients can be in touch with researchers and scholars to get the treatment plans and solutions to medical drugs depending on medical history.

Education

Blockchain has spread its wings in the field of education also. In education system it is mandatory to store the student record by the particular school management. Hence blockchain is the better and most secure option to maintain student records for a longer period of time (Saberi, S et al., 2019). Blockchain can be used to store infrastructure related issues such as CC photo coverage which are very important.

It is very important and primary thing to preserve transcripts of postsecondary students securely. Blockchain gives the solution to this, so that a student can access his transcripts at any time. This may avoid over heads in missing of transcripts.

Government

Blockchain technology is a great barrier to improve the government services and to make more transparent government citizen relationship. This distributed technology can be used to drastically reduce business process through more efficient and secure data sharing. Blockchain has numerous applications in public sector. With this technology government can improve the way they deliver services to public; they can prevent tax fraud and reduce waste. Digital cash transactions can help reshape financial transactions between government and public citizens.

The existing manual way is an inefficient way which will create the Hallmark (corruption) to the government. Public will loss the trust on the government and problems will not be solved effectively and efficiently. The decentralization technologies of blockchain give hope to the government to achieve streamlined operations and pare down back office operations like corruption, bureaucracy.

Cryptocurrency

Cryptocurrency is an online digital form of money developed using blockchain technology. In order to secure transactions online cryptocurrencies, use cryptograph algorithms. After cryptocurrencies came into existence, many issues in the financial sector. It gave solutions to double spending problems and hacking of accounts (Zibin Zheng and ShaoanXie, R, 2017). There are thousands of cryptocurrency technologies exist in the world, but Bitcoin became most popular because of using decentralization network instead of centralized one. Cryptocurrencies function similar to that of fiat currencies. Previous the acceptancy of cryptocurrencies in most of the business are very limited, but it became mainstream because of its continuous growing awareness.

Real Estate

Real estate is the most trending business in the present world. But most of scams will happen in real estate because of not proper maintenance of records and documents of the land. Still we are following the old method of recording the survey values of land, because of this one survey number may match to two or more property holders. This is mainly because of not maintaining the history of documents properly. Blockchain technology shows way to this kind of problems. With the features like transparency, decentralization blockchain gave solution to the problems in real estate. Blockchain can record the documents of the properly and there is a less chance of creating illegal documents of land as the blockchain technology is decentralized technology.

CONCLUSION

This chapter has tried to demonstrate the basic concepts of blockchain such as what is blockchain? How it works? and its applications. We didn't confine the concept of blockchain in this chapter to cryptocurrency technology, and we extended its features to different areas such as health care, real estate, education etc. Like any other trending technology blockchain also initially disrupts and the days pass on it will develop. In the near future we can expect blockchain will definitely improve its performance and scalability and also in terms of innovation. Blockchain will occupy almost all the market space in future because of its interesting and attractive features like decentralization, transparency, immutability.

REFERENCES

Berryhill, J., Bourgery, T., & Hanson, A. (2018). Blockchains unchained: Blockchain technology and its use in the public sector. *OECD Working Papers on Public Governance*, (28), 1-53.

Chen, G., Xu, B., Lu, M., & Chen, N. S. (2018). Exploring blockchain technology and its potential applications for education. *Smart Learning Environments*, 5(1), 1. doi:10.118640561-017-0050-x

He, P., Yu, G., Zhang, Y. F., & Bao, Y. B. (2017). Survey on blockchain technology and its application prospect. *Computer Science*, 44(4), 1–7.

Pilkington, M. (2016). Blockchain technology: principles and applications. In *Research handbook on digital transformations*. Edward Elgar Publishing. doi:10.4337/9781784717766.00019

Saberi, S., Kouhizadeh, M., Sarkis, J., & Shen, L. (2019). Blockchain technology and its relationships to sustainable supply chain management. *International Journal of Production Research*, *57*(7), 2117–2135. doi:10.1080/00207543.2018.1533261

Seebacher, S., & Schüritz, R. (2017, May). Blockchain technology as an enabler of service systems: A structured literature review. In *International Conference on Exploring Services Science* (pp. 12-23). Springer. 10.1007/978-3-319-56925-3_2

Wang, J., Wang, S., Guo, J., Du, Y., Cheng, S., & Li, X. (2019). A summary of research on blockchain in the field of intellectual property. Retrieved from. *Procedia Computer Science*, *147*, 191–197. doi:10.1016/j.procs.2019.01.220

Zheng, Z., & Xie, R. (2017). An Overview of Blockchain Technology: Architecture, Consensus, and Future Trends. *2017 IEEE 6th International Congress on Big Data*.

Chapter 8
Consequent Formation in Security With Blockchain in Digital Transformation

Shanthi Makka
 https://orcid.org/0000-0002-0387-3160
Birla Institute of Technology, Ranchi, India

Gagandeep Arora
ITS Engineering College, India

B. B. Sagar
Birla Institute of Technology, Mesra, India

ABSTRACT

Blockchain technology makes use of a centralized, peer-to-peer (P2P) network of databases, also called nodes, to validate and record digital transactions between individual users located anywhere across the globe. These transactions often take place through the exchange of cryptocurrencies such as bitcoins, Ethereum, and Ripple, etc. The security and transparency that is inherently present in digital transactions place blockchain technology in high demand across various industrial applications. Each node updates its database in real-time as and when transactions occur. The transaction gets authorized only when a majority of the nodes in the network validate the transaction. Once the verification is complete, a block, consisting of hash and keys, is generated for each new transaction and is linked to previous transactions in every database. Every node updates its database with the new block. A hacker would have to break down every node in the system to commit fraud. Blockchain could play a major role in maintaining the cyber security of digital transactions in the future.

DOI: 10.4018/978-1-7998-2367-4.ch008

INTRODUCTION

This chapter deals with how Blockchain Technology guarantees security in digital transformation. Blockchain technology create consume of a centralized, peer-to-peer (P2P) collaborate of databases is called nodes, to validate and record digital transactions between individual users located anywhere across the globe. These transactions often take place through the exchange of Cryptocurrencies such as bit-coins, Ethereum and ripple etc. A Cryptocurrency (or crypto currency) is a integral advantage outline to pursue as a midway of trade that benefit powerful cryptography to protect commercial transactions, force the establishment of further units, and confirm the dispatch of credit.

The security and transparency that is in inherently present in the digital transactions place Blockchain technology in high demand across various industrial applications. Each node updates its database in real-time as and when transactions occur. The validation of transaction is depends upon the criteria that majority of nodes in network gives approval. Once the verification is completed the hash address and keys will be generated for the new transaction and further it linked to previous nodes in database and all nodes in network will get updated with this new block of values. If any hacker wants to commit any fraud activity he or she has to breakdown all the nodes in network and all the nodes are located globally and it is visible to everyone in the network would increase difficulty to commit fraud Blockchain could hit a considerable act in maintaining cyber security of digital bond in the future.

WHAT IS BLOCKCHAIN?

Blockchain is an open-source, scattered ledger proficient of reporting and accumulate facts that is then achieve by unique crypto graphical designs. This unique and innovative design makes Blockchain a safe space for data and the data cannot be deleted, modified, manipulated, or misused in any way. Another crucial form of Blockchain technology is that it is consensus-oriented which further reduces the possibility of data being manipulated or misused. Its design is such that a large number of computers (nodes) are connected over a network.

So, whenever the Authors wish to enumerate a transaction to a Blockchain, The Authors must clarify or clarify a mathematical test, the outputs of which are communal with every machine linked to the network. Only when all other computers on the network reciprocally acknowledge with the output, then only user can the add transactions to the chain. Moreover, in Blockchain, data is never gathered (Yaga, D., et al., 2019) at one peculiar location, which makes cybercriminals to access the data all most impossible.

Figure 1. Blockchain Technology
(https://blockgeeks.com/wpcontent/uploads/2016/09/blockchaintech.jpg)

Blockchain is, hence, the first technology that expedites the pass on of digital proprietorship in a decentralized manner. All these aspects make Blockchain so imploring to the capitalist of the technical world. As the name proposes, the Blockchain framework is made up of various 'blocks,' each of which contains the transaction data, a timestamp, and the link (cryptographic hash) to the previous block. A Blockchain is a collection of documents that are known as blocks. These blocks of records are covered and obtain by cryptography. Blocks in database (Lindman, J., 2017) connect stable and include information from other blocks, deal data, and time space.

A Blockchain preserve the data from adaption. It also transcript bonds between two distinct affairs that allocate as a ledger. These ledgers are unchangeable. There's no distinct bit where these analog credit can be form or incensed. Blockchain technology is being worn in a collection of methods containing Bitcoin, Economic, Technology, Healthcare, and Insurance industries as a way to guard cyber data. They are augmenting in reputation because you can install any digital asset or transaction into a Blockchain. It doesn't matter what corporation you're a part of.

Figure 2. Data Protection using Blockchain
(https://i.pinimg.com/originals/61/4a/68/614a68c360a0e91f84972b1ff6247325.jpg)

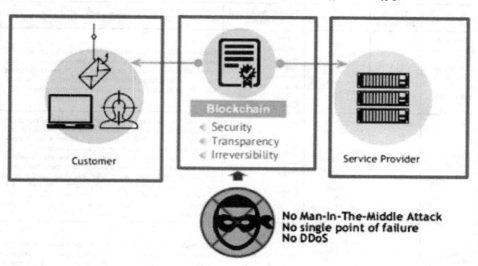

LITERATURE REVIEW

The Literature survey is presented in the form of table.

Table 1. Literature Survey

Authors	Year of publication	Title	Name of the Journal /Conference	Findings
Hawlitschek, F., Notheisen, B.,& Teubner, T.	2018	The limits of trust-free systems: A literature review on blockchain technology and trust in the sharing economy.	Electronic commerce research and applications, 29, 50-63.	The Authors discussed about how the adversity of approaches may be determine and investigate the future of blockchain technology for diffuse the concern of faith in the sharing economy. Through the literature review Authors found that: The perception of reliance varies extensively between the background of blockchain and the sharing economy, Blockchain technology is to some degree appropriate to redeem faith in platform providers, and that trust-free systems are barely conveyable to sharing economy communications and will essentially confide on the expansion of credible combination for blockchain-based sharing economy ecosystems.
Seebacher, S., & Schüritz, R.	2017	Blockchain technology as an enabler of service systems: A structured literature review.	In International Conference on Exploring Services Science (pp. 12-23). Springer, Cham.	The blockchain technology is mainly focused on peer-to-peer network; facultative concert among different parties and service system is selected as unit analysis to observe its capacity. Authors have recognized a group of attributes that guarantees trust and Fragmentation, promoting the creation and strategy of a service system.
Karafiloski, E., & Mishev, A.	2017	Blockchain solutions for big data challenges: A literature review.	In IEEE EUROCON 2017-17th International Conference on Smart Technologies (pp. 763-768). IEEE.	Blockchain Technology gives great significance when we search for efficient way to store, manage, and process Big Data. Authors' demonstrated possible ways about decentralized mainframe of private data, digital property resolution, communication with IoT and public institutions' amend are having compelling force on how Big Data may develop. In this paper Authors discussed about various Big Data areas that can be entrust by the Blockchain technology.

continued on following page

Table 1. Continued

Authors	Year of publication	Title	Name of the Journal /Conference	Findings
Calvaresi, D., Dubovitskaya, A., Calbimonte, J. P., Taveter, K., & Schumacher, M.	2018	Multi-agent systems and blockchain: Results from a systematic literature review.	In International Conference on Practical Applications of Agents and Multi-Agent Systems (pp. 110-126). Springer, Cham.	Intended to provide a broad overview in application concerns and Authors evaluate impetus, hunches, necessity, durability, and constraints granted in the present state of the art. Moreover, explaining the expected disputes and advances their perception on how MAS and BCT could be connected in various application aspects.
Brandão, A., São Mamede, H., & Gonçalves, R.	2018	Systematic review of the literature, research on blockchain technology as support to the trust model proposed applied to smart places.	In World Conference on Information Systems and Technologies (pp. 1163-1174). Springer, Cham.	The agile places are exposed with perverted or compose data, with the deceitful combination of new tools, and tools with firmware versions uncertain. These possibilities damage with the expanding capacity and variety of data, tools, framework, and end users linked to the Web. The systematic study of the article is picked 190 documents, which deals with the increasing interest on the theme of Blockchain technology with 14 publications in 2014 to about 100 already in 2017. The articles focused on the areas bitcoin (about 40%), IoT (about 30%), financial (about 15%), cryptocurrencies, electronic government (about 12%), smart contracts, smart cities, Business (with about 10% each) and health (about 5%).
Zhang, N., Zhong, S., & Tian, L.	2017	Using Blockchain to Protect Personal Privacy in the Scenario of Online Taxi-hailing.	International Journal of Computers, Communications & Control, 12(6).	The Authors have make use of permanent decentralized and Ability of the blockchain to suggest a blockchain based personal authenticated security protocol, which employs Online taxi-accost as the application scenario.
Jaffe, C., Mata, C., & Kamvar, S. *International Symposium on Wearable Computers* (pp. 81-84). ACM.	2017	Motivating urban cycling through a blockchain-based financial incentives system. In *Proceeding s of the 2017 ACM*	International Joint Conference on Pervasive and Ubiquitous Computing and Proceedings of the 2017 ACM	This thesis explains a Blockchain based financial catalyst system where closets can influence their bustle and district data to collect financial rectification from industries that would like to sponsor closet activity.
Bazin, R., Schaub, A., Hasan, O., & Brunie, L.	2017	Self-reported verifiable reputation with rater privacy.	In IFIP International Conference on Trust Management (pp. 180-195). Springer, Cham.	The Authors designed a new reputed system, which is decentralized, secured, and efficient and can be applicable to practical context. Through his reputation system user's can easily obtain the accurate reputation score of the service provided within a constant amount of time. User can also provide their feedback without their own credentials.
Król, M., Reñé, S., Ascigil, O., & Psaras, I.	2018	ChainSoft: Collaborative software development using smart contracts.	In CRYBLOCK 2018-Proceedings of the 1st Workshop on Cryptocurrencies and Blockchains for Distributed Systems, Part of MobiSys 2018 (pp. 1-6). ACM.	Authors presented ChainSoft - a podium for deploy software advancement and self-moving remittance amid parties that mistrust each other, by means of blockchain technology. ChainSoft permits any developer to built software and comply software, involves automatic code authentication and accomplish users' appropriate behavior. They invented a tool for their system using Ethereum Smart Contracts and Github/Travis CI and present first decision examining its protection and deep control cost.
Choi, Jindae; Shin, Sungjung. Choi, J., & Shin, S.	2016	Propose of smart place IoT systems for strengthen security of the smart grid environment.	International Information Institute (Tokyo). Information, 19(5), 1509.	Authors designed a new model for security verification as previous step operation maintenance of smart place IoT environment. Power energy catch benefit of ICT blend technology.
Barbosa, L. S.	2017	Digital governance for sustainable development.	In Conference on e-Business, e-Services and e-Society (pp. 85-93). Springer, Cham.	Authors demonstrated the effect of digital revolution of administration structure as a mechanism to improve continual evolution and more broad associations, in the resolve of the United Nations 2030 Agenda. Three primary disputes are inscribed: the inquiry of *scope, adherence* of software foundation, and the system to accomplish more limpid and *liable* public academy.

continued on following page

Table 1. Continued

Authors	Year of publication	Title	Name of the Journal /Conference	Findings
O'Dair, M., & Beaven, Z.	2017	The networked record industry: How blockchain technology could transform the record industry.	Strategic Change, 26(5), 471-480.	Blockchain technology may have reframing promising for those music industries correlate with listed music, and for the suitability of music progress. While forecast of extensive fragmentation may have been abortive, blockchain technology does present to have the capability to convert the act of third affair and to make musicians' course more feasible. Blockchains could advance the efficiency and opportunity of ownership data, expedite near-imperative repayments for authority, and necessarily boost the clarity of the key chain.

HOW BLOCKCHAIN WORKS

The Blockchain is very popular as the fundamental technology of Bitcoin. Essentially it purposes a peer-to-peer structure of computers to approve transactions (Peters, G. W., et al., 2016). Blockchain is a data structure to design and receive delivered ledger of transactions amidst a chain of computers. It permits customer to generate and confirm transactions instantly without a central power. The Blockchain technology can be classified into two divisions, one is Public Blockchain and other one is Private Blockchain.

Public Blockchain

A public Blockchain network or license less Blockchain system of connections is entirely open-ended and anybody amenable to perform in this gentle of grid can play without any consent. This is the dominant divergence among private and public Blockchain network. Anybody can battle in the formal network, execute the confer protocol, and conserve the trivial open public ledger. The benefit of Public Blockchain is greater defended than private network. But, it gives less secrecy and enormous computation potential and intensity is necessary, less ecological.

Private Blockchain

A Private Blockchain Network deserves an proposal to aid in the network. The confirmation of the challenge must be accomplished either by network discoverer or by the order determined by the author of the network. Permissions Blockchain Network puts restriction to the entry of participant and allows only the kind of participant that is required in the network. The Advantages of Public Blockchain is expanded isolation and Environmentally safe, as less computation competence is prescribed to conclude the harmony as in the case of Public Network. But, it is less protective as distinguished to public network.

Figure 3. Transaction using Blockchain
(https://dzone.com/storage/temp/7930704-blockchain-workflow.png)

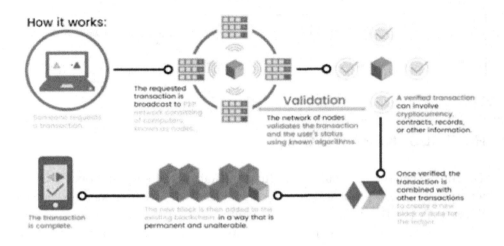

BLOCKCHAIN ARCHITECTURE

When working with Blockchain technology, it is needless to say that, you must possess a thorough understanding of Blockchain and its innate architecture. User has to competent with concepts such as Cryptography, Hash address generation,

Figure 4. Blockchain Network Architecture
(https://www.altoros.com/blog/wp-content/uploads/2017/04/Everledger-Blockchain-IBM-High-Security-Business-Network.png)

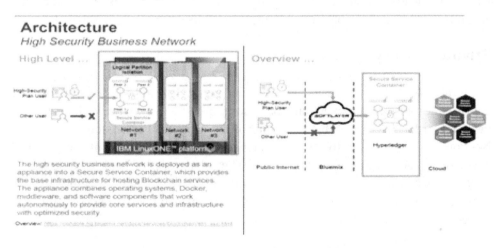

distributed ledger technology, consensus, decentralized consensus, smart contracts, and authorized computing, and many more. This first step is crucial to building a strong foundational knowledge in Blockchain technology.

Technical Architecture And A High Level View of Blockchain

Basically the Structure of Blockchain subsists of several of knobs, avouch has a provincial model of a **ledger**. In outmost scenario in the network, the knobs pertains distinct framework. The nodes broadcast with each other in authorize to obtain reconciliation on the essence of the ledger and do not depend upon a main authority to integrate and substantiate transactions. The method of obtaining this license is called consensus, and there are multiple algorithms have been constructed for this purpose. Customers dispatch their request for the transaction to the Blockchain to fulfill the working of the chain is constructed to implement. Formerly a transaction is finished, a file of the transaction is combined to one or more of the ledgers, and it cannot be updated or removed. This phenomenon of the Blockchain is said to be immutability discussed earlier.

Figure 5. Technical Architecture of Blockchain

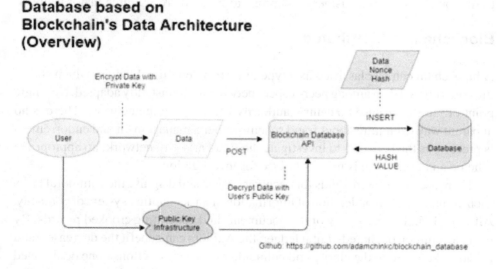

*(https://miro.medium.com/max/700/1*Vn97Zi2c12AADRfUuanyIw.png)*

Figure 6. Architecture for Security

Delivering a new architecture for security

Property of Rivetz Corp.

FEATURES OF BLOCKCHAIN

Every year many organizations suffer from 5% of dividends to fraud as per the survey done by company of verified and authorized deception Investigators. Fraud in career or field can be undetected for longer pan of time in fact sometimes it is hard to find out. To limit the business less prone to fraud, there are three major features:

Blockchain is Distributed

A blockchain can be classified as a type of distributed digital ledger, which shares the transactional data among peer-to-peer network and constantly adapted. No single point of failure because no central authority is present in the network. There is no apparent way to enquire about fraud scheme rather a management and endorsement is precarious the network, to investigate the fraud arises in network, no appropriate scheme and even there is no exact place for investigation.

There are different methods for deceivers to use and disguise their immoral tasks such as modification or deletion of information of an accounting system of company. Altering digital or hard copy of the documents and generating crooked records. By using a common or shared digital ledger, the Authors can benefit the decrease fraud because it escalerate the clarity and pellucidity of the transactions done deliberated supply chain (Pflaum, A., 2017) and between members of a business network. The identification of fraud transactions can be done easily because every participant in the network can see the history and transfer of capitals and a member or a group of members in a network controls the majority of network.

Blockchain is Immutable

The registered transactions on Blockchain Network are immutable or unchangeable because we cannot remove or alter them. Consensus is the process in which ahead a "block" of transactions are attached to the blockchain, all the associated members of the network must concede the transaction is valid. The block is assigned a timestamp, insured using Cryptography, and allied to the preceding block in the chain. Yet we can generate a fresh transaction to alter the state of a service, it will candidly be inserted to the chain, and the primitive transcript of the file will still be accessible. So, by adopting Blockchain you can draw the authority of a benefit, comprehensive of where, it has arrive from, where it is been, and who had control of it.

Reproduction is a Universal problem that influences an ample scope for organizations like extravagance of goods, apparel, foodstuff, medical stock, and many more products. Confirmation of the accuracy and endowment of a resource can be a threat because conventional inventory chains are high, complicated and inadequacy of pellucidity. Nonetheless, if an owner or Producer's equipment are implanted on Blockchain, that equipment will have inception due to their constant transaction antiquity, and that will make it crucial to gap off hoax equipment as original. The Authors have al the information, which is there on the Internet and the Authors don not promote other people access on it, whether it may be an email or a Facebook account, or a confidential bank transactions and any other social media. The problem with bringing information on the Internet has a chance of being hacked, duplicated, or penetrated. Immutability is a fundamental phenomenon that Blockchain lead to the table. It anticipates everything that is taped in a ledger from being composed and you no need to worry about your transaction information is safe or not because the way the Blockchain operates it keeps your data safe and secure by attaching to the multiple vulnerabilities. Even any hacker wants to attempted to hack it can't be done because of unreliability of blockchains. Blockchains ledgers begin with a one or array of transactions, which involves capitals, crypto-currency, data, accord, or values. Once the transaction is verified then it executes and transaction will be recorded. In Blockchain the created object cannot be altered. The effect of network provides immutability in Blockchain. The efficiency of a network is dependent upon the frequency of usage of network. The key feature of Blockchain is based on the ability to be immutable and secure. Let's take a look at how it's changing things in the cyber security world.

Blockchain can be Permissioned

The best deal with confidential data in Businesses cannot tolerate the access of someone to it. So there should ne some way out to safeguard the data from outsiders' and insiders for not corrupting the files of data. In this way, the permissions become major role. But distinct former features we have discussed, not all the Blockchain networks are permissioned. The permissioned networks can be enormous for deceit forestalling because they impede who acquiescing to participate and under what capacity along with their limitation. The contribution by the members of a permissioned network can be started once they are invited and authenticated.

In a permissioned network, management of Identity and controlling network access takes major role. In Linux Foundation the framework of Blockchain is implemented, all the participants issued a cryptographic membership cards for their Identity Proof with Hyper ledger Fabric. The assigned membership card permits them to access the transaction that belongs to them. Even prudential users cannot insert a record to the Blockchain without consensus and they cannot damage any records because all the records are encrypted. We cannot neglect any sort of fraud as per operational risks of 2017; it would be very costly and also reduces morale of employee and generate an ambiguous business atmosphere in addition to blunt your business and customer relationships.

SECURITY THROUGH BLOCKCHAIN

A Blockchain network is more secure as its framework, especially while establishing a private Blockchain, you must establish outdo of stage for classification. Still the Blockchain has instinctive resources that support security by soring data in cloud (Park, J., et al., 2017), those with ill intent can manipulate known vulnerabilities in your infrastructure. Exquisitely, you must have groundwork with unified security that can forbid anyone, including core users and supervisors from penetrate confidential data, contradict unauthorized attacks to alter data or functionality in network. Rigorously escort encrypted keys with high-level security standards without any misappropriation. With this competence, your Blockchain network will have the further shelter that required inhibiting attempts from within and without. The Authors can also design absolutely unified industry ready Blockchain framework to promote the evolution, administration, and applications of a multi organizational business network.

As mentioned in previous sections Blockchain is nothing but a sequence of blocks which has transactions as set of records and every block is linked to rest of all other blocks with previous and next hash pointer. It makes it impossible to damage any record by any hackers because they need hash address of that Block along with all other blocks linked to it. This alone might not seem like much of deterrence, but Blockchain has some other essential features, which provides supplementary security.

Figure 7. Security Levers in Blockchain
(https://blog.sodio.tech/wp-content/uploads/2018/06/Secure-Blockchain-based-Cloud-framework.png)

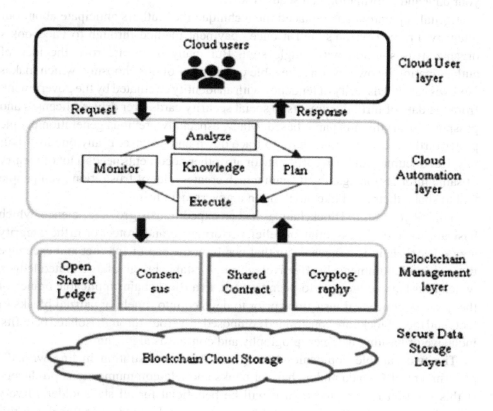

The records on a Blockchain (Aitzhan, N. Z., et al., 2016) are secured through cryptography. All the participants in the network are assigned with private keys with transactions they make and it also requires their won digital signature. If there is any change in records, the digital signature becomes shut-in and concerned authority in the network will get an alarm about fraud attempt. New proclamation is critical to preclude additional contamination. Grievously for enthusiastic hackers, Blockchains are broadcasted and allocated over peer-to-peer networks, which are updated continuously and preserved in synchronized. As a result they are not placed in central position, Blockchians never have single point of failure and information cannot be changed on a single computer. It requires huge amount of computational efficiency to reach each instance of an assured Blockchian and modify them at the same time span. There is some confusion whether small Blockchian networks can easily be accessible to attack or not. The bigger the network is more it is the more challenging it is. By default the Blockchain networks has certain features to protect your data and information in a secured way.

Digital separation has replaced the technique the Authors anticipate about our integrity. From Amazon's "tell it once" payment method through to Facebook's organized as solution with single sign. But many of us are rock the idea of authenticating by own over a relievable online prior of our choosing, which makes our lives easier. Disparity of tendency with an identity circulated by the government, from the date of birth documents to social security cards over driver's licenses and passports, everything is paper based. Many, especially previous generation people prefer birth certificates must hard to trace down and achieve. If any one lost their physical document of birth certificate or any other documents needs a lot of reentry of same information again and again which creates a lot of frustration even people feel to shake their head like anything in a government forms.

Indulge yourself to Blockchain as it is an expeditiously growing science, which basically focus on the essential for belief, performance, and protection in the integrity arena. Blockchain is a mechanism that perch on the cap of Internet and exchange the information immensely effectively through establishment of distributed ledger, which runs beyond the peer-to-peer network. In a Blockchain, applicable branch of the network concede transactions prior to devoted into timely organized blocks of facts and these blocks are constrained composed in a group through isolated benefits, inclusive of hashing using cryptography and consensus algorithms.

The two capable companies have given the demonstration in line with the government of Canada and a chain of banks and tele-communications producers. If this solution is accepted then it will be beneficial for all stakeholders. Every individual will enter the details about themselves only once and after doing this who so ever is interested people has to enter their details only once.

Concurrently, Blockchain identity using a Mobile App based facilitates identity customers to have the equal guarantee as conventional identity issued by the government without the requirement for inconvenience created for documented applications, registrations through online, and entry of data in various places. Concurrently, the confidential services and smart contract empower them to contact required information to authenticate integrity beyond negotiation of the safety and purity of confidential consumer data, the conceivable advantages never block there. Once the label of an identity of Blockchain citizen becomes completely achievable to dream of the world where every citizen is capable of building, controlling and maintaining a complete and credible analysis of their own life travel from their birth to death can be carried through a smart phone. If anyone choses to register their birth through travel records, history of employment, educational certificates uploaded through Blockchain, it creates secured, easy accessible digital identity and also it can be controlled in entire their lives.

It is very early to be sure of Blcokchain technology and still we have to do a lot to bring advanced version of Blockchain for digital identity for reality. Anyhow the people and industries are recovering the full capable of this metamorphic technology the experts need more and more ambitious government about the world must examine the same capability in the integrity scope in Canada and abutment of networks of their own and deal outshine the practice.

DATA SAFETY USING BLOCKCHAIN

To secure transactions distributed ledger technology popular in Blockchain Technology. Recognize and regulation of individual integrity is best of mind, disposed current actions, including the European Union's General Data Protection Regulation. Most of our identity (Liang, G., et al., 2018) is communal without our specific approval, brings reserved in districts the authors are doped of, and when composed amazing obstacles. A Decentralized approach enable us to deal with difficulties such as fraud where people use expiry documents for usage which puts everyone in network risk and it also reduces risk associated with user credentials used for personal interactions and virtual interactions through instruments and it also keeps users at other side to verify very critical to who is and what is at alternative oblique of the cover.

Just imagine loans sanctioned to the people so quickly by the banks by sharing related information by the users without manual verification process would reduce the cost and time and also if you get medical treatment at hospitals with your global identification card also reduces time and to proceed. Through this global identification card you are able to present yourself along with your medical history so doctors can know what exactly is the problem and what medicine to be given.

The Blockchain technology has framed a space to transform bonding between the users and industries are established and driven with various public flaws for identity. Blockchain permits point-to-point digital trade of identity at the peaks of the network, at the equipment. If people would control their identity by themselves, then the scope of digital permit would not have been at that extreme level with public key infrastructure (PKI) associate with certified authorities.

BLOCKCHAIN TECHNOLOGY WITH IoT

Let us consider an IoT network with centralized authority the authors like to call through devices, probably they treat them, as smart using sketches are not permitted to compose protective decisions by themselves without the central authority. In Blockchain model, the entire set of data is accumulated along with each tool and data also depicted and stocked. Prior to any information insertion to the network the hacker has to assemble all necessary resources for DNS attack and it must be confirmed and certified by every node present in the network. Since it permits deposit to be completed without any bank or any negotiator (Zheng, Z. et al., 2017). A Blockchain can be owned in desperate financial benefits like electronic assets, reimbursement, and payment through online. In addition to this it can also used in other fields like IoT, smart investments and services useful for public. Apparently, an IoT (Kumar, N. M., et al., 2018) is no longer conceded to a single node.

In the universe of an IoT, an advanced and it might have imply earlier, is in the amorphous step of growth that might be a good idea for those who can see the capability in merging Blockchain security from grounded. Actually, an IoT produces a rigid threat than the Cryptocurrency in which the distributed network assigned with affecting currency from one unidentified owner to another. There is a necessary need of complex structure to authenticate, protect, and manage all the layers of an entire network. There are many frameworks are built to handle such technical issues and an appropriate framework must be able to identify illegal interruptions and to reduce the spread of malware it has to crumb hacked devices from the network. It would require a protocol to insert and delete equipment from Blockchain without bring out a protective reaction.

In addition, the Blockchain technology must beat a problem such as reasonable result is 51% of attack problem is enforced to tiny, substantially limited to an IoT networks and to obtain the control of a Blockchain expects to compromise a bulk of network equipment a complex task, when the network is spread over a globe, then it inclines and augmented easily when it is directed to a home network. Specialists have resolve to an idea of a dumped on Blockchain converge that promotes greatly more safeguard than centralized version, but doesn't absolutely accommodated aggregation as a developed Blockchain.

The configured Internet is currently not designed to shaft the size and difficulties occurred while handling recent transactions, because it is made up with old technologies where security issues are very huge and happens very frequently. Achieving a Blockchain technology to an IoT directly moderate and subsequently would be a great idea. Bring it to its place and then adjust it subsequently. A defeat to an address the cavernous protective space will convince a global difficulty for millions of householders later.

CYBER SECURITY IN BLOCKCHAIN TECHNOLOGY

The first thing in our mind that "what is the role of cyber security in Blockchain Technology?"

Blockchain technology is creating a path for future. This is beyond panel for abundance organizations depending on immense Cybersecurity conservation. It abolishes flaws and deceptive data and computerizing factual and credible files. This can mark property and it is not sensitive to cyber interventions. The Industries that are associated with Blockchain technology will assure the safety of digital transactions, confidentiality of data and timestamps and it is also a smart choice. Let's see how Blockchain is related to Cybersecurity: the enhancement of Cyber defense is improved using Blockchain technology and it also averts crime and identifies interfere with data. It encrypts data and built it crystalline and agitable.

Cybersecurity (Ahram, T., et al., 2017) outbreaks and data crack have been a reason of main burden for every character. Frequently the hackers abduct confidential information of users such as a PAN number and Aadhar number to employ it for forged transactions. However, blockchain as described above actively verifies and authenticates the identity of a user without expecting any sort of confidential data. Even name of the user is also not required. The Blockchain Technology could play a major role in maintaining Cybersecurity and digital transactions in future.

Blockchain guarantees confidence and efficiency between parties, they may use private and public applications. It not only to encrypt data and all given transactions and here everything is decentralized. When a hacker tries to breakdown the data and crucial information this technology alerts an entire system. There is no single point

Figure 8. Blockchain in CyberSecurity
(https://3.bp.blogspot.com/t72wwwUXHfA/XDn0KT_ZR6I/AAAAAAAAAZ8/
J5wxgTBQ7CkITsaUTUZTdg2cIgfSc0wSQCLcBGAs/s1600/Blockchain%2Bin%2BCybersecurity.png)

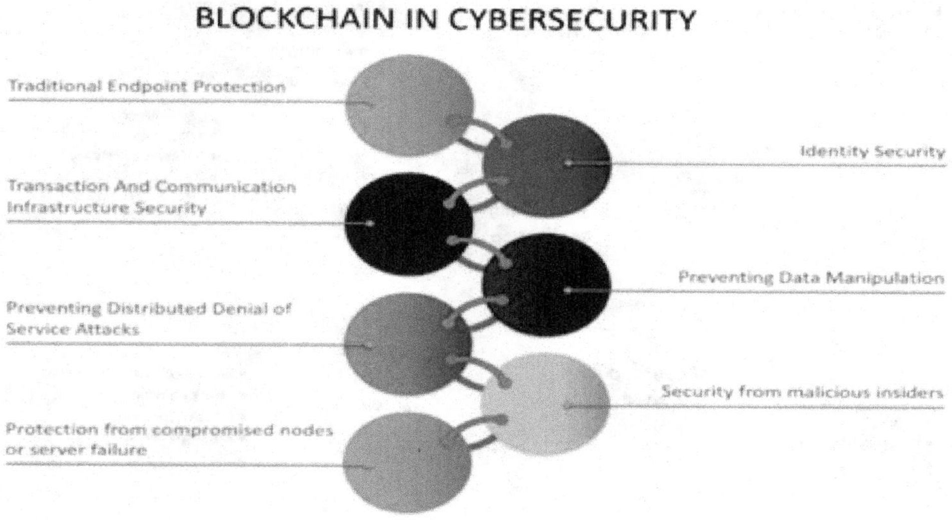

BLOCKCHAIN IN CYBERSECURITY

Traditional Endpoint Protection

Identity Security

Transaction And Communication Infrastructure Security

Preventing Data Manipulation

Preventing Distributed Denial of Service Attacks

Security from malicious insiders

Protection from compromised nodes or server failure

of failure in Blockchian, which can be hacked. Blockchain technology (Shackelford, S. J., et al., 2017) is using Cyber security because it provides an approach to secure everything more than transactional structures. Blockchain (Mylrea, M., et al., 2017) is also currently engaged in prevention of identity theft. The digital identification and actions you are receiving online can be verified by using Blockchain. To reduce the chance of identity theft Blockhain technology provides high-level degree of privacy for Internet users.

DIGITAL IDENTITY USING BLOCKCHAIN TECHNOLOGY

IBM is presently trying to find a solution that integrates (Eling, M., 2018) can be characterized with detectable or materialistic characteristics. The digital identity packaged will be provided with their social and temporal aspects. They desire to convince that every individual character has an integrity and they have to endorse others expectations in Blockchain technology system. This intent acceptation was taken away after huge data rupture in past that arises fellow citizen's perception disclosed. Alternatively in place of centralized system, the distributed ledgers in Blockchain technology can give immense security guarantee. All parties involved are verified users, and the ledgers verify an authenticity and certainty of the transactions.

Figure 9. Digital Identity using Blockchain
(https://www.researchgate.net)

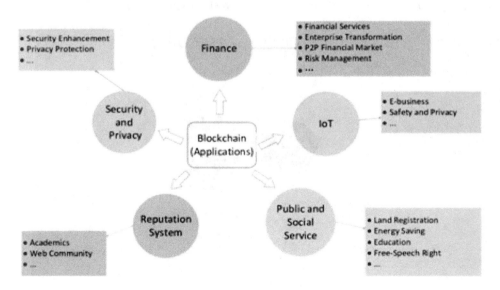

BLOCKCHAIN IN BANKING SECTOR

Currently the usage of Blockchain technology is very slow. As per survey of IBM in 2017, approximately 200 healthcare centers and only 16% of the defendants are conceded to choose Blockchain technology. The promising future that Blockchain (Guo, Y., et al., 2016) influences the healthcare organizations can be fulfilled only if healthcare centers exhibits readiness to accept this technology and accumulate the essential technical framework for it. As of now, authors can say that the acceptability is very slow, but Blockchain will definitely develop a deep-rooted froce on the healthcare industries and may other industries in the future. Since Blockchain's star application is cryptocurrency (Bitcoin) (Vujičić, D., et al., 2018), you must know how the system works. There are numerous platforms such as Coinbase and Coinmama where you can learn how to handle cryptocurrency (7, I. 2016) and digital transactions. You need to register on any of the mentioned platforms that are accessible in your country and then buy coins and start with the process after buying few coins and make your own folder to proceed.

The core objective is to focus to learn process, so we no need to purchase huge amount of coins. Online wallets are the best decision for small transactions, as you persist to make acquires utilizing your wallet, the concept of how digital financial transactions are organized using crypto currencies will constantly become fair choice to you. Just as data structures are a necessary aspect of coding, so it is also a important part of Blockchain technology. It employs a consolidation of data structures and cryptography to develop secure and vigorous surroundings for data. Thus, to incline a Blockchain proficient you must constitute a solid grip on data structures and cryptographic designs and operations consisting hash functions like MD5, CRC32, and SHA1.

BLOCKCHAIN IN HEALTH CARE

This is an industry where blockchain can radically transform lives (Mettler, M. 2016). If patient data is uploaded to a centralized server, doctors can access their patient's real-time medical condition to make the most appropriate diagnoses. This permits prompt, profitable, and productive treatment for compensating lives and also to help and guard the medical records of patients. Increasingly industries are moving forward to adapt Blockchain technology and realize the extensive advantages of expanding a blockchain system. Thus, there is a sharp demand (Korpela, K., et al., 2017) for professionals who have the knowledge to develop, manage, implement, and execute this technology.

Figure 10. Health Care using Blockchain

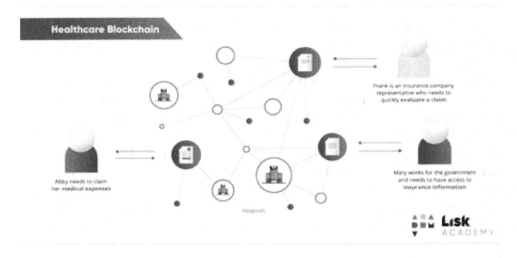

BLOCKCHAIN IN EDUCATION

Deployment of Blockchain technology in Education sector can give an advantage for verification of academic credentials of students in very secured and effective manner. Manuscripts and other related materials can be uploaded through online system that using Blockchain technology. Even though it is deployed in centrally and it is accessible by all concerned departments and can also be verified easily. Every alteration is recorded and linked with prior entry in the network. In this way no student will get any incorrect or invalid data such unearned degrees since it cannot passed through Blockchain verification process (Cai, Y., et al., 2016). It also provides new designing opportunities for the prominence system and it is also very effective in preclude targeted information such as crucial information like loan application's data where the deceitful information is fact based. Still their capability is bounded in instinctive information fraud like valuation fraud, where the validation of ground-truth is not easy. These systems are efficient in inhibit bad mouthing and conceal attack, but they are restricted in discover poll padding under sable attack, perpetual charges and disguise attack.

SUMMARY

The Blockchain Technology is the fundamental mechanism behind Crypto currencies such as bit-coins, Ethereum and ripple etc. This is a very secured, trusted, efficient technology while dealing with confidentiality of transfer of currency from one place to other. In this chapter we discussed what is Blockchain Technology, how the data can be protected or secured using Blockchain technology, Different types of Blockchain Architectures, Crypto currencies and their applications, various properties of Blockchain Technology, How the Blockchain is associate with IoT and it's benefits along with applications of Blockchain in Health Care, Education, Banking, Cyber security, and digital identification of the user.

REFERENCES

Ahram, T., Sargolzaei, A., Sargolzaei, S., Daniels, J., & Amaba, B. (2017, June). Blockchain technology innovations. In *2017 IEEE Technology & Engineering Management Conference (TEMSCON)* (pp. 137-141). IEEE. doi:10.1109/TEMSCON.2017.7998367

Aitzhan, N. Z., & Svetinovic, D. (2016). Security and privacy in decentralized energy trading through multi-signatures, blockchain and anonymous messaging streams. *IEEE Transactions on Dependable and Secure Computing, 15*(5), 840–852. doi:10.1109/TDSC.2016.2616861

Barbosa, L. S. (2017, November). Digital governance for sustainable development. In *Conference on e-Business, e-Services and e-Society* (pp. 85-93). Springer.

Bazin, R., Schaub, A., Hasan, O., & Brunie, L. (2017, June). Self-reported verifiable reputation with rater privacy. In *IFIP International Conference on Trust Management* (pp. 180-195). Springer.

Brandão, A., São Mamede, H., & Gonçalves, R. (2018, March). Systematic review of the literature, research on blockchain technology as support to the trust model proposed applied to smart places. In *World Conference on Information Systems and Technologies* (pp. 1163-1174). Springer. 10.1007/978-3-319-77703-0_113

Cai, Y., & Zhu, D. (2016). Fraud detections for online businesses: A perspective from blockchain technology. *Financial Innovation, 2*(1), 20. doi:10.118640854-016-0039-4

Calvaresi, D., Dubovitskaya, A., Calbimonte, J. P., Taveter, K., & Schumacher, M. (2018, June). Multi-agent systems and blockchain: Results from a systematic literature review. In *International Conference on Practical Applications of Agents and Multi-Agent Systems* (pp. 110-126). Springer. 10.1007/978-3-319-94580-4_9

Choi, J., & Shin, S. (2016). Propose of smart place IoT systems for strengthen security of the smart grid environment. International Information Institute (Tokyo) Information, 19(5), 1509.

Eling, M., & Lehmann, M. (2018). The impact of digitalization on the insurance value chain and the insurability of risks. *The Geneva Papers on Risk and Insurance. Issues and Practice, 43*(3), 359–396. doi:10.105741288-017-0073-0

Eyal, I. (2017). Blockchain technology: Transforming libertarian cryptocurrency dreams to finance and banking realities. *Computer, 50*(9), 38–49. doi:10.1109/MC.2017.3571042

Guo, Y., & Liang, C. (2016). Blockchain application and outlook in the banking industry. *Financial Innovation, 2*(1), 24. doi:10.118640854-016-0034-9

Hawlitschek, F., Notheisen, B., & Teubner, T. (2018). The limits of trust-free systems: A literature review on blockchain technology and trust in the sharing economy. *Electronic Commerce Research and Applications, 29*, 50–63. doi:10.1016/j.elerap.2018.03.005

Jaffe, C., Mata, C., & Kamvar, S. (2017, September). Motivating urban cycling through a blockchain-based financial incentives system. In *Proceedings of the 2017 ACM International Joint Conference on Pervasive and Ubiquitous Computing and Proceedings of the 2017 ACM International Symposium on Wearable Computers* (pp. 81-84). ACM. 10.1145/3123024.3123141

Karafiloski, E., & Mishev, A. (2017, July). Blockchain solutions for big data challenges: A literature review. In *IEEE EUROCON 2017-17th International Conference on Smart Technologies* (pp. 763-768). IEEE. 10.1109/EUROCON.2017.8011213

Korpela, K., Hallikas, J., & Dahlberg, T. (2017, January). Digital supply chain transformation toward blockchain integration. *Proceedings of the 50th Hawaii international conference on system sciences.* 10.24251/HICSS.2017.506

Król, M., Reñé, S., Ascigil, O., & Psaras, I. (2018). ChainSoft: Collaborative software development using smart contracts. In *CRYBLOCK 2018-Proceedings of the 1st Workshop on Cryptocurrencies and Blockchains for Distributed Systems, Part of MobiSys 2018* (pp. 1-6). ACM.

Kumar, N. M., & Mallick, P. K. (2018). Blockchain technology for security issues and challenges in IoT. *Procedia Computer Science, 132*, 1815–1823. doi:10.1016/j.procs.2018.05.140

Liang, G., Weller, S. R., Luo, F., Zhao, J., & Dong, Z. Y. (2018). Distributed blockchain-based data protection framework for modern power systems against cyber attacks. *IEEE Transactions on Smart Grid, 10*(3), 3162–3173. doi:10.1109/TSG.2018.2819663

Lindman, J., Tuunainen, V. K., & Rossi, M. (2017). *Opportunities and risks of Blockchain Technologies–a research agenda.* Academic Press.

Mettler, M. (2016, September). Blockchain technology in healthcare: The revolution starts here. In *2016 IEEE 18th International Conference on e-Health Networking, Applications and Services (Healthcom)* (pp. 1-3). IEEE.

Mylrea, M., & Gourisetti, S. N. G. (2017, September). Blockchain for smart grid resilience: Exchanging distributed energy at speed, scale and security. In 2017 Resilience Week (RWS) (pp. 18-23). IEEE.

O'Dair, M., & Beaven, Z. (2017). The networked record industry: How blockchain technology could transform the record industry. *Strategic Change, 26*(5), 471–480. doi:10.1002/jsc.2147

Park, J., & Park, J. (2017). Blockchain security in cloud computing: Use cases, challenges, and solutions. *Symmetry, 9*(8), 164. doi:10.3390ym9080164

Peters, G. W., & Panayi, E. (2016). Understanding modern banking ledgers through blockchain technologies: Future of transaction processing and smart contracts on the internet of money. In *Banking beyond banks and money* (pp. 239–278). Cham: Springer. doi:10.1007/978-3-319-42448-4_13

Pflaum, A., Bodendorf, F., Prockl, G., & Chen, H. (2017). *Introduction to the digital supply chain of the future: technologies, applications and business models minitrack.* Academic Press.

Seebacher, S., & Schüritz, R. (2017, May). Blockchain technology as an enabler of service systems: A structured literature review. In *International Conference on Exploring Services Science* (pp. 12-23). Springer. 10.1007/978-3-319-56925-3_2

Shackelford, S. J., & Myers, S. (2017). Block-by-block: Leveraging the power of blockchain technology to build trust and promote cyber peace. *Yale JL & Tech., 19*, 334.

Vujičić, D., Jagodić, D., & Ranđić, S. (2018, March). Blockchain technology, bitcoin, and Ethereum: A brief overview. In *2018 17th International Symposium INFOTEH-JAHORINA (INFOTEH)* (pp. 1-6). IEEE. 10.1109/INFOTEH.2018.8345547

Yaga, D., Mell, P., Roby, N., & Scarfone, K. (2019). *Blockchain technology overview.* arXiv preprint arXiv:1906.11078

Zhang, N., Zhong, S., & Tian, L. (2017). Using Blockchain to Protect Personal Privacy in the Scenario of Online Taxi-hailing. *International Journal of Computers, Communications & Control*, *12*(6), 886. doi:10.15837/ijccc.2017.6.2886

Zheng, Z., Xie, S., Dai, H., Chen, X., & Wang, H. (2017, June). An overview of blockchain technology: Architecture, consensus, and future trends. In *2017 IEEE International Congress on Big Data (BigData Congress)* (pp. 557-564). IEEE. 10.1109/BigDataCongress.2017.85

Chapter 9
Network Security Evaluation and Threat Assessments in Enterprise Systems

Sam Goundar

iD https://orcid.org/0000-0001-6465-1097
The University of the South Pacific, Fiji

Abraham Colin Chongkit
The University of the South Pacific, Fiji

Shalvendra Kumar
The University of the South Pacific, Fiji

Akashdeep Bhardwaj

iD https://orcid.org/0000-0001-7361-0465
University of Petroleum and Energy Studies, India

ABSTRACT

Companies have realized the need to have the competitive edge over their rivals. Enterprise systems provide this competitive edge. But with implementing enterprise system software (ESS), companies have to invest in the networking of their various business offices to interconnect to ESS. This chapter investigates the various ways two companies in Fiji do this and the various disadvantages they face from lack of knowledge of ESS to infrastructure limitations and issues faced in a developing country like Fiji. This chapter focuses on the network security issues of enterprise systems deployed in two companies in Fiji. It compares the information gathered to published papers on network infrastructure, network security issues, and threat assessments. It also proposes solutions to mitigate the security issues faced by enterprise systems networks.

DOI: 10.4018/978-1-7998-2367-4.ch009

INTRODUCTION

The exponential rise and extensive use of information and communications technology (ICT) has changed how an organization works (Taylor. P, 2015). ICT consists of hardware, software, telco and information systems which to process and analyze information and extract intelligence (Taylor. P, 2015). It is noted that Enterprise Systems Software implementation costs are significantly higher, five to 10 times the cost, of software licenses (Argawal & Sambamurthy, 2003). The benefits they provide outweighs the costs and are multidimensional (Lorenzo, 2004). The complexity of installation and implementation (Brodbeck et al., 2010). This chapter focuses on an aspect of ICT, which has seen an exponential increase in use for large enterprises, which is Enterprise Systems (ES). Vendors have been noted to focus their ES solutions targeting small to medium enterprises (SME) (Mehta. A (2010)) since most large enterprises have or are currently in implementation stages. The adoption of Enterprise Systems in companies in Fiji is limited. This research focus on two companies that have successfully implements ES. The authors further focus on the network security components of said implementations. According to (Markus et al., 2000), ESS are complex software designed to integrate transactional data and business processes in the entire business. This integrations cuts through the "islands of ideation" or departmental silos of information, gathering them all in one repository for better analysis, consistency of data, data integrity. This ultimately leads to better Business Intelligence and top-level decision-making.

The rise of new technologies and increase cybercrimes bring in many challenges to an Enterprise Systems Network. The costs associated with vulnerabilities are very devastating for any organization as a large amount of cost and time is being associated with it. According to (CSIS, 2018) "Cybercriminals at the high end are as technologically sophisticated as the most advanced information technology (IT) companies, and, like them, have moved quickly to adopt cloud computing, artificial intelligence, Software-as-a-Service, and encryption". This research seeks to find out the security issues in an enterprise systems network in Fiji, finding out solutions that organizations need to encounter in the daily operations and give recommendations for a secure and better platform in addressing the cyber-attacks. Limited or no research approaches are taken about this topic in Fiji. Our research will be one of the first and will seek to address the issues and give solutions to a secure enterprise systems network. Due to limited research, we seek to use conceptual framework.

RESEARCH SURVEY

The authors performed research that includes Literature Survey and Face-to-Face Interviews regarding the issues and concepts on Enterprise systems network. The research was done on three companies enterprise systems; i.e. Bizxxe, Sage. Interviews and questionnaires were done with IT managers and staffs to find out the security issues faced by the Enterprise Applications. We have used both qualitative and quantitative approach to collect data. Conceptual framework is used to complete our research and quantitative analysis is done with the data gathered. Face to face interviews was held and information was gathered on the security issues faced by organizations on managing ERP applications and their on their network. In addition, the security was analyzed according to different modules of the ERP application. As this research was based on the core application of the enterprise and their network, management did not fully reveal full information on the security breaches due to privacy. However, result gathered was sufficient to complete our research.

"Enterprise networks have become essential to the operation of companies, laboratories, universities, and government agencies". (Munir & Disso & Awan, 2013). As Enterprise network scale increase, their security issues starts to become critical. Organization starts to spend more on security to minimize the risk of enterprise failure due to attacks. To find out the Enterprise network security issues we have evaluated a Fiji company, which has several subsidiaries. Each subsidiary has operating systems with a complete network structure. The parent company has an Enterprise system, which is being used by all these subsidiaries to achieve goals and decision-making process. The parent company when it took over all the subsidiaries company decided to implement an ERP system so that all systems are integrated. This bought up a solution of integrating all subsidiaries operation in one system, which will be hosted and controlled by parent company IT team. The ERP system was than customized upon the management required where the certain IT experts' team developed it. The name of the Enterprise system was "Bizzxe" This system went live early in 2000 and it interacted all modules of subsidiary companies. ERP systems consisted of IT, Human Resource Module, Accounts, Sales, Purchasing, Inventory, and Global modules as

- Accounts consisted of Chart of Account, Journal Entries, Debit/ Credit, Receivables, Banking, Payables, Bank Reconciliation, Set-off, Finance Budgets, Configure, Report modules.
- SALES consisted of Customers, Quotations, Sales Orders, Sales Returns, Invoices, Pricing, Sales Discounts, and Reports.
- PURCHASING consisted of Suppliers, Purchase Orders, Goods/Services Receipts, Purchase Returns, Terms and Costs.

- INVENTORY consisted of Products, Picking Slips, Dispatch Slips, Stock Transfers, Stock Takes, Lot/Batch Maintenance, Store Setup, Item Location Setup, Reports.
- Human Resource consisted of Payroll, Recruitment, Training and Attendance.
- IT consists of Inventory, Purchase, Helpdesk, and Report.

This system is a web-based ERP system where end users can update their work from anywhere as long as they have good internet connection. This system is live now and upon our research, we found out that the system is facing legacy system.

An interview with the IT managers we found that the encryption standard RSA (4096 Bits) has let is to legacy system as it has issues with support with browsers. Adonix, a software firm in 1979, established sage. Company Y chose to use this ERP to perform its major business processes. The modules includes Accounting, Manufacturing, Customer Relationship management and Human Resource management. During our interviews with management on some of the security issues, we found that there were some malware and phishing attacks on the ERP to gain access to the ERP system. The company hosts this software and the external company provides technical support.

DATA COLLECTION

A set of questions were prepared for questionnaire and face-to-face interviews. We categorized the three most common attacks, DDoS, Phishing and Malware attacks. These we further investigated the attacks on the different modules of the ERP applications. In addition, data was collected on how organizations managed to mitigate these vulnerabilities on the network as a whole. These results are tabulated and then analyzed.

RESULTS

The data collected from interviews and questionnaires, quantitatively assessed the Enterprise network security issues of two organization in Fiji, which uses an ERP system. The security issues are represented as Phishing, malware, DDoS. These can be represented as P, M, D. Suppose N represents the company name, which had been analyzed to get data.

Figure 1. Threats for Bizzxe ERP Application Modules for Organization X

| Modules | Organsation x ERP (Bizzxe) | | | |
| | Attacks | | | |
	Phishing	Malware(Ransomware)	DDos	Total
IT	2	3	1	6
Accounts	6	5	2	13
Managemnet	5	3	1	9
Sales	3	4	1	8
HR	6	5	1	12
	22	20	6	48

Figure 2. Types of Attacks on Different ERP Modules Organization X

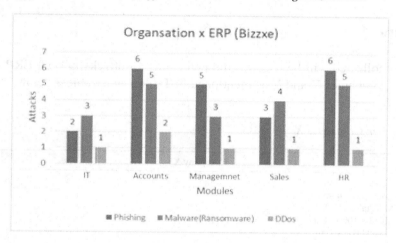

Figure 3. Threats on Bizzxe ERP Application Modules for Organization Y

| Modules | Organsation Y ERP (Sage) | | | |
| | Attacks | | | |
	Phishing	Malware(Ransomware)	DDos	Total
IT	1	1	0	2
Accounts	3	4	0	7
Customer Relationship	2	2	1	5
Manufacturing	2	4	1	7
HR	2	5	1	8
	10	16	3	29

Figure 4. Types of Attacks on the Different ERP Modules of Organization Y

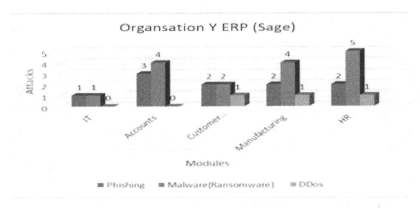

Scenario 1:

The data collected will be used to find percentage of attacks in each ERP system for both Companies X and Y as mentioned in Table 1 and Table 2 below.

Table 1: For Company X

Company X
$\%_x(P) = P/\text{Total (P)} \times 100$ $\%_x(P) = 22/48 \times 100 = 45.83\%$ $\%_x(M) = M/\text{Total (M)} \times 100$ $\%_x(M) = 20/48 \times 100 = 41.66\%$ $\%_x(D) = D/\text{Total (D)} \times 100$ $\%_x(D) = 6/48 \times 100 = 12.5\%$

Table 2: For Company X

Company Y
$\%_y(P) = P/\text{Total (P)} \times 100$ $\%_y(P) = 10/29 \times 100 = 34.48\%$ $\%_y(M) = M/\text{Total (M)} \times 100$ $\%_y(M) = 16/29 \times 100 = 55.17\%$ $\%_y(D) = D/\text{Total (D)} \times 100$ $\%_y(D) = 3/29 \times 100 = 10.35\%$

Figure 5. Organization of X-Attacks

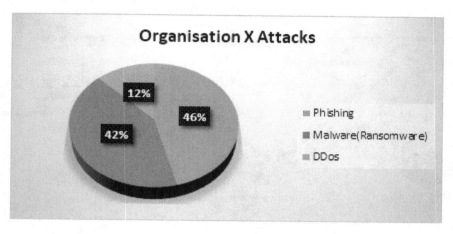

Figure 6. Organization of Y-Attacks

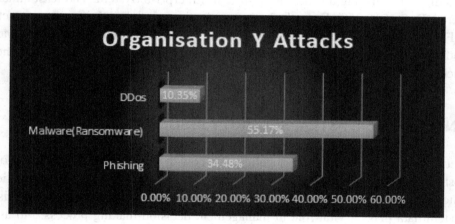

The data collected and analyzed from two companies X is shown above in graphical form. Upon analyzing the data. In this company Phishing, attack was 46%, which was highest. The ERP system in this organization has mainly been attacked through phishing emails. Malware also was high as it was 42% in overall attacks. The least attacks were DDoS of 12% this is mainly because the fact Fiji is developing nation and other companies host most of the ERP in

Figure 7. Phishing Attacks

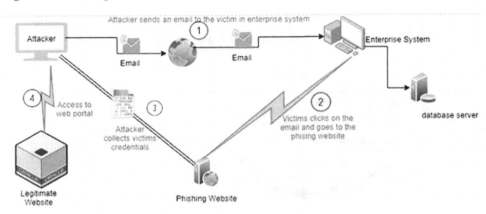

The data collected and analyzed from two companies Y is shown above in graphical form. Upon analyzing the data. In this company Malware, attack was 55.17%, which was highest. Phishing attack was 34.48% in Enterprise System. The least attacks were DDoS of 10.35%. From the both organizations analyzed the common attacks in Fijis Enterprise Network system is Phishing and Malware. Phishing and Malware both spread through internet where people are unaware of these attacks when they click of phishing emails and Malware.

ENTERPRISE SYSTEM SECURITY ISSUES

Network security is activities or policies on how to protect an enterprise network system. Security refers to a broader area of research, which ensures an organization enterprise network reliability, usability and safe network and data. In any enterprise, system data plays a vital role in management decision-making process. Fiji as a developing nation is still trying to cope up with technologies from other developed nations. Therefore, security issues arise in enterprise network system often. Enterprises are eventually investing in different types of security devices and protocol to make their network secure but still hackers tend to exploit the enterprise network with different types of attacks. Enterprise system continuously have issues as it is connected through network system. In Fiji, technology will have a potential issue, as Fiji is developing nation in terms of Enterprise system.

Phishing

"In phishing, an automated form of social engineering, criminals use the Internet to fraudulently extract sensitive information from businesses and individuals, often by impersonating legitimate web sites". Business use web-based ERP systems, which are subject to phishing attacks. In Fiji this attack most of end-users are unaware about scammers intention and what it cause in Enterprise System environment.

Attacker sends email to victims these could be users or anyone in enterprise

Figure 8. Phishing Email

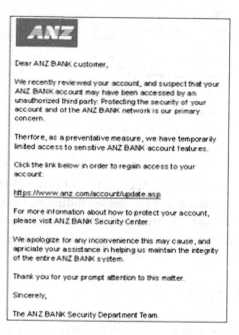

network system. Nowadays email phishing is more vigilant as most enterprise system users use company emails to communicate with stakeholder or mostly passwords are stored in emails of users. Victim than clicks the email and is directed to legitimate website without user's knowledge. The user enters credential and the data goes to attacker with victim login details. An example of a hoax email is shown below:

The above example compromises the user Pin, ID, and username thus in Banks Enterprise System it has major effects as customer detail and money are taken away without customer knowledge what has happened. In Fiji, phishing is a major issue in any enterprise network system because of lack of understanding on how credential

Figure 9. Malware Infection

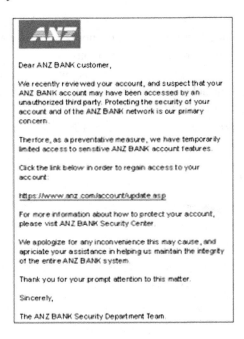

is stolen on one click of a mouse. According to Financial Intelligence Unit (Fiji Sun, 2018), there was an increase of businesses falling victim of email phishing and frauds. As a result, personal information was stolen and another login credential. Fiji FIU presented a case where there was biggest fraud of amount totaled $845,000.

COUNTERMEASURES

Users are generally the most important aspect of any enterprise system thus educating users on how phishing works and what are the potential risks that phishing can case on end users in enterprise network. Educating users on to verify the URL address and not to reveal confidential information to phishers. This can reduce many fraud aspects in Fiji when end users are educated about potential threats in Enterprise network system.

Malware Infection

"Malware infection occurs when malware, or malicious software, infiltrates your computer. Malware is a type of software created with the intent of damaging the victim's computer, stealing private information or spying on a computer without the consent of the user." Comodo, 2019. Trojans, viruses, spyware, ransomware, adware, rootkits and worms are popular malware that affects many organizations in Fiji. ERP systems in Fiji face these attacks and as a result, system slows down causing ERP software to not fully functional.

Most systems are nowadays are victims of Malware Infection in Enterprise Systems. End user tend to get pop- up, emails and all adware over internet that can cause operating system to behave weird in most cases freezes. Enterprise system software usually work on platforms where systems are integrated. This malware tends to cause interference between end-user and the system itself.

Types of Malware

- **Ransomware** is a type of malware that prevents or limits users from accessing their system, either by locking the system's screen or by locking the user's files unless a ransom is paid". (Deo, 2016). The attacks are directly on enterprise system as database files can be encrypted without able to decrypt. (Lena Fuks, 2019) explains about Ransomware attacks that users in enterprise system end users should be aware.
- **Bad Rabbit:** Is a type of attack with malicious code usually disguised as an adobe flash installer. It spreads via "drive -by download". If a person, clicks on the malicious installer their computer locks. The demand to decrypt the files is $280 from the attacker in Bitcoin.
- **Cerber:** This ransomware id distributed (RaaS) ransomware-as-a-service, which is a sort of cybercriminals. Its main target is cloud- based Office 365 users and has affected millions of users. This is spreads through an email with Microsoft Office document attached, which is already infected. Once the user opens are silently run in the background during encryption phase. Its uses RSA encryption and there are no free decryptions available.
- **Dharma:** It is a crypto virus that will affect the enterprise system via email and uses random combination of letters to encrypt the files. It struck the world in 2016 and uses AES 256 algorithm to encrypt files while simultaneously deleting shadow files. In 2019, it has files extension such as GIF, USA, AUF.
- **Grand Crab:** The most popular ransomware of 2018. It mainly relies on Microsoft Office, VBScript, and PowerShell.

Figure 10. DDoS Attack

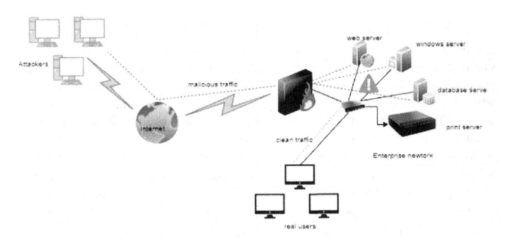

Ransomware continues to grow all over the world in top five treat. This is major concern all over the world as less developed nation such as Fiji can pay a heavy cost on these types of attacks.

COUNTERMEASURES

- Ransomware spreads in Enterprise mainly through user interaction by clicking malicious cites or URL link. User education could be most important preventable measure to avoid these attacks to occur in Enterprise network system.
- Firewall rules and polices needs to continuously review by Network administrators to prevent these malwares to enter the network of organization.
- Use Endpoint security solution to protect the enterprise network system. A huge number of endpoint security exits for example Kaspersky, Sophos. These security controls will enable or prevent the opening of suspicious sites.

DDoS Attacks

"A distributed denial-of-service (DDoS) attack is one in which a large number of compromised systems attack a single machine, thereby service is getting denied for users of the targeted system." (Anjali, 2014). The attack is done by sending syn request to ERP system. This type of attack is hard to differentiate from network traffic and Dos attack traffic. Today's ERP system is mainly hosted either on cloud and DDoS attack can cause deny of service.

DDoS attack is where attackers target the webserver with malicious traffic or syn request to the port. Its main target is to overload the server with malicious request to bring down the resources available with the enterprise network system. DDoS attack is mainly targeted to bring in down certain service that a particular module provides in Enterprise system. This module is Accounting, Production, Finance, Human Resource, IT many other.

According to our finding, the organization had Accounts, Sales, Purchasing, Inventory, Human Resource and IT modules in ERP software. DDoS attack is simply trying to attack certain service and bring it down so that other modules cannot access that.

NETWORK SECURITY MEASURES

Firewall and web proxy must be used to protect the intranet and to keep unwanted people out. Licensed Antivirus software must be installed and Internet security software package should be installed. For authentication, a strong password must be used to access GUI in Enterprise based software and kept confidential and password needs to be changed on a weekly or monthly basis to keep hackers guessing what will be the password. For wireless connection, use of robust password is required. Network analyzer and network monitoring tool need to be used to differentiate the types of traffic in enterprise network system.

Network Security Tools

- Nessus one of the top free network vulnerability scanner.
- N-map Security Scanner is free and open source security tool that can be used to scan enterprise network system.
- Wireshark network protocol analyzer can be used to analyses network traffic for UNIX and Windows
- Many other tools can be used in Fiji to monitor the network traffic flow and detect vulnerability in Enterprise systems.

Network Infrastructure Management

In today's organization, unmanaged and mismanaged use of infrastructure and network creates traffic issue to an enterprise system. Avoiding and managing proper information flow needs a Network infrastructure management. To avoid traffic congestion and bottleneck issues it manages and optimizes the network infrastructure. It includes the management of hardware and software resources of the organization, which allows communications management of the enterprise network and connectivity. It also provides the path of services and communications amongst processes, applications, services, users and external networks. Rapid demand for faster, secure and safe networks is a key aspect of any organization. Rapid increase in cybercrimes and frequent network breaches has made enterprises to adapt approaches that can encounter such instances. Server management and data storage, data integrity management, end management and operating system for servers needs to be managed by organizations. Advanced ip address management solutions with network security solutions are available. Furthermore, it provides end-to-end network management and accessibility including performance management and real time faults. This also helps proactive and predictive network management as it encounters network issues and future faults. The innovative time saving technologies in large network management also helps in organizational efficiency and growth.

Network infrastructure is one of the crucial part of IT infrastructure, which has been supporting IT environments. The entire communication including internal and external is connected with the entire network infrastructure. Network infrastructure management is being segmented based on solutions, network hardware, services, type of industry and size. Hardware includes selection of routers, switches, LAN cards, firewalls, end devices, servers etc. The solution is segmented into management and network operations, operating systems, ip address management and network security applications. Services include integration and support services. The enterprise size incudes small, medium and large enterprises. Large enterprises often adopt proper network infrastructure management to manage the network flow that is interconnected or distributed at various locations. The types of industries include government, income tax industry, water industry, healthcare, manufacturing, telecom, electricity and others. Network infrastructure management is not only about developing new solutions but is also about managing and maintaining the current infrastructure, making decisions on when and why to replace any hardware and software. Grochow, (2015) For instance making decisions on whether to choose wired or wireless connections for an enterprise application. It also includes proper wiring and cabling which does not distort communications. Figure below illustrates the factors for different types of infrastructure:

Figure 11. Factors for different types of Infrastructure

	Initial Implementation	Maintenance and Upgrade	Reimplementation	Technology Migration
Capabilities	Basic capabilities	Additional capabilities	New design	Old capabilities vs. new capabilities
Benefits	To different constituencies	Use of anecdotes	Reliability and performance improvements	Capability, reliability, and performance improvements
Risks	New technology acceptance	Impact of upcoming technology shift	Impact on related infrastructure and systems	New technology acceptance
Costs	Maintaining prior infrastructure	Cost changes with maintenance frequency Maintenance costs vs. replacement	Impact on related infrastructure and systems	Phased cost model Migration costs

Design & Implementing System and Network Security

- **Security services and processes:** This includes physical protection of IT assets such as switches, COMMS rack, servers, firewall etc. Adequate authentication to be implemented to access network services, such as file shares. Proper authorization to certain resources to certain groups of employees or users. Passwords not to be identical so that users do not access others content, that is confidentiality. Data integrity should be always there as it protects data from malicious modifications. Making all services available to staffs at all times ensuring adequate replication of services is there in times of a primary node or services being down.

- **End devices and Operating systems:** Ensuring that users to have their operating systems updated and having an optimal device to work on. The devices must also have an updated antivirus software to protect it against viruses and malicious attacks.
- **Active directory services:** In a windows server platform active directory manages the entire user accounts, permissions and policies that allows enforcing any administrative permissions. Making sure that there is a replication of the primary AD in case it fails.
- **Servers:** This is the main area of concern, as it is the core to any enterprise. Servers that we came across were Exchange server, Database server (Oracle), Active directory server, File
- Server, Application Server, Veam Server. These powerful machines are capable to process user's requests at maximum speed without much latency. There is also replication of these servers locally and on the DR site in case of any disaster or failure.
- **Security Devices:** With the use of firewall and proxy server, traffic is filtered. Inbound and Outbound traffic is thoroughly analyzed before entering and exiting the network.
- **Network devices:** This includes the powerful cisco router and switches to route traffic from the source to destination network. Cisco 4000 series router are used to router packets. Cisco catalyst 9000 series of switches are also preferred as core to forward frames.

OVERVIEW OF COMPANY X's INFASTRUCTURE

Figure 12. Company Infrastructure

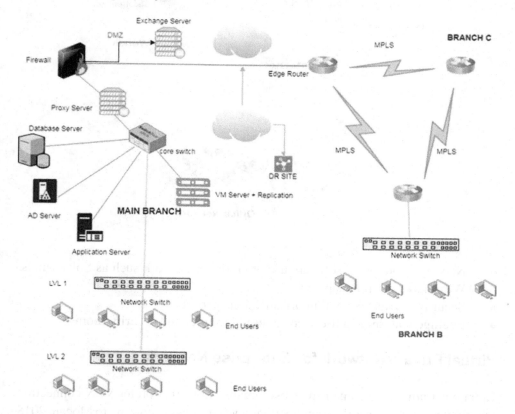

Security Measures

We have found out that organizations have the following measures to secure their networks:

- A robust proxy and firewall is used to encounter unwanted attacks
- An updated antivirus software package and internet security software package installed in end devices such as Eset endpoint and McAfee LiveSafe
- Strong passwords are used for authentications, and which is changed on a monthly basis
- Physical security for server rooms and COMMS rack is secure; unauthorized access is not permitted.

Figure 13. Remote Access VPN

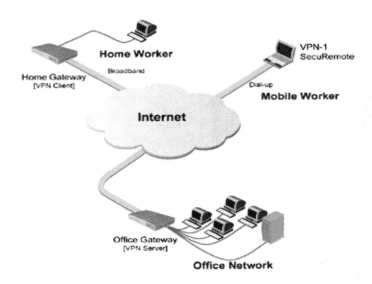

- Network monitoring software used to monitor network such as Solar winds, Wireshark, snort, Nmap
- Security barriers set within organizations perimeter
- Intelligent alarm and fire security used in server and security rooms

Virtual Private Network for Enterprise Network

Upon our finding, we came across two organizations that prefer VPN connection for remote sites to access their applications and services. According to Mocan, 2018 VPN concept started in 1996 by a Microsoft Employee, by developing a Peer-to-Peer Tunneling Protocol. This technology was developed for large organizations for their goals. Companies needed a secure communication when needed critical file or application access from a remote location. As the evolution of new threats and rise in cybercrimes, organizations tend to use this technology more often. A VPN establishes a secure and encrypted communication that utilizes combination of other technologies via a trusted network.

Type of VPN that Organizations Prefer are

- **Remote Access VPN - Client VPN:** allows users to connect to a private network and access services remotely. In this type of VPN, the client software is installed to users end devices to initiate a connection from a remote site.

This access is only given to users who work of premises and is vital for him/her to access services.

- **Site to site VPN:** is mostly used to connect corporate branches in a Wide Area Network. This VPN is based on router-to-router communication where one becomes a client while other router becomes a server. Communication is established once authentication process is done. Organizations that we came across use MPLS to connect their remote sites, as a result do not need a site-to-site VPN. It was also found out that companies had switched their dedicated fiber links to MPLS.

- **IP Sec Protocol:** This allows authentication, confidentiality and data integrity for an established connection. It operates in two modes: Transport and Tunneling mode. Transport mode encrypts data in the data packet and tunneling mode encrypts the whole data packet while communication takes place. It has a high level of security as encryption ensures confidentiality and authentication. IP sec is implemented in the firewall and provides a strong security.

- **Firewall:** A firewall is one of the most important component of a firm's network security. It is designed to block or restrict unauthorized access to and from a company's private network. According to our research, we found out that organizations prefer to use Fortinet as their main firewall.

Types of Firewalls:

- **Packet Filtering Firewall:** works on traffic based on IP location and or port number and IP protocol. For a specific service the packet is intended for, TCP/IP ports are used. For instance, port number for http is 80. Any incoming packet intended for http server is going to specify port 80 as the destination port. The filtering of information is based on layer three source and destination address; layer three, four-protocol information, and the interface where traffic is sent and received. Packet filtering firewall is one of the least expensive firewall and has number of flaws that hackers can exploit, as it does not remember the state of the previous packet (ebrary.net, n.d.)

Figure 14. Zero Trust Network Architecture

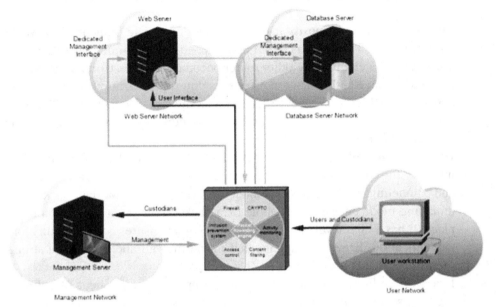

(Source: Drs. Albert Spijkers)

- **Stateful firewall:** the state of connection is been tracked in times of data initiation, transfer or termination process. It is useful when denying external devices and allowing your users to establish connection to these devices. In the OSI reference model from a transport layer perspective the layer three packets and layer four segments headers are examined. According to (Imran, Algamdi & Ahmad, 2015)"You have comprehended the built up association issue depicted above, yet despite everything you can't differentiate in the middle of good and terrible web activity. You require interruption counteractive action to identify and piece web assaults."

- **Circuit-Level Gateways:** This firewall is fast to approve or deny traffic without using much of the resources. It works through inspecting the TCP handshake. Due to its efficiency in packet inspection, it sometimes allows malware packets to pass thorough, as a result not a good solution for an enterprise systems network.

- **Proxy Firewalls:** works at the application layer to inspect and filter incoming packets between the networks. The proxy inspects the source traffic first before allowing direct traffic. It performs deep layer scanning and makes sure there is no malware attached to packets before entering the network. It creates an extra layer of protection as a result preferred by organizations.

- **Next-Generation Firewall:** one of the recent release. It has a feature of surface level packet inspection and deep packet examination of TCP handshake checks. It also includes other technologies such as intrusion prevention system, which automatically works to prevent attacks.

The Zero Trust Model

Created in 2009 by Forester, this model introduces a new way of thinking for a network security. This model declares that all network traffic be deemed untrusted. It implemented three concepts; organizations should ensure that all resources to be accessed securely, access control to be strictly enforced and principle of least privilege to be adopted and lastly all network traffic must be logged and inspected. The zero trust security requires a strict identity verification for each person that is trying to access an organizations network either from intranet or extranet. Traditional IT network security has a trust within the internal network users; however, it is hard to gain access from outside. One drawback of this approach is that once an attacker gains access to the network, they have a free access to the internal network.

Principles and Technologies Behind Zero Trust Security

The philosophy behind this approach is that there can be attackers, or hackers from inside and outside the network, as a result no users or devices to be automatically trusted. Moreover, least privilege access is given to users, where only needful access is given. This reduces the user's exposure to sensitive parts of the network. The security perimeters are divided into small zones to maintain different parts of the network. For instance, a network with files from a single data center may contain separate secure zones. A user or program trying to access one of these zones will not be able to access other zones without proper authorization. This process of breaking security perimeters into zones is called micro segmentation. Multifactor authentication is one of the core features in a zero trust security. It has a two-factor authentication where an access code is sent for verification. The zero trust model also requires device authorization as well, which limits the attacks.

Zero Trust Architecture Benefits

According to Alexander, 2018. "Zero Trust information security model has been gaining popularity lately. Over the years, we have been taught a certain security model that protects our business network. I will refer to it as the Trusted Network model." This requires less cost, skillset and management. This also helps organizations to help securely adopt to cloud and mobile solutions. It leaves no opportunity for attack penetration that ranges from users to endpoints, resources and networks. (Akamai, 2018)

Cloud Computing Data Security

In simple terms cloud computing refers to using resources as a service via internet on demand. This availability mechanism of being anywhere at any time provided you have an internet connection makes this a popular amongst business and it users. This reduces the infrastructure and management cost, however it also has drawbacks. Since data is outsourced to cloud, infrastructure it can become more vulnerable than storing it on a server-based environment within organizations premises. Three reasons why it is vulnerable are that different users share same physical infrastructure, service provider hosts data in their infrastructure and anytime from anywhere data is accessible through the internet. (Kacha, L & Zitouni, 2018)

CONCLUSION

Upon our findings, we came to find out that organizations do encounter security challenges when managing their enterprise systems network. They also have security mechanisms to protect their resources. There was no research done on the security issues of Enterprise Systems in Fiji. We found out that some organizations are not using ERP, rather has functional Information Systems that are not integrated as an ERP solution. In addition, some companies are not aware of the benefits that is derived from ERP. Breaches occur due to lack of security and loopholes within an organizations network and infrastructure setup.

RECOMMENDATION

The following research done on Enterprise Systems Network Security Issues shows that threats still occur even though there is security methods implemented. Time limitation was one of the flaws that affected the research, no previous research were done in Fiji about this topic. We also found out that no proper consulting service done during ERP implementation. Lack of understanding about ERP importance by non-technical staffs and not a proper budget allocation kept aside to reengineer business process and ERP maintenance and implementation. Some improvements that this research could have made was approaching on more companies and analyzing threats encountered by them. We would like to focus more on our findings if extended in future. In addition, we would like to extend our research on SME's across the pacific. Others can use this research and ICT standards; also, they can use it to base other research work on Enterprise Systems in Fiji and Across the Pacific. Also from this research, others can base their research focus on Enterprise System on a cloud platform, and find the challenges and benefits.

REFERENCES

Agarwal, R., & Sambamurthy, V. (2003). Principles and Models for Organizing the IT Function. *MIS Quarterly Executive*, *1*(1), 1–16.

Akamai. (2018). *Enforce a Zero Trust Security Model in Today's Hostile Environment*. Academic Press.

Alexander, Z. (2018). *Zero Trust Security Model – A Framework for a Different Approach*. Academic Press.

Anjali, M., & Padmavathi, B. (2014). DDoS Attack Detection based on Chaos Theory and Artificial Neural Network. *International Journal of Computer Science and Information Technologies*, *5*(6), 7276–7279.

Barba-Sánchez, V., Martínez-Ruiz, M., & Jiménez-Zarco, A. I. (2007). *Drivers, Benefits and Challenges of ICT Adoption by Small and Medium Sized Enterprises (SMEs): A Literature Review*. Problems and centrify.com.

Cisco Summits. (2018). *Zero Trust Security: A New Paradigm for a Changing World*. Retrieved from: https://www.ciosummits.com/wp-zero-trust.pdf

CSIS. (2018). *Economic Impact of Cybercrime- No Slowing Down*. CSIS.

Dosal, E. (2018). *The Different Types of Firewall Architectures*. Academic Press.

Fuks, L. (2018). *10 Ransomware Attacks You Should Know About in 2019*. Retrieved May 13, 2019, from https://www.allot.com/blog/10-ransomware-attacks-2019/

Grochow, J. (2015). *IT Infrastructure Projects: A Framework for Analysis*. Academic Press.

Kacha & Zitouni. (2018). *An Overview on Data Security in Cloud Computing*. Academic Press.

Lorenzo, O. (2004). *A Comprehensive Review of the Enterprise Systems Research*. Academic Press.

Markus, M. L., & Tanis, C. (2000). The Enterprise System Experience — From Adoption to Success. Academic Press.

Mehta, A. (2010). *A Study on Critical Success Factors for Successful ERP Implementation at Indian SMEs*. Bangalore: Christ University.

Mocan, T. (2018). *VPN History & The Future of VPN Technology*. Academic Press.

Munir, R., Diss, J., Awan, I., & Rafiq, M. (2013). *Quantitative Enterprise Network Security Risk Assessment*. Academic Press.

Parno, B., Kuo, C., & Perrig, A. (2006). Foolproof Phishing Prevention. In Lecture Notes in Computer Science: Vol. 4107. *Financial Cryptography and Data Security. FC 2006*. Berlin,: Springer.

Shang, S., & Seddon, P. (2002). Assessing and managing the benefits of enterprise systems: The business manager's perspective. *Information Systems Journal, 12*(4), 271–299. doi:10.1046/j.1365-2575.2002.00132.x

Williams, S., & Schubert, P. (2010). Benefits of Enterprise Systems Use. *Proceedings of the Annual Hawaii International Conference on System Sciences*, 1 - 9. 10.1109/ HICSS.2010.82

Chapter 10
Intellectual Property Rights Protection in Cyberspace:
An Indian Perspective

Manjula Raghav
Indira Gandhi National Open University, India

Nisha Dhanraj Dewani
(iD) https://orcid.org/0000-0002-8178-7188
Maharaja Agrasen School of Law, Guru Gobind Singh Indraprastha University, India

ABSTRACT

Development and advancement in information technologies have paved the path for many challenges for the intellectual property rights holders. There are several forms of cybercrimes such as pornography, stalking, cyber fraud, cyber terrorism, etc., that are affecting people, hurdling e-commerce, challenging law, and disturbing the channel of information and communication. No doubt that cybercrimes are offences where the computer is the means of the commission of the offence as well as a target of the offence. Apparently, such offences are generated through electronic means where mens rea has no role to play. This unruly horse is creating several problems in the world of intellectual property, which has the capacity to affect global commerce. This chapter will focus on Indian case laws to showcase the interface between IPR and cyberspace. Also the dealing of issues like cybersqatting, cyberbullying, cyber theft will be discussed in order to check the competency of IPR.

DOI: 10.4018/978-1-7998-2367-4.ch010

INTRODUCTION

Intellectual Property is the creation of intellect or mind. It is considered a valuable asset or reward to the creator for inventions, artistic work and literary expression in the form of rights. It comprises many areas such as Copyright, Trade Mark, Patent, Geographical Indications, Semiconductor, Designs, Utility Models and Trade Secrets.

The concept of property is different in cyberspace because it differs in nature from the actual tangible property. Cyberspace covers a vast geographical area; in fact it is a borderless domain which increases the possibility of trespass to intellectual property in cyber world. There are various aspects of the digital world which have deep impact on intellectual property. In today's worlds computers networks are interconnected on large level that is not subject to specific region or territory which aggravates the problem of Intellectual Property Rights infringement and causes damage to the value of intellectual property. Owing to the advancement of technology, easy ways are available in which people get engaged to cyber-crimes especially with regard to denting intellectual property. Cybercrimes is a criminal act committed using computers and internet. Such crimes can be committed easily from any place of the world and it is difficult to detect as well as almost impossible to prove them. The identification of the culprit is also not easy. Consequently, cyberspace is a vast stage for the cyber offenders to invade it and commit crimes. Moreover, it also creates a hurdle in deciding the jurisdiction of the court in the virtual world of internet.

INTERNATIONAL INSTRUMENTS FOR PROTECTING INTELLECTUAL PROPERTY RIGHTS IN CYBERSPACE

There are several international treaties and conventions have taken place for the protection and progress of intellectual property rights. However, there is no specific or particular treaty or convention on IPR in Cyberspace although these treaties can be applied in this context. They are capable of providing international standards for protection and progress of IPR in Cyberspace. These treaties as follows:

1. The Paris Convention was adopted in 1883 for protecting industrial property.
2. The Berne Convention was adopted in 1886 to provide protection to literary and artistic works.
3. WIPO Copyright Treaty (WCT) and WIPO Performance and Phonograms Treaty (WPPT) are known as WIPO Internet Treaties.
4. Patent Cooperation Treaty (PCT).
5. Trade Related Aspects of Intellectual Property (TRIPS).

Issues and Protection of Patent in Cyberspace

Patent is a form of intellectual property. It links with invention. It is an exclusive right provided by the authority to the inventor to exploit its invention for the limited time period. In India, Patent Act, 1970 governs and regulates this field of Intellectual Property Rights. As per *Halsbury's Law of England,* patent provides a monopoly right in respect of an invention. This monopoly provided by the Patent is a reward to the inventor excluding unlicensed users from the property and thus, creating a legal liability upon the wrong full user. However, it is to know that Patent is optional. It is not mandatory on the part of the inventor to register the Patent. The inventor of such invention can keep it closed to him. In such case, if the invention is used by some other person, that person is not having any remedy to protect his right. In this regard, The Allahabad High Court clearly stated, in *Shinning industries v. Shri Krishna Industries*, that an invention would be a property right only if it is registered and patented. So it is better to get it patented always (Ahuja, 2015) Though, every invention is not a subject matter of patent. In order to make any invention patentable, it should fulfil some criteria as it should be novel, non-obvious, inventive steps, having industrial potential, not falling under the provisions of sections 3 and 4of the Patent Act. Patent is provided for 20 years term in India if fulfils the criteria properly (Duggal, 2014).

Computer technology includes hardware, software and related aspects dealing with intellectual property. Any invention in the field of computer technology which is new, non- obvious, capable of industrial use, innovative steps is subject to patent protection. As per the past practice, generally, patents were provided to industrial process and practice and innovations in information technology were not included in the domain of patent protection. Business models were not part of patent. However, gradually, the position got changed and the invention in computer technology has been started taking recognition in the form of patent. In U.S., such innovations are recognised and provided patent. Initially, The U.S. Patent and Trademark Office (PTO) was reluctant to grant patent to inventions related to computer technology. Till 80s, it considered them comport programmes as mere mathematical calculations. But in *Diamond v. Diehr,* the Supreme Court ordered the PTO to grant patent to computer technology innovations. Further, in *State Street Bank & Trust v. Signature Financial Group*, The US Federal Court made the position clear for providing patent to computer software. In this case, the court upheld the patent provided for business methods. Consequently, in US a number of patents are provided to business models eligible for e- commerce for example, Demand collection system- Priceline.com, auction broker- eBay.com, virtual marketplace- amazon.com etc. (Sople, 2016).

In India, computer software is not subject matter of patent but such computer soft wares are protected under the umbrella of Copyright Act covered under the head of literary works. Such computer software covers artistic work, musical work, literary work and related programmes in this regard. Mathematical algorithm or related computer programs are not included in the category of inventions as they can be performed with profession skills. Section 2(ffc) of the India Copyright Act, 1957 defines computer programmes. As they fall under the head of literary works and comes under copyright protection as per section 2(o) of the Copyright Act, 1957. However, an amendment in the India Patent Act that took place in 2003 created a path for bringing computer technology subject to patent protection (Duggal, 2014). In short, it means that a computer programme or software which is capable of technical application in any industry or which can be formulated in the form of hardware can be patented in India. In this way, it covers two aspects first is that business methods (separately not patentable) and the other one is technical effect on the device which makes it patentable (Seth, 2013). Thus, computer software is protected under the both copyright and patent. There are some examples of patent protection provided by the India Patent office for software inventions as to Ebay for the method and system scheduling transaction listings at a network based facility, Google for automatically targeting web based advertisements. Oracle for tracking space usage in a database and many more examples are there in this regard (Sople, 2016).

In the context of business methods, divergent views are expressed. As per some critics, patent should not be provided for business methods as it will hamper innovation in cyberspace. Internet is itself in a developing stage and a lot more is to be explored in cyberspace. It should be left free from patentability to grow more and benefit more. On the other hand, different view is opined in this regard and favour patentability of business methods and software (Seth, 2013).

In this regard, the matter of jurisdiction and protection of rights are also relevant to be discussed. As internet has created several issues and one of them is patent protection has territorial limitation, it depends country to country. These days patent is originated at one place and sold at other place globally with the help of internet in such situation patent infringement issue arises in cyberspace as well as it also creates an issues of jurisdiction. However, to handle the matter more appropriately and to provide protection to patent in cyberspace is sound to strengthen international co-operation and in this regard, WIPO is trying to fulfil a positive role and addressing such issues.

Patents Protection in India

Any invention which qualifies the parameters of the provisions provided in Indian Patent Act will be protected. The same concept applies to any invention in cyberspace that will also be protected under the Act. As per section 2(1) (j), any invention in the field of computer technology, if it qualifies the definition of the term "invention, would be subject to protection under the Patent Act, 1970. In case of patent violation, the court can provide injunction and damages as remedial measure. In India, patent law is still in the process of development with the development of technology and e-commerce. A long path is yet to be covered and more judicial contribution is to be delivered in this domain.

Issues and Protection of Copyright in Cyberspace

Copyright plays a vital role in the development of the country. It is one of the intellectual properties. It ensures protection to the original expression of the author, artist or the creator of that artistic, literary, musical, dramatic and cinematographic work. It secures as well as motivates the creator to produce more creative and intellectual work. It provides full liberty to the owner of the right to use his work for commercial gain. It prohibits other from illegally using the work of the owner. The law provides protection to published as well as unpublished works. In short; it enhances cultural, literary, economic and social development. The copyright law ensures protection to the copyright owner for his rights as well as secures public interest in the present time.

Copyright work is an intangible and incorporeal work in nature. The whole idea is that it originates in mind first and then transforms into a material form. It is to be noted that idea is not protected under the copyright law but expression is guarded. Copyright over the work provides exclusive rights to the owner of the property. It is also considered a negative right because it excludes others from the usage of the property and only the right owner has exclusive right over that intellectual property. However, copyrights are provided to the owner for the limited time period or after the settled time period or the expiry of the prescribed time period, the property transfers in to the public domain. Copyright protection is provided for the life time of the author/owner and after his death it remains for sixty years.

Section 13 of The Copyright Act, 1957 deals with works in which copyright does subsists. Section 13(3) states in which copyright does not subsist. The Indian Copyright Act, 1957provides the protection to all kinds of original, literary works, musical works, artistic work, dramatic work, pictorial works, motion pictures, sculptural works, sound recording and computer programmes etc. Literary work not only counts the books, articles but includes computer programmes, tables and databases also. Computer programmes are also protected under The Copyright Act, 1957.Section 2(o) defines literary work which includes computer programmes, database and compilation etc. Computer program has been defined under section 2(ffc). The same principle of infringement of literary work is applicable on computer programs. Likewise; musical work includes any form of musical work. Artistic works includes different forms of artistic work as painting, sculptures, drawing, map, photograph etc. In the virtual world, digitalisation of work is also taking place and consequently, anything published on the website or any web page is to be considered as a copyrightable work under the head of literary work. It protects the material available on the webpage in any form, written, graphic, picture, sound, audio, video etc. Copyright guards everything in this regard available on the website (Sharma, 2015).

Copyright law covers a wide variety of human creativity to provide protection. The present IPR laws are especially being crafted to take care the needs of cyber space. Technology has enabled the transmission of copyrighted material in digital form in cyber space. Digital technology helps to convert and disseminate the content or material to World Wide Web or internet and further which can be stored and copied very easily. Thus on the one hand, technological advancement is paving path for new possibilities to provide recognition to copyrightable work but on the other hand, it is creating new challenges by raising modes of infringement of copyright on internet. It has become a common phenomenon in the present world. Technological progress has widened the problem of infringement. Technological advancement has made it easy to download copy and commit intellectual theft in the several forms on internet. Not only this, dissemination of the stolen material is boundary less. It is also too difficult to catch the wrongdoer and trace the place of the commission of the offence. In no time the protected and exclusive work can fall prey of infringement. Domestic or territorial IPR laws cannot be applied on cyber space due to the boundary less information technology. There are chances of involvement of various intermediaries in accessing copyright violation. Hence, most of the countries, including India, have introduced relevant changes in IP laws on cyberspace to tackle the situation. Liability has been constituted upon the Internet service providers, bulletin board service and private users in case of copyright infringement (Jaybhaye, 2016).

There are several issues of copyrights infringement in cyberspace like downloading or uploading of material on the website, caching, linking, framing and file sharing. There is a need of understanding them and finding proper solution to protect the rights of the owner pertaining to IP in cyberspace. Downloading or uploading of software programme on internet without the prior permission of the rightful owner is a punishable offence under the Copyright law in India. Downloading includes copying and reproduction of the copied software or the material. In *Playboy Enterprises Inc.*

case, the court held the defendant liable for operating a subscription bulletin board service that provided subscribers to download electronic pictures that made public display and dissemination of the pictures that were under the copyright protection of the plaintiff (Seth, 2013).

In India, illegal downloading and uploading of software is a punishable offence. In *Super Cassettes Industries Ltd. v. Myspace Inc. & Anr.*, the court provided temporary injunction against the defendant for displaying copyrighted songs and sound records of the plaintiff on the website (Seth, 2013).

Caching stands for the storage of file or content temporarily. The purpose of caching is to store a copy for future use as well as it can be viewed and accessed easily, quickly and without network traffic. Cache applies to hardware and software both. It can be seen in web browser where websites' images and html are formed temporarily so that it can be appear rapidly with one go. Thus it gets generated by the RAM. Caching can affect the commercial value of that website page which is not updated due to it. In *Apple Computer* v. *Formula International*, the court stated that copies stored in RAM are not permanent in fact temporary and a copy or program getting operated from RAM is not an infringing copy. It is to be noted that Google's caching methodology has been put several times under the scrutiny of copyright issues but in many cases it has been protected under the head of fair use (Seth, 2013).

Linking on internet connects the user to secondary website transgressing the primary website or the original site on which the user was. Thus, linking links one website to another website. It browses another website without browsing it in URL. Such act of linking on the internet can have legal consequences. It can mislead the user from the actual content. It can affect the advertising available on the original page.

MP3 revolution started off peer to peer music file sharing in the cyberspace. Due to it, music industry suffered a lot because it enabled downloading and sharing of music files freely from websites very easily. In a very famous *Napster Case,* A & M sued Napster for infringing the copyright of the music recordings. Napster provided a server to the users for peer to peer file sharing which worked as a search engine to download music files. The court found the violation by the Napster of the copyright material of the plaintiff.

Framing of websites also leads to infringement of copyright. Framing refers to incorporating the contents of one website from another website to frame or create of its own and it has been fabricated to appear as an original site. In *Midway Manufacturing Co.* v. *Artic International*, the court held that the derivative work of the defendant is an unauthorised adaptation and infringes the right of the plaintiff.

Doctrine of Fair Use in India

The copyright law provides protection to the rightful owner of the material .Similarly; on the other hand, the copyright law permits the users to make use of copyright work in certain situations. Thus, the law strikes a balance between the rights of the copyright owner and public interest. Such exception is provided for the purpose of research, private study, criticism and teaching etc. Section 52 of the Copyright Act, 1957 provides a list of permitted usage of the copyright material. These permitted acts fall under the head of "fair dealing" or" fair use". In the internet age, information cannot sustain in water tight compartment, there is a need of free flow and dissemination of information and data so that society at large can be benefitted. In India, Judiciary has also come forward with justified use of fair dealing. Under the head of fair use, reverse engineering is also permitted under section 52 of the Act (Ahuja, 2015).

In *Syed Asifuddin and Ors.* v. *the State of Andhra Pradesh &Anr*, the court stated that tempering of code done by Tata Indicom employees is a punishable offence under section 65 of the IT Act, 2000. Such tempering cannot be covered under fair dealing or reverse engineering under section 52 of the copyright Act, 1957.

Infringement of Copyright and Legal Remedies

The Copyright Act, 1957 applies to copyright infringement in cyberspace. There are provisions which define "computer", computer programme" and "literary work". Moreover, related to this context, Section 13 and 14 directly deal with copyright protection in cyberspace. In dealing with infringement, section 51 of the Copyright Act deals with violation of copyright and defines when copyright will be deemed to be violated by the unauthorised user. It is to be noted that in case of infringement of copyright, there are certain remedies are provided to the owner of the copyright. For this purpose, civil and criminal remedies are provided to the author or owner of the copyright. Section 55 provides civil remedies in case of infringement of copyright. It provides protection to the owner in form of injunctions and damages. On the other hand, the owner can take protection under criminal remedies or proceedings. It is to be noted that criminal remedy is distinct, independent and can be applied simultaneously to protect from further infringement and punish the wrongdoer. In this regard, *mens rea* is the main element to constitute the offence. Section 63 to 70 of the Act handles offences related to copyright. Section 63 deals with the offence of infringement of copyright. In a case, " *Dhiraj Dharam Das* v. *Sonal Info Systems Pvt. Ltd*. The court stated that registration is necessary if the owner of the copyright wants to avail the remedy under civil and criminal proceedings before the district court instead of a civil court.

Information Technology Act, 2000

Information Technology Act was enacted by the Indian Government to provide a legal framework to handle the issues regarding e-commerce and governance in India. With the development of technology, it is pertinent to keep Indian legal framework up to date so that issues related to cybercrime can be dealt by the Government. However, IT Act in itself is not sufficient to deal with issues related to Intellectual property rights in cyberspace (Jay bhaye, 2016). With regard to the copyright protection, Section 1(2) read with section 75 of IT Act, 2000 are relevant. It provides copyright protection in case of violation of copyright material by any person (including a foreign person) using computer system available in India would be liable under the Act (Sople, 2016).

Issues and Protection of Trade Mark in Cyberspace

Industrialisation has led to the development of industries and production and distribution of goods. Further, with the development of competitive environment, entrepreneurs and manufacturers started to provide recognition and identity to their products through some symbols, marks, pictures, words, image etc. and that could be easily differentiated with the similar genre of products of other manufacturers. A trademark represents the quality of the certain product as well as carries the reputation and goodwill in the market. No doubt trademarks are valuable assets in the competition era. They are having economic relevance and, consequently, subject to trademark violation. There are several instances of trademark infringement, competitors are keen to use deceptive trademark to uplift their business and earn more profit. Such threat to trademark and commerce led to the adoption of trade mark laws not only in India but worldwide. The main purpose and function of trade mark is to provide identity, origin, quality and source of the particular good. It advertises the product in the competitive world. Trade mark law helps the public identify the product from other similar products available in the market and protect from confusion and deception. Not only this, it also guards the trade and goodwill of the owner to which the trade mark is attached. Thus, trade mark is having grave importance in the field of Intellectual Property Rights and having huge economic value in the national as well as in the international market.

In India, the Trademarks Act, 1999 ensures protection to trade marks. The present Act repealed the Trade and Merchandise Act, 1958 after taking into consideration the requirements of trade and business since the adoption of globalisation and liberalisation policies in India. Most importantly, to keep up with the international standards and bring the Indian law in conformity especially with TRIPS (Trade related Aspects of Intellectual Property Rights), the Act was transformed. Section 2(1) (zb) defines what shall be included in the definition of "Trade mark". Trademarks should be capable of graphical representation as well as carry distinctiveness from others. Trademark owner automatically gets the trademark rights once he starts using a mark on the product or service. Thus registration is not mandatory to avail the protection of trademark laws; however, registration is always beneficial and provides edge on the trademark in case of dispute. The term of trade mark registration is ten years but it has to be renewed during that time period. An affidavit has to be filed after the certain time period for the continuous use of trademark. It can be cancelled in case of non-filing of the affidavit.

Trademarks are having high economic potential and simultaneously having high chances of passing off. There are several ways of infringement of trademark in cyberspace. Due to internet, trade and business is blooming in the virtual world where the face to face interaction is not necessary. Consumer believes and repose faith in the authenticity of the trademark of the goods or services that he wishes to avail. This trust and business transaction is needed to be protected trough the trade mark law. By which the consumer as well as the owner of the trademark can be protected from the fake and deceptive representation of the product. In the digital ecosystem, several ways have been originated to dent the e-commerce and earn fraudulent profit. Such practices in this regard are known as Trade mark as **meta tagging, cybersquatting, framing, hyperlinking** etc. Further, they can be discussed in detail.

Cybersquatting

Domain names provide a web address to the business in cyberspace. It helps in identifying business on internet. It establishes an address for communication in virtual world. Domain names work as trade mark as they create a link with the source and identify with the particular company. The protection which is provided to trade marks in case of passing off is also extended to domain names under the trade mark law. Thus, domain names carry economic value in the market. However, there are unfair practices leads to domain name disputes which is known as cyber squatting or cyber trafficking. Under such practices exploitation is being committed by registering the trademarks of others as their own domain names and further sells these domain names to the concerned trademark owner on high rate. Such disputes related to the Intellectual property in cyberspace are constantly high. Thus, cyber squatting steals the identity belongs to other person or brand or company on internet.

On the question of applicability of trade mark law on domain names and especially with regard to passing off, the court in *Satyam Infoway Ltd.* v.*Sifynet Solution (P) Ltd.,* held that "it is apparent that a domain name may have all the characteristics of a trade mark and could find an action for passing off (Ahuja, 2015)." In *Tata Sons*

Ltd. v. MonuKosuri and others, the court provided an injunction to the plaintiff against the defendant for deceptively registering the resembling domain name carrying the word "Tata".

Meta Tagging and Hyper Linking and Framing

Meta tags are used by a person on the website to tag the competitor's trademark to mislead the users and fulfil unfair means. Through this process traffic is promoted towards that particular site whenever search is made of that particular word. In this way accessibility of that particular site is increased that lead to legal dispute for misusing trademark.

In hyper linking by accessing one website the user can access the other connected website by just clicking on the available location. If someone wants to link a website with another then permission should be taken from the owner of the website before linking it otherwise it will be considered infringement. Linking happens without mentioning any location address or typing on search engine. Through linking process, the user accesses the other electronic address on internet without knowing the actual source behind it.

Framing is used to create deception to the user by framing or appear to link the other site on the same webpage through some html format. Through framing another website is connected and displayed to appear in the same window that creates an impression that it belongs to the same page. It leads to misleading of content as the user remains unaware about the actual source of the contents on the webpage. It constitutes trademark violation as the website owners frame the trade mark of other owner on their website to create a false impression in the mind of the user regarding the belongingness of goods or services. Thus, framing can lead to confusion about the actual trademark website and its products.

Protection Under Trade Mark Law

Legal remedies are provided to the trade mark infringement or passing off under section 135 of the Trade Mark Act, 1999 in the form of injunction, damages or transferring of infringing good or destruction of trafficked goods. Section 103proves penalty for applying false trademarks and trade descriptions that will be punishable with imprisonment for a term not less than 6 months, but may extent to 3 years and fine of not less than Rs50,000/- which can be extended to Rs. 2 Lacs. Section 104 states Penalty for selling goods or providing services to which false trade mark or false trade description is applied which is punishable with not less than six months imprisonment and it can be extended to Rs. 2 Lacs. If the trade mark is not registered as per the legal provisions, in such situation the common law remedy is available to the owner of the trade mark but if the trade mark is registered, the owner of the trade mark in case of infringement can apply for the remedy under the Trade Marks Act, 1999.

Protection Under ICANN

The WIPO established the online domain name dispute resolution system for domain name disputes which is also known as ICANN policy. The remedy which provided in this system is quick as well as inexpensive. It was adopted by ICANN on 24th October, 1999. The policy was adopted for settling disputes for registering and exploiting domain names. In *Tata Sons Limited v. Advance Information Technology Association,* the dispute was settled by WIPO in favour of Tata Sons Ltd., consequently, gained right over the disputed domain name created by the respondents. In other case of similar nature, in *NIIT Ltd* v. *Vanguard Design*, WIPO directed the respondent to transfer the domain name to the complainant who was held to be deceptive and has likelihood to cause confusion in the mind of the users (Seth, 2013).

SUGGESTIONS

1. Study should be conducted to perceive the behaviour of cyber criminals. The usage of technology depends upon the motives of the minds of the users. There is a need to know and understand the criminal aspect of cybercrimes and the psychology of the criminals.
2. There is a need to educate people about the misuse of intellectual property in cyberspace. Almost everybody is having access to computer or smartphones and internet so there is a need to provide a guide to protect from such issues. In this regard, seminars, workshops and conferences can play vital role in dissemination of knowledge and protection.
3. Information Technology Act, 2000 lacks to protect Intellectual property rights in cyberspace being a law dealing with cybercrimes. The Government should look in to the matter to strengthen the law specifically in this regard.
4. There is a need to keep up dated with the advancement of technology so that the authority which is dealing with such issues can handle them and keep themselves ahead of the criminals.

CONCLUSION

Cyberspace is the most vital domain for the purpose of e- commerce, entertainment, art, literary work, social networking, dissemination of information and many more activities. It becomes more important with regard to Intellectual Property. It supplements and compliments IP (Intellectual Property) and increases its value in the international market but on the other hand there are several ways to wrongly affect and dent such intellectual property in cyberspace. Such challenges can be tackled through awareness and care as well as there is a need on the part of the Government to keep laws ready with the advancement of technology to deal with them and, moreover, ardent implementation of law is of primary concern.

REFERENCES

A & M Records v. Napster 239F 3d 1004 (9th Cir 2001)

Ahuja, V. (2015). Law Relating to Intellectual Property Rights (4th ed.). Lexis Nexis Publication.

DhirajDharam Das v. *Sonal Info Systems Pvt. Ltd* 2012(52)PTC 458 (Bom) p.475

Diamond v. Diehr, 450 U.S. 175

Duggal, P. (2014). *Legal framework on electronic commerce and intellectual property rights in cyberspace*. New Delhi, India: Universal Law Publishing.

Jaybhaye, A. (2016). *Cyber Law and IPR Issues: The Indian Perspective*. Retrieved from http://docs.manupatra.in/newsline/articles/Upload/19A86CE4-2FBD-432B-B166-AFBA9087A834.pdf

Legal Service India. (2019). *Intellectual Property Rights in India*. Retrieved from http://www.legalservicesindia.com/article/1742/Intellectual-Property-Rights-in-India.html

Midway Manufacturing Co. v. *Artic International* (2006)1ALD(Cri)96

NIIT Ltd v. *Vanguard Design,* WIPO Case No. D2003–0005

Playboy Enterprises Inc. v. *Frena;* 839 F. Supp. 1552 (1993)

Satyam Infoway Ltd. v.*Sifynet Solution (P) Ltd* (2004)6SCC145

Seth, K. (2013). Computers, Internet And New Technology Laws. Lexis Nexis Publication.

Sharma, V. (2015). *Information Technology Law and Practice Law and Emerging Technology Cyber Law and E- Commerce* (4th ed.). New Delhi, India: Universal Law Publication.

Shinning industries v. Shri Krishna Industries; AIR 1975 All 231

Sinha, M., & Mahalwar, V. (2017). *Copyright law in the Digital World Challenges and Opportunity.* Springer Nature Singapore. doi:10.1007/978-981-10-3984-3

Sople, V. (2016). *Managing Intellectual Property the Strategic Imperative* (5th ed.). Delhi, India: PHI Learning Private Limited.

State Street Bank & Trust v. Signature Financial Group; 149 F.3d 1368 (Fed. Cir. 1998)

Super Cassettes Industries Ltd. v. Myspace Inc. &Anr; IA No. 3085/2009 in CS (OS) No. 2682/2008

Sweet and Maxwell (Thomas Reuters). (2013). *Intellectual Property: Patents* (8th ed.). Copyrights, Trademarks and Allied Rights.

Syed Asifuddin and Ors. V. the State of Andhra Pradesh &Anr; 2006 (1) ALD Cri 96

Tata Sons Ltd. v. MonuKosuri and others 2001 PTC 432

Chapter 11
Efficient and Secure Data Access Control in the Cloud Environment

Anilkumar Chunduru
Rajiv Gandhi University of Knowledge Technologies, India

Gowtham Mamidisetti
Presidency University, India

ABSTRACT

Cloud computing is a highly demanding zone in the present IT enterprise. The key characteristics are adaptability, productivity, pay-per-utilize, and cost viability. Access control and information security are the significant issues in cloud computing. Various access control strategies are present. The major problems of storing data in expandable access control and access rights from users are not used in this scheme. This chapter presents a generic survey on scalable and secure access control systems and schemes in cloud computing with a key focus on cloud security. Research gaps in the existing literature on cloud security are presented.

INTRODUCTION

Access Control is an authentication system that authorizes an authority or enables control for accessing. While accessing the facility, in general various steps like authentication, authorization, identification and accountability are performed in access control system (Yang, Y et al. 2014). Clients are allowed to use the facility based on their identity. There are three characteristics to verify the information with

DOI: 10.4018/978-1-7998-2367-4.ch011

respect to access control devices such as PIN, PWD and Pass-Phrase, and the client has access the reader, card reader, door lock, door phone, locks etc. Security and trust aspects are significant snags of an organization to utilize distributed computing. Efficient identity and access management (IAM) scheme is essential to reduce the security issue of distributed computing. The emerging demand of external information handling raises various objections for sectors that need to prolong access control approaches apart from their organization's firewall into the cloud especially for maintenance of outsourced information. The main features of identity and access management system is Single Sign-On (SSO) (Abdul Raouf Khan, 2012, pp. 613-615). Identities within the context are federated identities. Central Authentication Service (CAS) performs distributed identity and it also presents architecture on distributed identity services for cloud dependent technologies. In federated identity management design, such as OpenID Connect, it does not require registration in cloud for accessing. Certainly, these designs cannot solve the problem, since one user shares his identity across multiple clouds (i.e. Single Sign-On). By using Single Sign-On and OAuth Protocol on one user, users can able to share their content to several clouds and similarly, several users can share their content to single cloud.

RELATED WORK

Access control can be discussed as a system or mechanism that permits, denies or confines a client in information access from a framework (Yongdong Wu, Vivy Suhendra, & Huaqun Guo,2012). Users can use this system for choosing a particular framework, various assets and applications. An Access Control Standard (ACS) incorporates the strategy. (Xiao Wei Gao, Ze Min Jiang, & Rui Jiang, 2013) proposed an entryway based access control strategy in which a few private clouds are considered. Client of one private cloud can get the information from another private cloud. It gives a secured correspondence between clients by means of a third-party. But the principle issue of this scheme lies in accessing one association at any point of time. It does not support bi-directional access.

(David Ferraiolo, D. Richard Kuhn,& Ramaswamy Chandramouli, 2003)have proposed a plan for secure correspondence amongst the client and CSP. This plan settles the issue of replay assault and man-in-middle attack in the information retrieval stage. Issue in this method is DO should reliably stay online to access his data.

(Ryan Ausanka-Crues, 2001,pp. 20-25)proposed a mechanism for specific Role Based Access Control Model (RBAC). RBAC decides client's access to the framework in light of the activity part which is characterized as a base measure of authorizations that is important to finish a task. The primary issue emerges when RBAC is reached out crosswise over regulatory area of the association.

(Lili Sun & Hua Wang, 2010) proposed a procedure, which is a default control for desktop working frameworks. This gives a distinctive access arrangement to various client gatherings. This method enforces users to relay on cloud servers to access his data which becomes overhead from maintaining the whole system.

HIERARCHY OF EFFICIENT AND SECURE ACCESS MODELS

An Access Control Standard (ACS) can be characterized as a set of approaches of a framework administrator, which can be utilized to characterize client's access right. ACS guarantees that the exclusive approved clients can get the proprietor's delicate information. Access control procedures have a greater number of highlights than controlling the clients in getting the rights from a system (Suyel Namasudra, Samir Nath & Abhishek Majumder, 2014). Furthermore, ACS oversees and controls the information access of all clients. There are few issues with respect to information access and control.

1. Cloud servers face threats mainly from internal and external attackers. Internal attackers who tries to access from their own organizations and companies. Those attackers who can be any third parties are external attackers. Attackers of these two types try to access clients secure data from cloud data centers.

2. Existing methods does not concentrate on users revocation problems. User's revocations does not allow a revoked users to gain access to the system in future. Due to this revoked users face data access problems.

3. Overhead occurs when CSP are need to check the entire system for permitting users data access. This prolong the access time of the data as well as the processing time of the CSP.

4. Access time of the data is more.

5. Overhead occurs due to the need of data owners to stay online throughout the data accessing time.

6. Till now, there is no standard structure among CSP, information proprietors and clients that would guarantee to safeguard the classification of the client's delicate information.

7. In cloud computing the data are distributed in many data centers for security. Even if the data owners delete the entire data, they have possibilities to regain from the providers. Another major problem in cloud computing is Fine Grained access control.

Figure 1. Hierarchy of Access Control Models

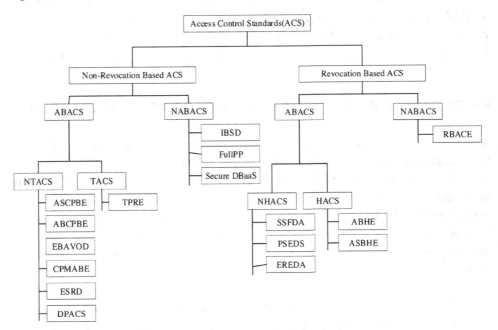

Non Revocation Based ACS

When the clients are less and their restrictions are less Non-revocation based access control is used. Here clients will not get revoked as they are settled by unchangeable data access priorities . Hence the security problems is also very less as compared to revocation methods. The following are two types of Non-Revocation based ACS: Non-attribute based ACSs and attribute based ACSs.

Non-revocation, non-attribute based ACS is divided into three types. They are IBSD, FullPP, and SecureDBaaS.

IBSD

There are numerous issues in the current access control plans, for example, the entrance strategy is dependably dictated by the CSP, where information are unsecured against the conspiracy assaults. Major advantage of this strategy is to support queries from inter and intra platforms.

Table 1. Acronym of access control models

Acronym	Access Control Models
IBSD	Identity Based Storage data scheme
FullPP	Full lifecycle privacy preservation scheme
SecureDBaaS	Secure database as a service access control
NTACS	Non-time based access control standards
TACS	Time-based access control standards
TPRE	Time-based proxy re-encryption scheme
ASCPBE	Attribute-set cipher text policy based encryption
ABCPBE	Attribute based cipher text policy based encryption scheme
EBAVOD	Encryption based attribute verifiable outsource decryption
CPMABE	Cipher text policy multi message attribute based encryption scheme
ESRD	Efficient and secure retrieval data scheme
DPACS	Data privilege access control standards
RBACE	Role-based access control encryption
NHACS	Non-hierarchical based access control standards
HACS	Hierarchical based access control standards
ABHE	Attribute based hierarchical encryption scheme
ASBHE	Attribute set based hierarchical encryption scheme
SSFDA	Scalable, secure and fine-grained data access control standards
PSEDS	Privacy-preserving scalable and efficient data sharing scheme
EREDA	Efficient, revocable and expressive data access control model
ABACS	Attribute Based Access Control Standards
NABACS	Non Attribute Based Access Control Standards

FullPP

In existing strategies, namely EBAVOD, CPMABE, IBSD, ASCPBE do not examine information after time expiration. This technique is similar to FullPP Distributed Hash Table (DHT) and Identity Based Encryption Time Release (IBETR) In this strategy, fewalgorithms, namely data extract, encryption, polynomial generation and system setup, Vanishing Data object (VDO) generation exists.

SecureDBaaS

A database is connected by a user to client. It generates metadata and is stored in cloud database. User can access those data by SQL command in suspicious database. SecureDBaaS is divided into three processes such as Setup phase, parallel SQL operations and Consecutive SQL operations.

Attribute Based Access Control Standards (ABACS)

ABACS is divided into two types. They are NTACS and TACS.

NTACS

In Non-time based ACS, at data encryption time, time is not a constraint. They are divided into following six attributes based on non-time ACS. They are ASCPBE, ABCPBE, EBAVOD, CPMABE, ESRD, and DPACS.

Attribute-set cipher text policy based encryption (ASCPBE): ASCPBE strategy does not support the combination of various attributes from various sets (Dongyoung Koo, Junbeom Hur & Hyunsoo Yoon, 2013)In this strategy there are four algorithms: Encryption, Decryption, Setup, and Key Generation. For setup, it takes'd' as a parameter for depth. It outputs (Pkey) public key and (Mkey) Master key.

Attribute Based Cipher Text Policy Based Encryption Scheme (ABCPBE)

In this strategy private key of clients is allowed by data owners and attributes encrypt the information with access plan (Clifford Cocks, 2001, pp. 360-363). Here to construct an access structure OR and AND gates are used. This strategy is divided into five algorithms. Encryption, setup, Decryption, key generation, and Authorization. The main intension of this strategy is secure collision resistance. Whenever clients revoke from the plan, this strategy does not support properly.

Figure 2. Example of encryption scheme attribute based outsource decryption

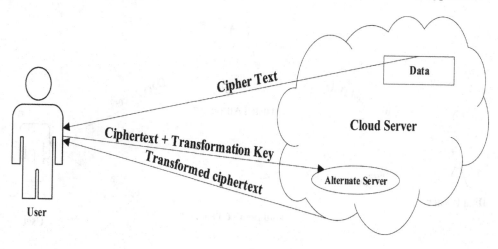

Encryption Based Attribute Verifiable Outsource Decryption (EBAVOD)

In ASCPBE strategy the main drawback is that, the decryption procedure associates many pairing operations that may lead to complexity. To overcome this EBAVOD is proposed. Clients can verify to ensure that all the transactions are correctly done. In this strategy, actual EBA scheme is updated without sourced decryption. Fig. 2 clearly shows encryption strategy attribute based outsource decryption. This strategy consists of seven algorithms: Encryption, Decryption, and Key generation, Setup, Generation of converted key, Encryption using converted key, and Decryption of converted encrypted data.

Cipher Text Policy Multi Message Attribute Based Encryption Scheme (CPMABE)

ASCPBE method is non-scalable and also resist large number of access policies. To overcome these issues a novel cipher text policy based on multi-message attribute based encryption scheme is proposed. This strategy is efficient, as encrypted text message as cipher text is followed. In this strategy, there are four groups: User, Attribute Authority (AA), Frontend Server, and Backend Server and four procedures namely Data packing, Data Unpacking, AB-setup, and AB-Key generation.

Figure 3. A Secure Data Retrieval Scheme

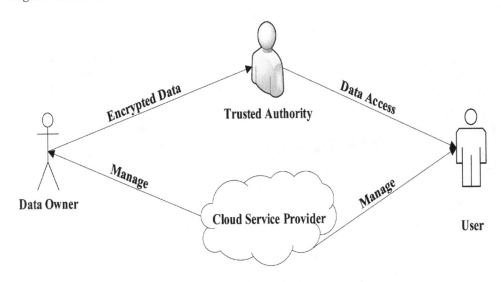

Figure 4. Privilege data access control system for message flows

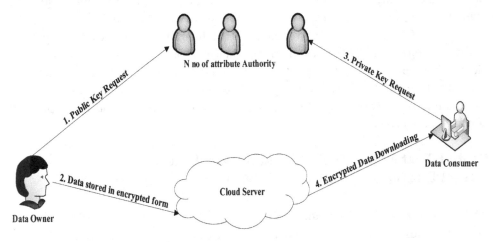

Efficient and Secure Retrieval Data Scheme (ESRD)

The main issue nowadays is data retrieval from the cloud servers. Secure and effective data retrieval scheme focus on reducing redundancy and secure data retrieval. This method shows better performance when there is huge amount of data.

Data Privilege Access Control Standards (DPACS)

The existing strategies, such as FullPP, ESDR, SecureDBaaS and ACSs pay awareness on information security. User's identity can easily get key issuers, but clients do not disclose identity of key issuers.

Time-Based Access Control Standards (TACS)

In ASCPBE, the CSP clearly knows the efficient time of accessing rights to clients, which may tend to leak private information. In present techniques the information owner must be present in online at the time of sending PRE keys. This method has five steps such as encryption, re-encryption, decryption, setup and key generation.

REVOCATION BASED ACCESS CONTROL STANDARDS

In revocation based ACSs, client's data are stored against untrusted users. Revocation based ACSs are effective in our plan.

Revocation Based Attribute Access Control Standards

In this section, revocation based attribute access control standards are discussed.

Revocation Non-Hierarchical Attribute Based Access Control Standards

Revocation based attribute based non-hierarchical ACSs are useful to users. It is divided into three types such as SSFDA, PSEDS, and EREDA.

Scalable, Secure and Fine-Grained Data Access Control Standards (SSFDA)

ASCPBE and ABCPBE strategies do not sustain scalability and flexibility. If the number of users increases, the strategy does not apply properly. One of the main issues in this strategy is user's revocation problem. This model is divided into four entities: Data owner, User consumer, Data consumer and CSP along with third parties. In this strategy eight algorithms are there: ADecrypt, AUpdateAtt, AKeyGen, AEncrypt, ASetup, AMinmalSet, AUpdateSK and AUpdateAtt4File.

Privacy-Preserving Scalable And Efficient Data Sharing Scheme (PSEDS)

SSFDA strategy increases more complexity at client side. In HACS and ABHE every user has private key. Those are critical issues to manage. To overcome those two issues PSEDS has proposed. There are four entities in this strategy: Data owner, Cloud Server (CS), PKG and Cloud customer. In this strategy, four algorithms are present: Encryption, system initialization, Key generation, and decryption.

Efficient Revocable And Expressive Data Access Control Model (EREDA)

In ASCPBE strategy the main important issue is attribute revocation. Computation cost also increases on account of attribute revocation. To overcome this issue an efficient revocable and expressive data access control model was proposed. Five entities are present: Cloud service provider, Data owner, User, Certificate authority, attribute authority.

Revocation Hierarchical Based Attribute Access Control Models

In revocation hierarchical based ACSs, a tree structure is maintained.

Attribute Based Hierarchical Encryption Scheme (ABHE)

The main issue of storing data in cloud server is access control and attribute revocation. ASCPBE failed to gain high performance and scalable client's revocation. ABHE consists of five operations: Domain, Domain Manager, Role master, CSP, and User. In this strategy, there are six algorithms: Creation of user, creation of domain, setup, Revocation, Encryption and decryption.

Attribute set based hierarchical encryption scheme (ASBHE): In cloud environment security and privacy issues on utilized data is growing gradually. Most of the present strategies are not giving guarantee for scalable, secure and flexible access control models. This strategy is an extension of ASCPBE. There are five entities in this strategy: Data consumer, Domain Authorities, Data owner, CSP and trusted authorities.

Revocation Based Non-Attribute Access Control Models

In Revocation based non-attribute access control model, users do not depend on the attributes.

Role-based Access Control Encryption (RBACE)

With the growth of cloud computing, large data storage utilizes the infrastructure of cloud. In ABHE and ASBHE, the identities of client become more in depth of hierarchy and long in length. To overcome this situation the RBACE is proposed. It is divided into four entities: CSP, User, Data owner, Role manager.

CONCLUSION

As the data stored in the cloud datacenters is rapidly increasing and is attempted to hack by the unauthorized users, providing security to data is becoming very important. Attackers try all possible ways to acquire the data. It is the responsibility of the CSP to provide security for the data from both insiders and outsider. A brief survey of data security is represented and analyzed in this paper. It is important to know the different methods used by the attackers to acquire data in unauthorized way and to prevent the future data attacks from them. As the possibilities pave different ways for the attackers, this field is always outstanding to resist all this new methods. Future issues can be like protecting data from the natural disaster and reducing the data access time from CSP.

REFERENCES

Ausanka-Crues, R. (2001). Methods for access control: Advances and limitations. *Harvey Mudd College*, *301*, 20.

Cocks, C. (2001, December). An identity based encryption scheme based on quadratic residues. In *IMA international conference on cryptography and coding* (pp. 360–363). Berlin: Springer. doi:10.1007/3-540-45325-3_32

Ferraiolo, D., Kuhn, D. R., & Chandramouli, R. (2003). *Role-based access control*. Artech House.

Gao, X. W., Jiang, Z. M., & Jiang, R. (2013). A novel data access scheme in cloud computing. *Advanced Materials Research*, *756*, 2649–2654. doi:10.4028/www.scientific.net/AMR.756-759.2649

Khan, A. R. (2012). Access control in cloud computing environment. *Journal of Engineering and Applied Sciences (Asian Research Publishing Network)*, *7*(5), 613–615.

Koo, D., Hur, J., & Yoon, H. (2013). Secure and efficient data retrieval over encrypted data using attribute-based encryption in cloud storage. *Computers & Electrical Engineering*, *39*(1), 34–46. doi:10.1016/j.compeleceng.2012.11.002

Namasudra, S., Nath, S., & Majumder, A. (2014, March). Profile based access control model in cloud computing environment. In *2014 International Conference on Green Computing Communication and Electrical Engineering (ICGCCEE)* (pp. 1-5). IEEE. 10.1109/ICGCCEE.2014.6921420

Sun, L., & Wang, H. (2010). A purpose based usage access control model. *International Journal of Computer and Information Engineering*, *4*(1), 44–51.

Wu, Y., Suhendra, V., & Guo, H. (2012, June). A gateway-based access control scheme for collaborative clouds. In *Proc. 7th International Conference on Internet Monitoring and Protection* (pp. 54-60). Academic Press.

Yang, Y., Chen, X., Wang, G., & Cao, L. (2014, December). An identity and access management architecture in cloud. In *2014 Seventh International Symposium on Computational Intelligence and Design* (Vol. 2, pp. 200-203). IEEE. 10.1109/ISCID.2014.221

Compilation of References

A & M Records v. Napster 239F 3d 1004 (9th Cir 2001)

Adesina, O. S. (2017). Foreign policy in an era of digital diplomacy. *Cogent Social Sciences*, *3*(1), 1297175. doi:10.1080/23311886.2017.1297175

Adler, M., & Gailly, J.-L. (2002). *An introduction to cryptography*. Available at: https://www.cs.unibo.it/babaoglu/courses/security/resources/documents/intro-to-crypto.pdf

Agarwal, R., & Sambamurthy, V. (2003). Principles and Models for Organizing the IT Function. *MIS Quarterly Executive*, *1*(1), 1–16.

Ahram, T., Sargolzaei, A., Sargolzaei, S., Daniels, J., & Amaba, B. (2017, June). Blockchain technology innovations. In 2017 IEEE Technology & Engineering Management Conference (TEMSCON) (pp. 137-141). IEEE. doi:10.1109/TEMSCON.2017.7998367

Ahuja, V. (2015). Law Relating to Intellectual Property Rights (4th ed.). Lexis Nexis Publication.

Aitzhan, N. Z., & Svetinovic, D. (2016). Security and privacy in decentralized energy trading through multi-signatures, blockchain and anonymous messaging streams. *IEEE Transactions on Dependable and Secure Computing*, *15*(5), 840–852. doi:10.1109/TDSC.2016.2616861

Akamai. (2018). *Enforce a Zero Trust Security Model in Today's Hostile Environment*. Academic Press.

Alam, M. G. R., Masum, A. K. M., Beh, L.-S., & Hong, C. S. (2016). Critical Factors Influencing Decision to Adopt Human Resource Information System (HRIS) in Hospitals. *PLoS One*, *11*(8), e0160366. doi:10.1371/journal.pone.0160366 PubMed

Alexander, Z. (2018). *Zero Trust Security Model – A Framework for a Different Approach*. Academic Press.

Alexander. (1996). *The Underground Guide to Computer Security*. Addison Wesley Publishing Company.

Almazán, D. A., Tovar, Y. S., & José, M. (2017). Medina Quintero, Influence of information systems on organizational results. *Contaduría y Administración*, *62*(2), 321–338. doi:10.1016/j.cya.2017.03.001

Anderson, J. G. (2007). Social, ethical and legal barriers to e-health. *International Journal of Medical Informatics, 76*(5-6), 480–483. PubMed

Andress, J. (2011). *The Basics of Information Security. Understanding the Fundamentals of InfoSec in Theory and Practice.* Elsevier.

Anjali, M., & Padmavathi, B. (2014). DDoS Attack Detection based on Chaos Theory and Artificial Neural Network. *International Journal of Computer Science and Information Technologies, 5*(6), 7276–7279.

Arora, S. (2017). *Digital India: Driving the Next Wave of Innovation.* Retrieved from https://snmpcenter.com/digital-india/

Ausanka-Crues, R. (2001). Methods for access control: Advances and limitations. *Harvey Mudd College, 301*, 20.

Authentication, E. (2013). *Network security, security services.* Available at:http://www.abcd.lk/sliit/eBooks/Data%20Communications%20and%20Networking/Chapter%2031.pdf

Ayatollahi, H., Bath, P. A., & Goodacre, S. (2009). Accessibility versus confidentiality of information in the emergency department. *Emergency Medicine Journal, 26*(12), 857–860. doi:10.1136/emj.2008.070557 PubMed

Baker, W. T. (2018). *U.S. Patent Application No. 10/055,791.* US Patent Office.

Barba-Sánchez, V., Martínez-Ruiz, M., & Jiménez-Zarco, A. I. (2007). *Drivers, Benefits and Challenges of ICT Adoption by Small and Medium Sized Enterprises (SMEs): A Literature Review.* Problems and centrify.com.

Barbosa, L. S. (2017, November). Digital governance for sustainable development. In *Conference on e-Business, e-Services and e-Society* (pp. 85-93). Springer.

Bazin, R., Schaub, A., Hasan, O., & Brunie, L. (2017, June). Self-reported verifiable reputation with rater privacy. In *IFIP International Conference on Trust Management* (pp. 180-195). Springer.

Belle Woodward, N. M. (2011, August). Expansion and validation of the PAPA Framework. *Information Systems Education Journal, 9*(3). https://isedj.org/2011-9/N3/ISEDJv9n3p28.pdf

Berne, E. S. (2008). Ethical and Legal Issues in the Use of Health Information Technology to Improve Patient Safety. HEC FORUMSpringer Netherlands. doi:10.100710730-008-9074-5

Berryhill, J., Bourgery, T., & Hanson, A. (2018). Blockchains unchained: Blockchain technology and its use in the public sector. *OECD Working Papers on Public Governance,* (28), 1-53.

Bjola, C. (2017). Trends and counter-trends in digital diplomacy. *The Soft Power, 30*, 126–129.

Boneh, D., & Shoup, V. (2016). *A Graduate Course in Applied Cryptography.* https://toc.cryptobook.us/

Brandão, A., São Mamede, H., & Gonçalves, R. (2018, March). Systematic review of the literature, research on blockchain technology as support to the trust model proposed applied to smart places. In *World Conference on Information Systems and Technologies* (pp. 1163-1174). Springer. 10.1007/978-3-319-77703-0_113

Brynjolfsson, A. (2014). *McAfee, The Second Machine Age: Work Progress, and Prosperity in a Time of Brilliant Technologies*. New York: W.W. Norton & Company.

Cai, Y., & Zhu, D. (2016). Fraud detections for online businesses: A perspective from blockchain technology. *Financial Innovation*, 2(1), 20. doi:10.118640854-016-0039-4

Calvaresi, D., Dubovitskaya, A., Calbimonte, J. P., Taveter, K., & Schumacher, M. (2018, June). Multi-agent systems and blockchain: Results from a systematic literature review. In *International Conference on Practical Applications of Agents and Multi-Agent Systems* (pp. 110-126). Springer. 10.1007/978-3-319-94580-4_9

Cathy Schoen, R. O. (2012). A Survey Of Primary Care Doctors In Ten Countries Shows Progress In Use Of Health Information Technology, Less In Other Areas. *Health Affairs*, 31(12). https://www.healthaffairs.org/doi/full/10.1377/hlthaff.2012.0884 PubMed

Chen, G., Xu, B., Lu, M., & Chen, N. S. (2018). Exploring blockchain technology and its potential applications for education. *Smart Learning Environments*, 5(1), 1. doi:10.118640561-017-0050-x

Choi, J., & Shin, S. (2016). Propose of smart place IoT systems for strengthen security of the smart grid environment. International Information Institute (Tokyo) Information, 19(5), 1509.

Cisco Summits. (2018). *Zero Trust Security: A New Paradigm for a Changing World*. Retrieved from: https://www.ciosummits.com/wp-zero-trust.pdf

Cocks, C. (2001, December). An identity based encryption scheme based on quadratic residues. In *IMA international conference on cryptography and coding* (pp. 360–363). Berlin: Springer. doi:10.1007/3-540-45325-3_32

Comodo. (2019). *COMODO creating trust online: Network security*. Available at: https://enterprise.comodo.com/blog/what-is-network-security/

CSIS. (2018). *Economic Impact of Cybercrime- No Slowing Down*. CSIS.

Dey, M. (2007). *Information security management - A Practical Approach*. Windhoek: AFRICON.

DhirajDharam Das v. *Sonal Info Systems Pvt. Ltd* 2012(52)PTC 458 (Bom) p.475

Diamond v. Diehr, 450 U.S. 175

Digdipblog.files.wordpress.com . (2019). Available at: https://digdipblog.files.wordpress.com/2017/08/the-digitalization-of-diplomacy-working-paper-number-1.pdf.

Diplo Foundation. (2018). *Digital Diplomacy, E-diplomacy, Cyber diplomacy*. https://www.diplomacy.edu/e-diplomacy

Diplo Foundation. (2019). *Social Media Fact Sheets of Foreign Ministries – Diplo Foundation.* https://www.diplomacy.edu/blog/infographic-social-media-factsheet-foreign-ministries

Doherty, N. F., Anastasakis, L., & Fulford, H. (2009, December). The information security policy unpacked: A critical study of the content of university policies. *International Journal of Information Management, 29*(6), 449–457. doi:10.1016/j.ijinfomgt.2009.05.003

Dosal, E. (2018). *The Different Types of Firewall Architectures.* Academic Press.

Duggal, P. (2014). *Legal framework on electronic commerce and intellectual property rights in cyberspace.* New Delhi, India: Universal Law Publishing.

Duncombe, C. (2019). *Twitter and transformative diplomacy: social media and Iran–US relations.* Available at: https://academic.oup.com/ia/article/93/3/545/3077244

Eling, M., & Lehmann, M. (2018). The impact of digitalization on the insurance value chain and the insurability of risks. *The Geneva Papers on Risk and Insurance. Issues and Practice, 43*(3), 359–396. doi:10.105741288-017-0073-0

Ernst & Young, L.L.P. (2004). *Information Security Survey.* Technical report. Author.

Eyal, I. (2017). Blockchain technology: Transforming libertarian cryptocurrency dreams to finance and banking realities. *Computer, 50*(9), 38–49. doi:10.1109/MC.2017.3571042

Ferraiolo, D., Kuhn, D. R., & Chandramouli, R. (2003). *Role-based access control.* Artech House.

Fessler, J. M., & Grémy, F. (2001). Opinion Paper: Ethical Problems in Health Information Systems. *Methods of Information in Medicine, 40*(04), 359–361. doi:10.1055/s-0038-1634432 PubMed

Fuks, L. (2018). *10 Ransomware Attacks You Should Know About in 2019.* Retrieved May 13, 2019, from https://www.allot.com/blog/10-ransomware-attacks-2019/

Gao, X. W., Jiang, Z. M., & Jiang, R. (2013). A novel data access scheme in cloud computing. *Advanced Materials Research, 756*, 2649–2654. doi:10.4028/www.scientific.net/AMR.756-759.2649

Goel, S., & Chengalur, I. N. (2010, December). Metrics for characterizing the form of security policies. *The Journal of Strategic Information Systems, 19*(4), 281–295. doi:10.1016/j.jsis.2010.10.002

Goswami. (2012). *Network Security.* Available at: https://bhg2.files.wordpress.com/2012/08/ch1.pdf

Grochow, J. (2015). *IT Infrastructure Projects: A Framework for Analysis.* Academic Press.

Gunjal, B. (2019). Knowledge management: Why do we need it for corporates. *Malaysian Journal of Library & Information Science.*

Guo, Y., & Liang, C. (2016). Blockchain application and outlook in the banking industry. *Financial Innovation, 2*(1), 24. doi:10.118640854-016-0034-9

Hare, C. (2001). Information Security policies, procedures, and standards: Establishing an essential code of conduct. CRC Press LLC.

Hart, J. (2010). *Globalization and Digitalization.* Academic Press.

Haux, R. (2006). Health information systems–past, present, future. *International Journal of Medical Informatics, 75*(3-4), 268–281. doi:10.1016/j.ijmedinf.2005.08.002 PubMed

Hawlitschek, F., Notheisen, B., & Teubner, T. (2018). The limits of trust-free systems: A literature review on blockchain technology and trust in the sharing economy. *Electronic Commerce Research and Applications, 29,* 50–63. doi:10.1016/j.elerap.2018.03.005

Haynal, G. (2011). Corporate diplomacy in the information age: Catching up to the dispersal of power. *Diplomacy in the digital age: Essays in honour of Ambassador Allan Gotlieb,* 209-224.

Health Information Unit. Ministry of Health. (2009). Health metric network. In Fiji Health Information System: Review and Assessment. Ministry of Health, Suva.

Heeks, R. (2006). Health information systems: Failure, success and improvisation. *International Journal of Medical Informatics, 75*(2), 125–137. doi:10.1016/j.ijmedinf.2005.07.024 PubMed

Henriette, E., Feki, M., & Boughzala, I. (2015). The shape of digital transformation: a systematic literature review. *MCIS 2015 Proceedings,* 431-443.

He, P., Yu, G., Zhang, Y. F., & Bao, Y. B. (2017). Survey on blockchain technology and its application prospect. *Computer Science, 44*(4), 1–7.

Holloway, R. (2009). *Network Security hierarchy. University of London Kenny Paterson's Lectures for: M.* Sc. in Information Security.

Holmes, M. (2013). *What is e-Diplomacy?* In 7th European Consortium for Political Research General Conference, Bordeaux.

Ifinedo, P. (2014, January). Information systems security policy compliance: An empirical study of the effects of socialisation influence and cognition. *Information & Management, 51*(1), 69–79. doi:10.1016/j.im.2013.10.001

Ismail, W. B. W., Widyarto, S., Ahmad, R. A. T. R., & Ghani, K. A. (2017). A generic framework for information security policy development. *4th International Conference on Electrical Engineering, Computer Science and Informatics (EECSI),* 1-6. 10.1109/EECSI.2017.8239132

Jaffe, C., Mata, C., & Kamvar, S. (2017, September). Motivating urban cycling through a blockchain-based financial incentives system. In *Proceedings of the 2017 ACM International Joint Conference on Pervasive and Ubiquitous Computing and Proceedings of the 2017 ACM International Symposium on Wearable Computers* (pp. 81-84). ACM. 10.1145/3123024.3123141

Jaybhaye, A. (2016). *Cyber Law and IPR Issues: The Indian Perspective.* Retrieved from http://docs.manupatra.in/newsline/articles/Upload/19A86CE4-2FBD-432B-B166-AFBA9087A834.pdf

Kacha & Zitouni. (2018). *An Overview on Data Security in Cloud Computing.* Academic Press.

Kaka, N., Madgavkar, A., Kshirsagar, A., Gupta, R., Manyika, J., Bahl, K., & Gupta, S. (2019). *McKinsey Global Institute, Digital India: Technology to transform a connected nation.* Retrieved from https://www.mckinsey.com/business-functions/mckinsey-digital/our-insights/digital-india-technology-to-transform-a-connected-nation

Karafiloski, E., & Mishev, A. (2017, July). Blockchain solutions for big data challenges: A literature review. In *IEEE EUROCON 2017-17th International Conference on Smart Technologies* (pp. 763-768). IEEE. 10.1109/EUROCON.2017.8011213

Kauf, S. (2019). Smart logistics as a basis for the development of the smart city. *Transportation Research Procedia, 39,* 143–149. doi:10.1016/j.trpro.2019.06.016

Kayikci, Y. (2018). Sustainability impact of digitization in logistics. Procedia manufacturing, 21, 782-789.Impact of digitization in logistics. *Procedia Manufacturing, 21,* 782–789. doi:10.1016/j.promfg.2018.02.184

Khan, A. R. (2012). Access control in cloud computing environment. *Journal of Engineering and Applied Sciences (Asian Research Publishing Network), 7*(5), 613–615.

Kondo, K., Sasaki, Y., Todo, Y., & Iwata, T. (2018). On the design rationale of SIMON block cipher: Integral attacks and impossible differential attacks against SIMON variants. *IEICE Transactions on Fundamentals of Electronics, Communications and Computer Science, 101*(1), 88–98. doi:10.1587/transfun.E101.A.88

Koo, D., Hur, J., & Yoon, H. (2013). Secure and efficient data retrieval over encrypted data using attribute-based encryption in cloud storage. *Computers & Electrical Engineering, 39*(1), 34–46. doi:10.1016/j.compeleceng.2012.11.002

Korpela, K., Hallikas, J., & Dahlberg, T. (2017, January). Digital supply chain transformation toward blockchain integration. *Proceedings of the 50th Hawaii international conference on system sciences.* 10.24251/HICSS.2017.506

Kovacich, G. (1998). *Information Systems Security Officer's Guide.* Butterworth-Heinemann.

Król, M., Reñé, S., Ascigil, O., & Psaras, I. (2018). ChainSoft: Collaborative software development using smart contracts. In *CRYBLOCK 2018-Proceedings of the 1st Workshop on Cryptocurrencies and Blockchains for Distributed Systems, Part of MobiSys 2018* (pp. 1-6). ACM.

Kuhn, K. A., & Giuse, D. A. (2001). From hospital information systems to health information systems. *Methods of Information in Medicine, 40*(04), 275–287. doi:10.1055/s-0038-1634170 PubMed

Kumar, N. M., & Mallick, P. K. (2018). Blockchain technology for security issues and challenges in IoT. *Procedia Computer Science, 132,* 1815–1823. doi:10.1016/j.procs.2018.05.140

Kurbalija, J. (2017). Diplomacy in a Globalizing World. In Diplomacy in a globalizing world. Oxford University Press.

Lahiri, T. (2019). *Trump spent the hours before meeting Kim Jong Un tweeting about "Da Nang Dick" and Michael Cohen.* https://qz.com/1560926/trump-tweets-about-da-nang-dick-michael-cohen-in-hanoi/

Landler, M. (2019, April 11). *Trump Says He's Open to Third North Korea Meeting, and 'Smaller Deals' Are Possible.* https://www.nytimes.com/2019/04/11/us/politics/trump-north-korea-summit.html

Laudon, K. C., & Laudon, J. P. (2018). *Management Information Systems - Managing the Digital Firm* (15th ed.). Pearson.

Lebek, B., Uffen, J., Breitner, M. H., Neumann, M., & Hohler, B. (2013). Employees' information security awareness and behavior: A literature review. *Proceedings of the Annual Hawaii International Conference on System Sciences*, 2978-2987. 10.1109/HICSS.2013.192

Legal Service India. (2019). *Intellectual Property Rights in India.* Retrieved from http://www.legalservicesindia.com/article/1742/Intellectual-Property-Rights-in-India.html

Liang, G., Weller, S. R., Luo, F., Zhao, J., & Dong, Z. Y. (2018). Distributed blockchain-based data protection framework for modern power systems against cyber attacks. *IEEE Transactions on Smart Grid*, *10*(3), 3162–3173. doi:10.1109/TSG.2018.2819663

Lindman, J., Tuunainen, V. K., & Rossi, M. (2017). *Opportunities and risks of Blockchain Technologies—a research agenda.* Academic Press.

Lorenzo, O. (2004). *A Comprehensive Review of the Enterprise Systems Research.* Academic Press.

Manor, I. (2017). *The Digitalization of Diplomacy: Toward Clarification of a Fractured Terminology.* Working Paper. Exploring Digital Diplomacy.

Markus, M. L., & Tanis, C. (2000). The Enterprise System Experience — From Adoption to Success. Academic Press.

Marshall, K. P. (1999). Has Technology Introduced New Ethical Problems? *Journal of Business Ethics*, *19*(1), 81–90. doi:10.1023/A:1006154023743

Matt, C., Hess, T., & Benlian, A. (2015). Digital transformation strategies. *Business & Information Systems Engineering*, *57*(5), 339–343. doi:10.100712599-015-0401-5

McBride, T., Ekstrom, M., Lusty, L., Sexton, J., & Townsend, A. (2018). *Data Integrity: Identifying and Protecting Assets Against Ransomware and Other Destructive Events.* National Institute of Standards and Technology.

Mehta, A. (2010). *A Study on Critical Success Factors for Successful ERP Implementation at Indian SMEs.* Bangalore: Christ University.

Meingast, M., Roosta, T., & Sastry, S. (2006, August). Security and privacy issues with health care information technology. In 2006 International Conference of the IEEE Engineering in Medicine and Biology Society (pp. 5453-5458). IEEE. doi:10.1109/IEMBS.2006.260060

Mettler, M. (2016, September). Blockchain technology in healthcare: The revolution starts here. In *2016 IEEE 18th International Conference on e-Health Networking, Applications and Services (Healthcom)* (pp. 1-3). IEEE.

Midway Manufacturing Co. v. Artic International (2006)1ALD(Cri)96

Ministry of Health. (2008). *PATIS User Training Manual*. Suva: Author.

Ministry of Health. (2014). *PATISPlus User Manual, PMI, Appointments, ATD, and SOPD modules. In-service manual*. Author.

Mocan, T. (2018). *VPN History & The Future of VPN Technology*. Academic Press.

Munir, R., Diss, J., Awan, I., & Rafiq, M. (2013). *Quantitative Enterprise Network Security Risk Assessment*. Academic Press.

Mylrea, M., & Gourisetti, S. N. G. (2017, September). Blockchain for smart grid resilience: Exchanging distributed energy at speed, scale and security. In 2017 Resilience Week (RWS) (pp. 18-23). IEEE.

Namasudra, S., Nath, S., & Majumder, A. (2014, March). Profile based access control model in cloud computing environment. In *2014 International Conference on Green Computing Communication and Electrical Engineering (ICGCCEE)* (pp. 1-5). IEEE. 10.1109/ICGCCEE.2014.6921420

Network Security. (2000). *Cisco systems, Network Security, ISOC NTW 2000*. Available at: http://www.potaroo.net/t4/pdf/security.pdf

Network World. (2016). *Strong authentication methods*. Available at: https://www.networkworld.com/article/2296774/seven-strong-authentication-methods.html

NIIT Ltd v. Vanguard Design, WIPO Case No. D2003–0005

Noubir, P. G. (2004). *Fundamentals of cryptography*. Available at: http://www.ccs.neu.edu/home/noubir/Courses/CSU610/S06/cryptography.pdf

NPTEL. (n.d.). *Network Security, CSE IIT, Kharagpur*. Available at: https://nptel.ac.in/courses/106105080/pdf/M8L1.pdf

O'Dair, M., & Beaven, Z. (2017). The networked record industry: How blockchain technology could transform the record industry. *Strategic Change, 26*(5), 471–480. doi:10.1002/jsc.2147

OECD. (2019). *Digital Opportunities for Better Agricultural Policies*. Paris: OECD Publishing; doi:10.1787/571a0812-

Office of Information Technology (OIT) Division of Information Resource Management. (2009). *Resource and Patient Management System, Patient Information Management System (PIMS), Admission/Discharge/Transfer, Version 5.3 Patch 1009*. Albuquerque, NM: Author.

OUPblog. (2019). *How Twitter enhances conventional practices of diplomacy*. Available at: https://blog.oup.com/2017/10/twitter-diplomacy-practices-foreign-policy/

Pamment, J. (2016). Digital diplomacy as transmedia engagement: Aligning theories of participatory culture with international advocacy campaigns. *New Media & Society, 18*(9), 2046–2062. doi:10.1177/1461444815577792

Parimbelli, E., Bottalico, B., Losiouk, E., Tomasi, M., Santosuosso, A., Lanzola, G., & Bellazzi, R. (2018). Trusting telemedicine: A discussion on risks, safety, legal implications and liability of involved stakeholders. *International Journal of Medical Informatics, 112*, 90–98. doi:10.1016/j.ijmedinf.2018.01.012 PMID:29500027

Park, J., & Park, J. (2017). Blockchain security in cloud computing: Use cases, challenges, and solutions. *Symmetry, 9*(8), 164. doi:10.3390ym9080164

Parno, B., Kuo, C., & Perrig, A. (2006). Foolproof Phishing Prevention. In Lecture Notes in Computer Science: Vol. 4107. *Financial Cryptography and Data Security. FC 2006.* Berlin,: Springer.

Pawar & Anuradha. (2015). Network Security and Types of Attacks in Network. *International Conference on Computer, Communication and Convergence.* 10.1016/j.procs.2015.04.126

Peltier, T. (1999). *Information Security Policies, A Practitioner's Guide.* Academic Press.

Peslak, A. R. (2006). PAPA revisited: A current empirical study of the Mason framework. *Journal of Computer Information Systems, 46*(3), 117–123.

Peters, G. W., & Panayi, E. (2016). Understanding modern banking ledgers through blockchain technologies: Future of transaction processing and smart contracts on the internet of money. In *Banking beyond banks and money* (pp. 239–278). Cham: Springer. doi:10.1007/978-3-319-42448-4_13

Pflaum, A., Bodendorf, F., Prockl, G., & Chen, H. (2017). *Introduction to the digital supply chain of the future: technologies, applications and business models minitrack.* Academic Press.

Pilkington, M. (2016). Blockchain technology: principles and applications. In *Research handbook on digital transformations.* Edward Elgar Publishing. doi:10.4337/9781784717766.00019

Playboy Enterprises Inc. v. *Frena;* 839 F. Supp. 1552 (1993)

Popper, B. (2017, June 26). *New study explains why Trump's 'Sad' tweets are so effective.* https://www.theverge.com/2017/6/26/15872904/trump-tweet-psychology-sad-moral-emotional-words

Preneel. (2011). *Cryptographic algorithms.* Available at: https://handouts.secappdev.org/handouts/2011/Bart%20Preneel/preneel_cryptographic_algorithms_2011.pdf

Public Diplomacy. (2019). *Public Diplomacy Alumni Association. Diplo Foundation.* Available online at http://www.publicdiplomacy.org/1.htm

Rao, Rath, & Kabat. (2018). *Cryptography And Network Security Lecture Notes.* Veer Surendra Sai University of Technology.

Saberi, S., Kouhizadeh, M., Sarkis, J., & Shen, L. (2019). Blockchain technology and its relationships to sustainable supply chain management. *International Journal of Production Research*, *57*(7), 2117–2135. doi:10.1080/00207543.2018.1533261

Sandeep. (2010). *Need of network security*. Available at: https://www.indiastudychannel.com/resources/105777-Need-of-Network-Security.aspx

Sangchoolie, B., Folkesson, P., & Vinter, J. (2018, September). A study of the interplay between safety and security using model-implemented fault injection. In *2018 14th European Dependable Computing Conference (EDCC)* (pp. 41-48). IEEE. 10.1109/EDCC.2018.00018

Satyam Infoway Ltd. v.*Sifynet Solution (P) Ltd* (2004)6SCC145

Schneier, B. (1994). *Applied Cryptography*. New York: Publishers, John Kiley & Sons, Inc.

Schneier, B., Kohno, T., & Ferguson, N. (2013). *Cryptography engineering: design principles and practical applications*. Wiley.

Security services. (2013). http://www.idconline.com/technical_references/pdfs/data_communications/Security_Services.pdf

Seebacher, S., & Schüritz, R. (2017, May). Blockchain technology as an enabler of service systems: A structured literature review. In *International Conference on Exploring Services Science* (pp. 12-23). Springer. 10.1007/978-3-319-56925-3_2

Seth, K. (2013). Computers, Internet And New Technology Laws. Lexis Nexis Publication.

Shackelford, S. J., & Myers, S. (2017). Block-by-block: Leveraging the power of blockchain technology to build trust and promote cyber peace. *Yale JL & Tech.*, *19*, 334.

Shang, S., & Seddon, P. (2002). Assessing and managing the benefits of enterprise systems: The business manager's perspective. *Information Systems Journal*, *12*(4), 271–299. doi:10.1046/j.1365-2575.2002.00132.x

Sharma, V. (2015). *Information Technology Law and Practice Law and Emerging Technology Cyber Law and E- Commerce* (4th ed.). New Delhi, India: Universal Law Publication.

Shinning industries v. Shri Krishna Industries; AIR 1975 All 231

Shostack, A. (2014). *Threat modeling: Designing for security*. John Wiley & Sons.

Shunmugapriya. (2018). *Security Services and Mechanisms*. Available at https://eezytutorials.com/Cryptography-And-Network-Security/Security-services-and-mechanisms.php#.XLsqzugzbIU

Şimşek, M., & Şentürk, A. (2018). Fast and lightweight detection and filtering method for low-rate TCP targeted distributed denial of service (LDDoS) attacks. *International Journal of Communication Systems*, *31*(18), e3823. doi:10.1002/dac.3823

Sinha, M., & Mahalwar, V. (2017). *Copyright law in the Digital World Challenges and Opportunity*. Springer Nature Singapore. doi:10.1007/978-981-10-3984-3

Slaughter, A. M. (2009). *A new world order*. Princeton University Press.

Smith, N. M., DeLeeuw, W. C., & Willis, T. G. (2018). *U.S. Patent No. 9,860,057*. Washington, DC: U.S. Patent and Trademark Office.

Soomro, Z. A., Shah, M. H., & Ahmed, J. (2016). Information security management needs more holistic approach: A literature Review. *International Journal of Information Management, 36*(2), 215–225. doi:10.1016/j.ijinfomgt.2015.11.009

Sople, V. (2016). *Managing Intellectual Property the Strategic Imperative* (5th ed.). Delhi, India: PHI Learning Private Limited.

Specification for Information Security Management Systems. (1999). *Information security management, part 2*. Technical Report BS 7799–2.

Stallings, W. (2003). *Cryptography and Network Security. In Principles and Practices*. Prentice Hall.

State Street Bank & Trust v. Signature Financial Group; 149 F.3d 1368 (Fed. Cir. 1998)

Statista. (2019). *Retail e-commerce sales worldwide from 2014 to 2021 (in billion U.S. dollars)*. Retrieved from https://www.statista.com/statistics/379046/worldwide-retail-e-commerce-sales

Straub, D. W. Jr, & Collins, R. W. (1990). Key information liability issues facing managers: Software piracy, proprietary databases, and individual rights to privacy. *Management Information Systems Quarterly, 14*(2), 143–156. doi:10.2307/248772

Sun, L., & Wang, H. (2010). A purpose based usage access control model. *International Journal of Computer and Information Engineering, 4*(1), 44–51.

Super Cassettes Industries Ltd. v. Myspace Inc. &Anr; IA No. 3085/2009 in CS (OS) No. 2682/2008

Sweet and Maxwell (Thomas Reuters). (2013). *Intellectual Property: Patents* (8th ed.). Copyrights, Trademarks and Allied Rights.

Syed Asifuddin and Ors. V. the State of Andhra Pradesh &Anr ; 2006 (1) ALD Cri 96

Tata Sons Ltd. v. MonuKosuri and others 2001 PTC 432

The OSI Security Architecture. (n.d.). Available at: https://cgi.csc.liv.ac.uk/~alexei/COMP522_10/COMP522-SecurityArchitecture_07.pdf

Troshani, I., Jerram, C., & Hill, S. R. (2010). Exploring the Public Sector Adoption of HRIS. *Industrial Management & Data Systems, 111*(3), 470–488. doi:10.1108/02635571111118314

Turner, D. M. (2017). *Applying Cryptographic Security Services - a NIST summary*. Available at: https://www.cryptomathic.com/news-events/blog/applying-cryptographic-security-services-a-nist-summary

Ulas, D. (2019). Digital Transformation Process and SMEs. *Procedia Computer Science, 158*, 662-671.Process and SMEs. *Procedia Computer Science, 158*, 662–671. doi:10.1016/j.procs.2019.09.101

Vacca, J. R. (2009). *Computer and Information Security Handbook*. Morgan KaufmannSeries in Computer Security.

Vujičić, D., Jagodić, D., & Ranđić, S. (2018, March). Blockchain technology, bitcoin, and Ethereum: A brief overview. In *2018 17th International Symposium INFOTEH-JAHORINA (INFOTEH)* (pp. 1-6). IEEE. 10.1109/INFOTEH.2018.8345547

Wang, J., Wang, S., Guo, J., Du, Y., Cheng, S., & Li, X. (2019). A summary of research on blockchain in the field of intellectual property. Retrieved from. *Procedia Computer Science*, *147*, 191–197. doi:10.1016/j.procs.2019.01.220

Wang, Y., & Kogan, A. (2018). Designing confidentiality-preserving Blockchain-based transaction processing systems. *International Journal of Accounting Information Systems*, *30*, 1–18. doi:10.1016/j.accinf.2018.06.001

Ward, N. S. (2004). The accuracy of clinical information systems. *Journal of Critical Care*, *19*(4), 221–225. doi:10.1016/j.jcrc.2004.09.005 PubMed

Williams, S., & Schubert, P. (2010). Benefits of Enterprise Systems Use. *Proceedings of the Annual Hawaii International Conference on System Sciences*, 1 - 9. 10.1109/HICSS.2010.82

Winter, A., Haux, R., Ammenwerth, E., Brigl, B., Hellrung, N., & Jahn, F. (2010). Health information systems. In Health Information Systems (pp. 33–42). London: Springer; doi:10.1007/978-1-84996-441-8_4.

World Health Organization. (2012). *Management of patient information, Trends and challenges in Member States, Global Observatory for eHealth series*. Author.

Wu, Y., Suhendra, V., & Guo, H. (2012, June). A gateway-based access control scheme for collaborative clouds. In *Proc. 7th International Conference on Internet Monitoring and Protection* (pp. 54-60). Academic Press.

Xuan & Champion. (2017). *Threats and attacks*. Available at: http://web.cse.ohio-state.edu/~champion.17/4471/4471_lecture_2.pdf

Yaga, D., Mell, P., Roby, N., & Scarfone, K. (2019). *Blockchain technology overview*. arXiv preprint arXiv:1906.11078

Yang, Y., Chen, X., Wang, G., & Cao, L. (2014, December). An identity and access management architecture in cloud. In *2014 Seventh International Symposium on Computational Intelligence and Design* (Vol. 2, pp. 200-203). IEEE. 10.1109/ISCID.2014.221

Zafar, H., Randolph, A. B., & Martin, N. (2017). *Toward a More Secure HRIS: The Role of HCI and Unconscious Behavior*. Academic Press.

Zhang, N., Zhong, S., & Tian, L. (2017). Using Blockchain to Protect Personal Privacy in the Scenario of Online Taxi-hailing. *International Journal of Computers, Communications & Control*, *12*(6), 886. doi:10.15837/ijccc.2017.6.2886

Zheng, Z., & Xie, R. (2017). An Overview of Blockchain Technology: Architecture, Consensus, and Future Trends. *2017 IEEE 6th International Congress on Big Data*.

Zheng, Z., Xie, S., Dai, H., Chen, X., & Wang, H. (2017, June). An overview of blockchain technology: Architecture, consensus, and future trends. In *2017 IEEE International Congress on Big Data (BigData Congress)* (pp. 557-564). IEEE. 10.1109/BigDataCongress.2017.85

About the Contributors

Sam Goundar is an Editor-in-Chief of the International Journal of Blockchains and Cryptocurrencies (IJFC) – Inderscience Publishers, Editor-in-Chief of the International Journal of Fog Computing (IJFC) – IGI Publishers, Section Editor of the Journal of Education and Information Technologies (EAIT) – Springer and Editor-in-Chief (Emeritus) of the International Journal of Cloud Applications and Computing (IJCAC) – IGI Publishers. He is also on the Editorial Review Board of more than 20 high impact factor journals. As a researcher, apart from Blockchains, Cryptocurrencies, Fog Computing, Mobile Cloud Computing and Cloud Computing, Dr. Sam Goundar also researches in Educational Technology, MOOCs, Artificial Intelligence, ICT in Climate Change, ICT Devices in the Classroom, Using Mobile Devices in Education, e-Government, and Disaster Management. He has published on all these topics. He was a Research Fellow with the United Nations University. He is a Senior Lecturer in IS at The University of the South Pacific, Adjunct Lecturer in IS at Victoria University of Wellington and an Affiliate Professor of Information Technology at Pontificia Universidad Catolica Del Peru.

Bharath Bhushan has received his Ph.D. in Computer Science from VIT University, Vellore, India. He has pursued his M.Tech in Computer Networks and Information Security from JNTUA, India. He has received his B.Tech in Information Technology from JNTUA, India. Currently he is working as an Associate Professor in the Computer Science and Systems Engineering, Data Analytics Research Lab, Sree Vidyanikethan Engineering College, Tirupathi, India. He has authored many national and international journal papers and one book. Also, he has published many chapters in different books published by International publishers. He is holding membership in many professional bodies like CSTA, MCDM and IAENG. He is in the editorial board of international journals like IJFC, IJGR and is a reviewer of over 06 international journals. His areas of research include Cloud Computing, Multi Criteria Decision Making, Data Analytics, Networks, Internet of Things.

Vaishali Ravindra Thakare is an Assistant Professor at the Atria Institute of Technology in Bangalore, India in department of science and engineering. She is pursuing Ph.D at VIT University (TN), India.She was Research Associate in the School of Information Technology and Engineering, VIT University and received M.S (by Research) degree from VIT University (TN), India. She received Bachelor of Engineering in Information Technology from Rashtrasant Tukdoji Maharaj Nagpur University, Nagpur in 2012. She has published many research articles in peer-reviewed journals and in international conferences. Her area of interests includes cloud security and virtualization, security protocols in cloud computing, cloud computing architectures.

* * *

Gagan Deep Arora, an alumni of Berhampur University, Orissa, is a versatile academician, administrator and an effective education leader with over 17 years of comprehensive experience in the area of strategy planning and professional development and conscientious teacher and subject expert. He has numerous publications in both national and international journals to his credit. His area of Research includes Image Partitioning ,Theoretical Computer Science and Data Science.

Syed Basha completed, Ph.D. in School of computer science and Engineering, from VIT university in 2019, Vellore from the VIT (Deemed by the university), Vellore, India. In 2011, he joined the Department of computer science and Engineering, Mewar University, Rajasthan as an Assistant professor, and in 2012. Later, he joined the Information Science and Engineering, The Oxford College of Engineering, Bangalore, Karnataka, India as Assistant professor. Later, in the year 2013, he joined the Information Technology, SVCET-A, Chittoor as Assistant professor. His current research interests include BigData Analytics, BlockChain Management, Internet of Things. He has 30+ publications, which includes research papers - 18 (Scopus, SCI) and conferences (International)-7, Book Chapters-6, Letters-2. He is one of the editors for the textbooks - 4, Conducted Guest Lecture in various Engineering Colleges in India. He received Award for this contribution towards the number of publications in the year 2018 from VIT.

Akashdeep Bhardwaj achieved his PhD from University of Petroleum & Energy Studies (UPES), Post Graduate Diploma in Management (PGDM), Engineering graduate in Computer Science. He has worked as Head of Cyber Security Operations and currently is a Professor in a leading university in India. He has over 24 year experience working as an Enterprise Risk and Resilience and Information Security and Technology professional for various global multinationals.

Bettlylyn Chandra is an MBA student at The University of the South Pacific. This research project paper was written under the supervision of Dr. Sam Goundar.

Anilkumar Chunduru received his B.Tech. degree in Computer Science and Engineering from JNTU Kakinada, India in 2012. He received his M. Tech. degree in Computer Science and Engineering from JNTU Hyderabad, India in 2014. Currently, he is pursuing Ph.D. degree in Computer Science and Engineering as Part-time from Vellore Institute of Technology Vellore, Tamilnadu, India. Now he is working as an Assistant Professor in the Dept of CSE in Dr. APJ Abdul Kalam IIIT-Ongole, RGUKT-AP. His research interests include cloud computing, Information Security, Cryptography.

Nisha Dhanraj Dewani is an Assistant Prof. in Maharaja Agrasen School of Law, affiliated to GGSIPU. She worked for 8 years in Amity Law School Delhi. Her LLB and LLM is from the University of Jamia Millia Islamia. Currently she is pursuing Ph.D. from the same University. Her passion is in IPR, International Trade law and International Commercial Law. She has international and national publication in reputed journals.

J. Janet is the Principal of Sri Krishna College of Engineering and Technology, Coimbatore, a top 100 NIRF ranked autonomous Institution affiliated to Anna University. Being a distinguished academician with 25 years of experience, she has guided more than 12 doctoral candidates to completion with research thrust on Internet of Things, Artificial Intelligence and Medical Image Processing. She has over 120 SCI and Scopus Indexed Journal publications to her credit with research imprint of 450+ citations. She has a colossal Research funding grants to the tune of 6.51 Crores in diverse schemes of DST and AICTE ,10 IPR patent publications and 1 International patent. She has served as Convener and Program Chair for more than 50 International conferences and workshop program committees. She has authored an assortment of books and book chapters with leading publishers on emerging technologies. Her research articles regularly showcase the cover page story of CSI Communications magazine and Open Source For You Magazine(An EFY Group Publication). She is the recipient of Global Outreach Education Award 2019 for Excellence in Lifetime Achievement, Young Principal-Coimbatore Zone award 2018 and several Institutional awards for the establishment of Centre of Excellence and vibrant Academic-Industry Interfaces.

Parthiban K. is an Assistant Professor at Dept. of CSSE Sree Vidyanikethan Engineering College, Tirupathi.

Dasari Kalyani is working as Assistant Professor having more than 16 years of reaching experience. Published more than 10 papers in reputed journals and conferences.Cryptography and information security are the main focused areas with 8 years of research experience.

Pooja Kaplesh working as Assistant Professor (CSE) in Chandigarh University, Mohali.

A. Kousalya is an Associate Professor of Sri Krishna College of Engineering and Technology , Coimbatore. She received her Master Degree from SNS College of Technology, Coimbatore, in the year 2010 and the PhD from Anna University, Chennai in the year 2017. Her research interest includes Cloud Computing, Internet of Things, Security and Big Data Analytics.

Lavanya L. is working as Asst. Professor in IT department at Sree Vidyanikethan Engineering College.

Shanthi Makka has a total of 16 years of teaching experience in various Engineering colleges across India. Prior to this, She completed B.Tech from GITAM, Visakhapatnam, and M.Tech from Galgotia College of Engineering and Technology, G.B.T.U. and Ph.D. from Birla Institute of Technology (BIT), Ranchi. She published the number of research papers in various International Journals and International and National Conferences and She has a profound knowledge of Algorithms, Theory of Automata, Data Structures, Compiler Design, C, C++, Python, Parallel Algorithms, Blockchain Technology, and Java Programming along with other Computer Science and Information technology subjects. She has good academic skills and working with employees of different mindsets allows her to leverage the skill for imparting knowledge and experience to budding engineers. She is a Professional Member of ACM. Her research interests are Parallel Computing, Blockchain technology, theoretical computer science, and Distributed System.

Gowtham Mamidisetti is currently working as an Assistant professor in the Department of CSE, Presidency University, Bangalore. His research area is cryptography, Information security, and Cloud security. His research work is published in many national and international journals which consists of Scopus indexed journals.

Hima P. is a fellow Researcher in the discipline of Computer Science and Technology at S.K University, Anantapur, Andhra Pradesh. She has completed her graduation and as well as post-graduation from JNTU affiliated colleges Ananathapuramu. She is a member of International Association of Engineers (IAENG), Computer Science Teachers Association (CSTA). She has 4 years of experience in teaching. Her areas of interest are Cloud Computing, Information Security and Image Processing.

Ravi Kumar Poluru received M.Tech. from JNTU Anantapur, Anantapuram in 2014. Currently, he is a Research Scholar in the School of Computer Science & Engineering, Vellore Institute of Technology, Vellore and pursuing his Ph.D. work in the field of Internet of Things. His main areas of research include the Internet of Things, Wireless Sensor Networks and Nature Inspired Optimization Techniques.

Manjula Raghav has been pursuing Ph.D. from School of Law, IGNOU. She has also worked as an assistant professor of law at Amity Law School Delhi, affiliated to IP University. Her specialisation is in Constitutional Law. She has written many international and national papers in reputed journals.

Balakrishnan S. is a Professor and Head, Department of Computer Science and Business Systems at Sri Krishna College of Engineering and Technology, Coimbatore, Tamilnadu, India. He has 17 years of experience in teaching, research and administration. He has published over 15 books, 3 Book Chapters, 15 Technical articles in CSI Communications Magazine, 1 article in Electronics for You (EFY) magazine, 3 articles in Open Source for You Magazine and over 100 publications in highly cited Journals and Conferences. Some of his professional awards include: Data Science Writer of the Year 2019 - Artificial Intelligence, MTC Global Outstanding Researcher Award, Contributors Competition Winner July 2019, August 2019 and September 2019 by DataScience Foundation, with cash prize of £100, 100 Inspiring Authors of India, Deloitte Innovation Award - Cash Prize Rs.10,000/- from Deloittee for Smart India Hackathon 2018, Patent Published Award, Impactful Author of the Year 2017-18. His research interests are Artificial Intelligence, Cloud Computing and IoT. He has delivered several guest lectures, seminars and chaired a session for various Conferences. He is serving as a Reviewer and Editorial Board Member of many reputed Journals and acted as Session chair and Technical Program Committee member of National conferences and International Conferences at Vietnam, China, America and Bangkok. He has published more than 10 Patents on IoT Applications.

Bharat Sagar is currently working as an Assistant Professor in Department of Computer Science and Engineering, Birla Institute of Technology, Mesra Ranchi and posted at B.I.T. Noida Campus. He received his MCA from UPTU and Ph.D. (Computer Science) from SHUATS Allahabad. His research interests are in Software Engineering, Parallel Computing and Distributed System and Machine Learning. He had published more than 45 research papers in Prestigious Refereed Journals and Conferences of international repute like Web of Science, Scopus, Elsevier, Inderscience, IEEE and Springer. He is also co- author in 03 book chapters in edited books published by Springer and IGI Global publishers. Dr. Sagar is also reviewer of various reputed SCIE and Scopus International Journals and Chaired Several IEEE other International conferences. He is invited in various International summits and conferences as an invited Special Guest organized by Govt. of India and others. Recently, Dr. Sagar Honored by "Young Scientist Award" in JNU, New Delhi on 15th June, 2019. This is second time to recipient the same, previously he has been awarded by "Young Scientist Award" in Aalborg University, Denmark (Europe) in year 2016. Dr. B. B. Sagar is a Professional member of IEEE Computer Society (USA), IENG (Hong Kong), ACM (Canada) and He is also Fellow of IETE (India). Many Scholers are doing their research under his supervision, 4 Ph.D Degrees are awarded and 03 are ongoing.

K. John Samuel received the B. Tech. from Intell Engineering college, Anantapuramu in 2009, M. Tech. from JNTUA Anantapuramu in 2012. He is a part-time Ph.D. scholar from Vellore Institute of Technology, Vellore. He has nearly 9 years of teaching experience. He is currently working as Assistant professor at Srinivasa Ramanujan Institute of Technology, Anantapuramu. He has published 13 research papers in various peer-reviewed international journals and international conferences with majority of them are indexed in Scopus and Thomson Reuters.

D. Dharunya Santhosh is an Assistant Professor in the department of Information Technology at Sri Krishna College of Engineering & Technology, Coimbatore, Tamil Nadu. Dharunya was graduated with distinction from Anna University, Chennai in post graduation. Her areas of interest includes Software Engineering, Data Mining and Cyber Security.

Bhaskar Thota is a Professor in the department of Computer Science and Technology at S.K University, Anantapur A.P. He holds the post of Deputy Director of Distance education at S.K. University and He is the CSE Coordinator of Engineering at S.K. University. He has completed his M.Sc and Ph.D in computer science from S.K. University. He has acquired M.Tech from Acharya Nagarjuna University. He has been continuously imparting his knowledge to several students from the last 17 years. He has published 68 National and international publications, 10 International conferences. 13 National conferences. One UGC Major Research Project. Attended seminars in 3 countries. He has completed major research project (UGC).

Index

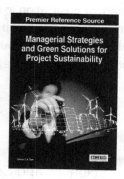

IGI Global Proudly Partners With eContent Pro International

Receive a 25% Discount on all Editorial Services

Editorial Services

IGI Global expects all final manuscripts submitted for publication to be in their final form. This means they must be reviewed, revised, and professionally copy edited prior to their final submission. Not only does this support with accelerating the publication process, but it also ensures that the highest quality scholarly work can be disseminated.

English Language Copy Editing

Let eContent Pro International's expert copy editors perform edits on your manuscript to resolve spelling, punctuaion, grammar, syntax, flow, formatting issues and more.

Scientific and Scholarly Editing

Allow colleagues in your research area to examine the content of your manuscript and provide you with valuable feedback and suggestions before submission.

Figure, Table, Chart & Equation Conversions

Do you have poor quality figures? Do you need visual elements in your manuscript created or converted? A design expert can help!

Translation

Need your documjent translated into English? eContent Pro International's expert translators are fluent in English and more than 40 different languages.

Email: customerservice@econtentpro.com

www.igi-global.com/editorial-service-partners

Printed in the United States
By Bookmasters